Financing State and Local Government
in the 1980s

Financing State and Local Government in the 1980s

Roy Bahl
THE MAXWELL SCHOOL
SYRACUSE UNIVERSITY

New York   Oxford
OXFORD UNIVERSITY PRESS

Copyright © 1984 by Oxford University Press, Inc.

Library of Congress Cataloging in Publication Data
Bahl, Roy W.
  Financing state and local government in the 1980s.

  Bibliography: p.
  Includes index.
   1. Finance, Public—United States—States.
2. Local finance—United States.   I. Title.
HJ275.B26 1984   336.73   82-22500
ISBN 0-19-503305-1
ISBN 0-19-503306-X (pbk.)

Printing (last digit): 9 8 7 6 5 4 3

Printed in the United States of America

To the Memory of

Richard Gustely
1945–1981

PREFACE

This book is a result of several years of thinking about public policy in the state and local government finance area. Though I prepared this material for classroom use, it is not meant to be a basic textbook and does not pretend to cover the underlying theory or describe the important institutions in any detail. Rather it is my version of the issues and problems currently facing the state and local government sector and the policies that have been proposed to confront these issues. I have long felt that a more focused public policy discussion was needed in this area.

One could not hope to cover, or even identify, the full range of important issues. I have limited the concern in this manuscript to some of those questions and policies that grow out of the relationship of the state and local government sector to changes in the national economy: the new economic role of state and local governments, the measurement of fiscal health and the effects of business cycles, inflation and regional shifts. The emphasis throughout, if I have done what I set out to do, is on what the data and past analytic work seem to be telling us about the prospects for the future. What I hope students will get from these pages is a feel for the analytic techniques necessary to enter the policy debate in a respectable way, the very great possibilities for using and misusing data to answer the important questions, the importance of understanding institutions before offering theories, and a kind of general reference point for studying state and local government finances.

Ours is an economy in the midst of very great changes, and the 1980s promise to be an important transition period. Much of this book is about the adjustments that will be required of state and local governments. A problem with any such effort is keeping ones perspective about the long-run, in spite of the current economic situation. Since I began working on these subjects, the U.S. economy has gone from recession to recovery, twice, high to low inflation, and oil crisis to oil glut. Indeed, as this manuscript is going to press, the U.S. economy is in the midst of a vigorous recovery. Nevertheless, my view of the next decade—which certainly colors the arguments below—is of a slower growing U.S. economy, with more uncertainty about the cycle and inflation, continued regional shifts, and more of the fiscal conservatism that characterized the late 1970s. Though some of my statistics will be dated by the time this book is published, I think that my view of the next decade will not.

I began thinking about putting this material into a book in connection with my course in U.S. state and local government finance. My students have suffered through several drafts with me, and their responses have been helpful in revising the material. I am likewise in the debt of colleagues in the Metropolitan Studies Program, from whom I am ever learning: Guthrie Birkhead, Jesse Burkhead, James Follain, David Greytak, Bernard Jump, Jerry Miner, and Larry Schroeder. My research assistant, Larry DeBoer, labored long and expertly over the data, and often made substantive contributions to the work. Evan Smith and Dana Weist did an equally thorough job of assisting me in final updates of the tables. This material was first put together for the Joint Economic Committee of Congress as part of its Special Study on Economic Change. Deborah Matz of the JEC gave me many early and good reactions to the manuscript, as did Fritz Stocker of Ohio State University. Esther Gray did her usual superb job of typing the manuscript and kept her good humor through what must have seemed like far too many revisions.

Despite all this good help and advice, the mistakes in these pages are my responsibility.

Syracuse, New York   R.B.
May 1983

CONTENTS

ix

Financing State and Local Government
in the 1980s

CHAPTER 1

INTRODUCTION

The United States economy has undergone dramatic changes during the past decade. Employment shifts from the more affluent Northeast and industrial Midwest to the Southeast and Southwest have eliminated much of the interstate variation in per capita income. National income growth has been unstable through three recessions and a prolonged period of price inflation, the growth rate in real gross national product (GNP) is down, and the relative costs of housing and energy are way up and likely to remain so. The rate of national population growth has slowed, the age distribution has been changing toward fewer school-aged children and more elderly, and the most rapidly growing counties in the nation are outside metropolitan areas. Perhaps the most significant trend, however, is a change that did not occur. Despite wars on poverty, model cities, new frontiers, new federalisms, and safety nets, the plight of the urban poor remains intolerable.

What are the implications of these changes in the national economy for the financial condition of state and local governments? There is surely some basis for arguing a negative impact.[1] Regional shifts reduce fiscal capacity far more than they reduce public expenditure demands in declining areas, and the pressures from population and income growth lead to fiscal adjustment problems in the growing areas. Recession has slowed

3

revenue growth for some state and local governments, compromised their budgetary position, and brought about an increased dependence on federal assistance. Particularly central city governments in the older regions were hurt by the business cycle, as they were hit hardest by the recessions and benefited least from the recoveries. While regional shifts and recession were dampening revenue growth, inflation was raising the cost of providing even a constant level of public services. Demographic changes may also have contributed to the revenue-expenditure imbalance of state and local governments. A growing concentration of the elderly and an increasing number of households may well increase expenditure requirements by more than they raise taxpaying capacity. On the other hand, the rapid population increases in the growing regions have pushed up expenditure requirements, especially in cases where substantial development of the basic infrastructure was required. This line of reasoning would lead one toward a conclusion that national economic and demographic changes have led to a deteriorating financial position for at least some state and local governments.

Others would argue that these national changes have not exacerbated the chronic fiscal problems of state and local governments. The temporary setbacks due to the 1975 recession were more than offset by national economic recovery, the buoyancy of state and local government taxes and federal aid flows, and a process of urban revitalization that is popularly referred to as gentrification. There is some evidence to support this position. The state and local government sector developed a substantial surplus by 1978, and tax reductions were the order of the day during 1978–81. Moreover, popular sentiment would seem to be on the side of the view that state and local budgets are more healthy than pressed—the current inclination to reduce taxes and limit government expenditures would seem less in line with John Kenneth Galbraith's fear of too many tailfins than with Ronald Reagan's or Howard Jarvis's implication that there are too few. Even the fiscal crises in New York City and Cleveland were labeled by some as unique and due mostly to financial mismanagement and politics. One observer has gone so far as to declare that the urban crisis is over.[2]

The truth, as always, is somewhere in between. Regional differences in economic structure make it possible for some states to benefit more than others during the same national recovery and for others to be more burdened during the same recession. Moreover, our complicated local government structure makes it possible for some central cities to deteriorate while their suburban neighbors thrive. In addition, there is great variation across the country in the distribution of taxing powers and expenditure responsibility between levels of government. Hence, what may be a city fiscal problem in New York is a county problem in Kentucky and a state problem in Hawaii. What all of this means is that the effects of changes in the United States economy on state and local government finances cannot be understood apart from an appreciation of the interstate diversity in changes in economic and demographic structure and in intergovernmental arrangement. Generalizations are just not easily made.

The objectives in this book are to begin a sorting out of the many and varied effects of recent national economic changes on state and local government finances and to consider the outlook for the state and local government sector in light of these findings. Chapter 2 is a description of the growth and changing economic role of the state and local government sector. The conventional wisdom that state and local governments should not engage in distribution or stabilization activities is questioned, and the allegation that state and local government taxes and expenditures have somehow become "too large" is considered. In Chapter 3, the evidence on the current fiscal health of the state and local sector is examined, with considerable attention paid to the meaning of the large sector surplus in the national accounts and to the methods of identifying urban fiscal distress. The focus then shifts, in Chapter 4, to an assessment of the more specific impacts of inflation and recession on state and local government revenues and expenditures. In Chapter 5, the fiscal effects of regional shifts in economic activity are considered. The intent in the final chapter is to pull these strands together to assess the outlook for state and local government finances in light of probable future changes in the national economic and demographic makeup and to consider the essential elements of a very needed national urban policy for the United States.

Readers should remain aware of three important limitations to this work. First, and always, data are too short and limited to allow a full telling of the story. For examples, there are not good measures of local area price level changes, no annual estimates of personal income or employment in cities, and little information about the characteristics of migrants. Second, there are areas where there is very little objective evidence about the impact of the changing economy on state and local government finances and where, consequently, this work is as much speculation as analysis. Finally, there is the issue of perspective, i.e., how to identify the most important of the long-term influences on state and local government budgets at a time when so much is changing, i.e., the inflation rate has gone from high to low, the economy has moved from sustained recovery to deep recession, and the oil situation has gone from shortage to glut. Such limitations, common to studies which attempt to assess the outlook, are flagged throughout this work.

CHAPTER 2

THE GROWING FISCAL AND ECONOMIC IMPORTANCE OF STATE AND LOCAL GOVERNMENTS

One might begin a study of state and local government finances by asking about the role of the state and local government sector in the national economy. How important is this sector as a contributor to economic growth, and what part has it played in carrying out the traditional allocation, distribution, and stabilization functions of government? In fact, the state and local government sector constitutes a significant share of GNP—13 percent in 1981—and about half of total government spending. This means that state and local government fiscal actions are an important force to be reckoned with in the formulation of national economic policy.

Policy analysts have long puzzled about the "proper" distribution, stabilization, and allocation objectives of state and local governments and the "proper" federal policy toward the state and local sector. Three important issues have caught the attention of scholars and policymakers:

The distribution question: are subnational governments

7

large enough to significantly influence the interpersonal distribution of income?

The stabilization question: could counter-cyclical behavior by state and local governments influence the pattern of national income growth, and compromise the effectiveness of federal macroeconomic policy?

The allocation question: has the state and local government sector become too large in the sense of discouraging private investment and retarding economic growth while vastly overpaying public employees relative to their productivity? Or is it too small in the sense of not providing an adequate level of public services?

This chapter focuses on these three questions, beginning with a description of the changing size and composition of state and local sector activities. Attention is then turned to a questioning of the conventional wisdom about what is and should be the economic role of state and local governments in the system of federal-state-local finances. Finally, we summarize the arguments that government—including state and local government—has somehow become too large and ought to be limited in its size and growth. Some perspective on these issues is an essential prerequisite to evaluating the fiscal health of subnational governments, a task taken up in Chapter 3.

GROWTH IN THE STATE AND LOCAL GOVERNMENT SECTOR

The development of the United States public sector between 1942 and 1976 can be characterized by three major trends: a growing importance of the state and local sector in the United States economy; a shift in public spending toward health, education, and welfare services; and a long-term trend of increase in state and local government dependence on federal intergovernmental transfers.[1] Since 1976, each of these three trends has been reversed. This abrupt change in the pattern of American fiscal federalism, if it continues, suggests a changing role for state and local governments.

A brief digression on how one goes about identifying such

trends and turning points would seem in order. Although the quality of the data available is relatively good, measurement of the size of this sector is not at all straightforward. Indeed, whether the state and local government sector has increased in size depends on whether we measure its growth against that of the federal sector or against GNP, whether we measure government activity in terms of employment or expenditures, whether intergovernment aids are counted as federal or state and local government expenditures, how transfer payments to individuals are treated, and what time period is chosen for study.

The two most commonly used indicators of government activity are employment and expenditures. If public employment is taken as the proper measure of activity, state and local governments have clearly dominated the growth in the public sector in the past twenty years. Between 1954 and 1980, state and local government employment increased by 174 percent while growth in the federal sector was only 22 percent.[2] Public employment may not be an appropriate comparative, however, because the functions of the state and local government sector make it quite labor intensive whereas transfers, debt repayment, capital outlays, and other nonlabor expenditures are much more important at the federal level. Total expenditure is probably a better indicator of the relative growth of the state and local sector.[3]

Growth of the Sector

The use of expenditures to measure the growth in government activity raises the question of whether federal grants should be counted as federal or state and local government expenditures. The former would imply measurement of size according to where the funds are raised, the latter according to where they are spent. If grants are counted as part of the federal sector, federal government domestic expenditures[4] are equivalent to a larger and increasing share of total public sector activity (Table 2-1). If federal grants are included in state and local rather than federal expenditures, then the state and local sector and the federal sector are about the same size but, surprisingly, the federal domestic sector is growing at a faster rate (Table 2-1). During the past quarter century, the federal government share of total public spending has increased from about 40 percent

Table 2-1. Government Domestic Expenditure

Calendar Year	Percent of Total Domestic Public Sector			Percent of GNP		
	Federal[a]	State[b]	Local[b]	Federal[a]	State[b]	Local[c]
	From Own Funds					
1954	45.6	25.4	29.0	6.2	3.5	4.0
1964	48.4	24.2	27.4	8.5	4.3	4.8
1969	48.7	26.2	25.1	9.9	5.3	5.1
1970	50.5	25.7	23.8	11.2	5.7	5.3
1971	51.9	24.9	23.2	12.1	5.8	5.4
1972	54.2	23.7	22.1	12.7	5.6	5.2
1973	54.3	24.3	21.4	12.8	5.7	5.0
1974	54.8	24.2	21.0	13.6	6.0	5.2
1975	57.8	23.0	19.2	15.7	6.2	5.2
1976	58.4	22.8	18.8	15.5	6.1	5.0
1977	59.2	22.2	18.6	15.3	5.7	4.8
1978	59.2	22.2	18.5	14.9	5.6	4.7
1979	59.1	22.5	18.4	14.6	5.6	4.6
1980[c]	61.0	21.6	17.3	15.9	5.6	4.5
1981	61.1	21.5	17.4	15.9	5.6	4.5
1982 (est.)	61.3	21.1	17.6	16.6	5.7	4.8
	After Intergovernment Transfers[d]					
1954	39.9	21.4	38.7	5.5	2.9	5.3
1964	39.7	22.4	37.8	7.0	4.0	6.8
1969	38.2	23.4	38.4	7.8	4.8	7.8
1970	39.3	22.9	37.8	8.7	5.1	8.4
1971	40.2	22.9	36.9	9.4	5.4	8.6

Year						
1972	40.6	22.8	36.6	9.5	5.4	8.6
1973	41.1	22.4	36.5	9.7	5.3	8.6
1974	42.5	21.9	35.6	10.6	5.4	8.8
1975	44.9	21.4	33.7	12.2	5.8	9.2
1976	45.0	22.2	32.7	12.0	5.9	8.7
1977	45.7	21.7	32.6	11.8	5.6	8.5
1978	45.1	21.7	33.2	11.4	5.5	8.4
1979	45.7	21.6	32.7	11.4	5.3	8.1
1980c	48.3	20.8	30.9	12.6	5.3	8.1
1981	50.0	20.5	29.5	13.0	5.3	7.7
1982 (est.)	51.3	20.0	20.0	14.0	5.4	7.8

a Excludes federal expenditure for national defense, international affairs and finance, and space research and technology and the estimated portion of net interest attributable to these functions. Includes Social Security (OASDHI) and all federal aid to state and local governments, including general revenue sharing payments.

b The National Income and Product Accounts do not report state and local government data separately. The state and local expenditure totals (National Income Accounts) were allocated between levels of government on the basis of ratios (by year) reported by the United States Bureau of the Census in the government finance series.

c Preliminary.

d All federal aid to state and local governments, including general revenue sharing payments, is included as state and local expenditure and excluded from federal domestic expenditure.

Source: Summarized from Advisory Committee on Intergovernmental Relation, *Significant Features of Fiscal Federalism, 1981–82* edition, Tables 1 and 2. Washington: USGPO.

of total public spending to over 50 percent, *even if defense expenditures are excluded and intergovernmental transfers are counted as state and local government expenditures.* This very important and long-term trend of centralization in the United States fiscal system has not been widely recognized.

A break in this pattern occurred after 1976. The state and local government sector began to decline relative to GNP, and its share of total public spending fell off rapidly. This decline was due in part to a reduced flow of federal assistance and in part to a resistance to tax increases by state and local governments. The latter would seem to be the more important cause, at least until the 1982 round of state and local government tax increases. The Advisory Commission on Intergovernmental Relations (ACIR) estimated that none of the $30 billion in real state tax increase during 1976–80 was due to "political actions,"[5] and the ratio of state and local government taxes to personal income fell from 12.8 percent in 1977 to 11.6 percent in 1980. The increased federal role in the United States fiscal system, then, is as much due to a slowdown in state willingness to tax as it is to federal grant retrenchment.

Increased Social Welfare Expenditures

A second dominant trend in the United States fiscal system has been the continuing increase in the budget claim of health, education, and welfare expenditures. The postwar increase in public expenditures at all levels of government, as well as the shift toward an increasing federal share, has been largely due to increased social welfare expenditures.[6]

At the federal level, the expenditure increases of the past two decades have been dominated by increased Social Security expenditures and by increased grants to state and local governments (Table 2-2). The Social Security share of federal domestic expenditures has more than doubled since 1954, and federal aid to state and local governments doubled between 1954 and 1978. Moreover, there was a marked shift toward social welfare services in the composition of this federal aid. Again, there would appear to be a structural break in the past five years. Assistance to state and local governments as a share of the total federal budget has been declining since it peaked at

Table 2-2. Sources of Growth in Federal Domestic Expenditures

Calendar Year	Percent Distribution			Percent of GNP		
	Social Security (OASDHI)[a]	Federal Aid[b]	All Other[c]	Social Security (OASDHI)[a]	Federal Aid[b]	All Other[c]
1954	16.2	12.7	71.1	1.0	0.8	4.4
1964	30.3	19.1	50.6	2.6	1.6	4.3
1969	36.4	21.7	41.9	3.6	2.2	4.1
1970	35.8	22.2	42.1	4.0	2.5	4.7
1971	35.2	22.4	42.3	4.3	2.7	5.1
1972	34.9	25.1	40.8	4.3	3.2	5.2
1973	36.9	24.3	38.7	4.7	3.1	5.0
1974	37.0	22.5	40.5	5.0	3.1	5.5
1975	34.3	22.4	43.2	5.4	3.5	6.8
1976	35.7	22.9	41.4	5.5	3.6	6.4
1977	36.6	23.0	40.4	5.6	3.5	6.2
1978	37.0	24.0	38.9	5.5	3.6	5.8
1979	38.2	22.8	39.0	5.6	3.3	5.7
1980	37.7	21.3	41.0	6.0	3.4	6.5
1981	39.7	18.8	41.5	6.3	3.0	6.6
1982 (est.)	41.3	16.4	42.3	6.9	2.7	7.0

[a] National Income and Product Account.

[b] Federal aid as reported in the National Income Accounts (used here) differs slightly from the federal payments (Census) series (used in Table 2.3). The major difference is the inclusion of federal payments for low-rent public housing (estimated at $3.5 billion in 1980) in the Census series but excluded by definition from the NIA series. Federal general revenue sharing is included in both series.

[c] Includes direct federal expenditure for education, public assistance and relief, veterans benefits and services, commerce, transportation, and housing, and others.

Source: Summarized from ACIR, *Significant Features, 1981–82*, Table 3.

13

24 percent in 1978, and the Social Security share of expenditures has slowed its increase in recent years.

The reversal has been much more dramatic at the state and local government level, where about 60 percent of the expenditure increase during the 1960–76 period was for health, education, and welfare purposes. This share fell to 56 percent between 1976 and 1981. Put another way, the average 1 percent increase in GNP between 1960 and 1976 generated a 1.56 percent increase in social welfare expenditures. Between 1976 and 1981, this income elasticity of social welfare expenditures was only 0.84. The implication seems clear enough. Federal assistance to state and local governments, largely for health, education, and welfare purposes, has been cut. State and local governments have responded relatively more by passing these cuts along than by raising taxes or redirecting expenditures from other areas. On the one hand, this response had undesirable distributional effects, but on the other it came at a time when the numbers of school-aged children and welfare recipients were on the decline.

Federal Aid Dependence

The third major trend of the past two decades has been the growing importance of federal aid flows in the public sector. For every 1 percent increase in GNP between 1954 and 1976, federal general revenues (including Social Security) grew by about 1 percent, state and local government revenues from own sources by about 2 percent, and federal aid by about 5 percent. With this trend came a growing reliance by state and local governments on federal aid. By 1978, federal aid accounted for 22 percent of total state and local government revenue and was a more important financing source than any of the property, sales, or income taxes (Table 2-3).

Between 1976 and 1980, federal revenue grew about 20 percent faster and state and local government revenues, both own source and federal aid, about 20 percent slower than did GNP.[7] The result is that federal grants have declined in importance as a financing source for state and local governments, reversing a two-decade trend of increase. The National Income Accounts (NIA) at the end of 1981 show that the federal fi-

Table 2-3. Reliance of State and Local Government on Federal Aid and Major Tax Revenue Sources

	Percent of Total General Revenue			
Year	Federal Aid	Property Taxes	Income Taxes	Sales Taxes
1954	10.3	34.4	6.6	25.1
1964	14.7	31.0	8.0	23.1
1974	20.1	23.0	12.3	22.2
1976	21.7	22.3	12.3	21.3
1977	21.9	21.9	13.4	21.2
1978	22.0	21.0	13.9	21.4
1979	21.8	18.9	14.3	21.6
1980	21.7	17.9	14.5	20.9
1981	21.3	17.7	14.3	20.3

Source: U.S. Bureau of the Census, *Governmental Finance*, Series GF No. 5. Washington, D.C.: GPO, various years.

nancing share has fallen to 21.3 percent of state and local government revenues.[8]

Increasing Centralization

Accompanying these three important trends has been a growing dominance of state government within the state and local sector. The state government share of total taxes collected rose from 56 to 64 percent between 1965 and 1981, and the states' share of direct expenditures increased from 43 to 46 percent (Table 2-4).[9] This trend is explainable by two considerations: state government income and sales taxes are more bouyant than local property taxes and there has been a move toward heavier state government financing of locally provided services.

This centralization of fiscal activity toward the state level is a relatively uniform trend that was not interrupted by the turnaround in 1976. As may be seen from the coefficients of variation reported in Table 2-4, states have become more alike in their division of fiscal responsibility between the state and local levels.[10] In fact, only fifteen of the fifty states had reductions in the state direct expenditure share between 1976 and 1980 (twelve of these were the less populous and more rural states). The increased state share of tax revenues is also a relatively

Table 2-4. Interstate Variations in Selected Indicators of Fiscal Importance

	Total Expenditures as Percent of State Personal Income			Federal Aid as Percent of Personal Income			Federal Aid as Percent of General Revenues		
	1965	1976	1981	1965	1976	1981	1965	1976	1981
Mean	17.0	18.9	21.3	3.4	4.5	4.2	18.9	23.5	22.2
Coefficient of variation	0.21	0.15	0.27	0.66	0.26	0.26	0.56	0.15	0.17

	Revenues from Own Source as Percent of Personal Income			State Government Percent of Direct Expenditures			State Government Percent of Tax Revenues		
	1965	1976	1981	1965	1976	1981	1965	1976	1981
Mean	13.4	14.5	15.6	43.1	44.4	46.3	56.0	62.2	64.1
Coefficient of variation	0.13	0.15	0.70	0.25	0.21	0.21	0.22	0.17	0.16

Source: *Governmental Finances*, 1980–81, 1975–76, 1964–65.

uniform trend, that is, states have become much more alike in terms of state government dominance of the tax system. Only thirteen states moved against this trend.

Other fiscal trends are not so uniform among the states. On average between 1965 and 1976, state and local governments increased their expenditure share of personal income, raised tax effort, and received federal grants that constituted an increasing share of state personal income. Whereas states became more homogeneous in terms of the share of personal income spent by state and local governments, there was no such narrowing of the interstate diversity in revenue effort, i.e., the gap between high- and low-taxing states widened. After 1976 the picture began to change. There was much more diversity in the average expenditure share of personal income in 1981 than in 1976, and dependence on federal assistance was down. The average revenue share of personal income (revenue effort) rose slightly, but there was an increase in interstate differences in tax burdens.[11]

THE ECONOMIC ROLE OF SUBNATIONAL GOVERNMENTS

What is the place of state and local governments in the formulation and implementation of national economic and social policy? Conventional thought holds that of the three functions of public budgets—stabilization, distribution, and allocation—only the last can be properly addressed by lower-level governments.[12]

State and local government stabilization programs may be quickly ruled out. Fiscal policies affecting the rate of increase of national income and prices require a coordinated effort that is beyond the reach of state and local governments. Certainly control of the size of the money supply could never be decentralized: the temptation to any one government to print enough to cover its deficit and then spread the inflationary effects over the nation would be too great. (Imagine the consequences if the New York City government had been permitted to print money in 1975!) Subnational government fiscal policy is equally improper. If state or local governments borrowed to stabilize national income growth, a heavy burden would be placed on future generations of local residents since most state debt is held by outsiders. Neither would increases or reductions in state spending be an effective stabilization measure because of "leakages" from the state economy, i.e., the typical state resident spends a significant share of his or her income on goods produced in other states, hence the employment-generating effects of such programs would spread to other areas and states. In short, the open-economy problem precludes the use of fiscal and monetary policy by state and local governments to alter national income and price level growth.

The conventional wisdom views income distribution policies in a similar light. This is because mobility may allow residents to offset the distributional intentions of governmental tax and expenditure policies, i.e., high-income taxpayers may migrate to other jurisdictions to avoid paying for redistributive programs while low-income families may migrate in to benefit from them. Some cursory evidence of this effect may be seen in the cases of New York City and New York State, i.e., in the extent to which their fiscal problems may be attributed to attempts to engage in redistribution through the provision of relatively large amounts of public service benefits and transfers to the poor.[13]

It is the allocation decision that is usually identified as the proper budgetary function of individual state and local governments, i.e., the decisions about which and how much local services will be provided and about how budgets will be financed. By leaving these decisions to our fragmented system of 80 000 local governments, the efficiency of the process is improved because the diverse preferences of local voters may be taken into account.

One might argue with this conventional thinking and take the position that the economic role of state and local governments is not so limited. With own-source revenues equivalent to about 40 percent of total federal, state, and local government revenues and with expenditures equivalent to about 13 percent of GNP, the fiscal activities of state and local governments can have an important influence on national income growth and the distribution of real income. Moreover, the traditional allocative function of state and local governments has been bent by any number of federal actions, e.g., reducing state and local autonomy through conditional grant programs, expenditure mandates, school finance issues, civil rights legislation, and so forth.

These considerations would seem to call for some rethinking of the traditional views about the proper economic role of state and local governments.[14] Accordingly, the sections below consider the potential role of the state and local government sector in the formulation and implementation of national economic policy and in the redistribution of income. We then turn to the broader allocation issue and particularly to the question of whether the state and local government sector has become, somehow, too large.

Macroeconomic Policy and State and Local Government Finances

One cannot question the traditional view that state and local governments are ill-equipped to formulate independent growth and stabilization policies. Yet events of the past decade have made it clear that the impact of federal macroeconomic policy on state and local governments, and the reaction of state and local governments to such policies, must be carefully considered. In this respect, two issues are of particular importance: (a) whether the budgetary decisions of state and local governments compromise or accentuate federal stabilization programs and (b) whether federal stabilization or economic growth programs which involve stimulating the state and local sector result in unintended changes in the system of fiscal federalism.

Effects on the Business Cycle. Two issues are important in determining whether state and local governments will reinforce or offset federal stabilization policies. The first is whether their fiscal actions are naturally countercyclical or procyclical and the second is whether federal grants stimulate spending in the state and local government sector.

With respect to the first, it has long been debated whether the discretionary fiscal actions of state and local governments tend to reinforce economic contractions and expansions or are countercyclical. Hansen and Perloff argued that there is a perversity in the fiscal behavior of state and local governments, that they increase spending in times of national expansion and curtail spending and raise taxes in times of national economic contraction.[15] Hence these authors see the fiscal actions of state and local governments as following the cycle and intensifying economic fluctuations. In a careful study of the post-war-to-early-60s period, Rafuse was unable to find evidence of the perversity hypothesis.[16] His results show that state and local government revenues had a stabilizing effect during every expansion and a perverse effect during every contraction and that expenditures had the opposite effects. "To note these conclusions is, of course, simply to spell out the stability implications of receipts and expenditures that continued to rise whatever the phase of the business cycle."[17]

More recent analyses show mixed results, partly because of ambiguities in the measurement of the impact of the state and local fisc. The consensus of studies by the ACIR,[18] Gramlich,[19] Vogel and Trost,[20] Reischauer,[21] and Jones and Weisler[22] is that the state and local government fiscal response is mildly countercyclical but probably differs markedly from state to state and from recession to recession. DeBoer makes the point that the deeper the recession is and the longer it lasts, the more likely is the state and local government sector to act in a countercyclical fashion, i.e., to raise taxes and cut expenditures.[23] This may explain why the destabilizing behavior observed by Hansen and Perloff during the depression has not been repeated in most of the post-World War II period.

The second question is whether federal grants can stimulate state and local government spending. The question is important: if a cornerstone of macroeconomic policy is to stimulate aggregate demand by increasing grants to state and local governments, one would want to be sure that state and local governments do not respond by substituting the new grant for what they had intended to spend from their own resources. Much depends on grant design. To the extent that grants are general purpose and lump sum one might expect such a substitutive result, and to the extent that they are matching one might expect a stimulative outcome.[24]

In fact, the federal government attempted to use the state and local government sector as kind of administrative agent for stabilization policy in the aftermath of the 1974–75 recession.

A major element of the recovery program was the Economic Stimulus Package, i.e., the CETA, Local Public Works, and Antirecession Fiscal Assistance grants. The idea was to stimulate the economy by pushing new grant moneys through the state and local government sector. However, the performance of the state and local sector during the 1975–78 recovery probably did not add significantly to the expansion. During this period, the federal government's budget deficits were in the $30 to $70 billion range while federal grants to state and local governments increased by $23 billion (42 percent). During this same period, state and local government construction expenditures increased only from $34.6 to $37.6 billion and the general account surplus of state and local governments grew from $6.2 to $27.4 billion.[25] The fact that the state and local sector had accumulated a surplus equivalent to about one third the size of the federal deficit by 1978 (and the fact that much of this accumulation was due to increased federal grants) suggests that the expansionary grant policies of the federal government were to some extent offset by the contractionary actions of state and local governments.

Another example of the need to consider state and local government response can be drawn from economic policy during the 1981–83 period of contraction. The success of the Reagan administration's economic program is affected by the state and local government sector fiscal response. The current version of the supply-side approach is to balance federal tax cuts with reductions in federal aid while assuming that competitive forces will restrain state and local governments from increasing taxes. If, instead, state and local governments attempt to make up for the losses with their own tax increases, some of the federal tax reduction advantages will be offset. This could be a particularly important problem in light of the investment disincentives thought to be associated with high state and local income and property taxes. By 1982 such tax increases had begun to take place.

The point in this discussion is that the fiscal actions of state and local governments have to be reckoned with in the formulation of national economic policy. The sector simply too large a share of GNP to be ignored.

Effects on Government Structure.   Federal policies instituted or expanded in the name of stabilization objectives may have important long-term effects on the structure of United States federalism. Because such effects can be unintended by-products rather than the result of reasoned policy, they may be inconsistent with the goals of other federal, state, and local government policies. A good example of such an effect is the aforementioned Economic Stimulus Package, which vastly increased the share of federal grants going directly to local governments. This in turn had two important consequences. First, it reduced the role of state governments in the federal-state-local fiscal system at a time when the state government share of total taxing and spending was on the increase. This policy ran counter to the trend of increased centralization and reduced the leverage of state governments in the state and local fiscal system. The second important consequence was a dramatic increase in the dependence of some large cities on direct federal assistance. Such dependence is not easily backed away from, particularly for cities whose economic base is growing slowly or actually declining. The important point here is that neither of these structural changes was an explicit objective of the stimulus package. Indeed, the phasing out of the stimulus package and the general reduction of federal grants created especially acute problems for those large cities that had become most dependent.

The Reagan administration's federalism program, which is designed to stimulate national economic growth, also introduced structural changes. The proposals for a restructuring of the grant system and the "swap" and "turnback" proposals would considerably strengthen the position of state governments.[26]

Federal macroeconomic policy, then, has introduced or porposed fundamental changes of direction in the federal system—twice in five years. In both cases the changes were consequences of broader economic policies rather than objectives of some thought-out national urban policy.

Distribution Policy and State and Local Government Finance

With state and local governments accounting for 40 percent of nondefense government spending and 13 percent of GNP, it stands to reason that this sector can have potentially important effects on the distribution of income.

State and local governments influence the distribution of income through the extraction of taxes and the provision of public services and assistance. Probably the more significant and certainly the most visible form of distributive influence is through participation in direct income transfers, e.g., public assistance payments. Though the federal government provides about half the funding for public welfare services, there are substantial interstate and even intercity variations in benefit payments. The consensus of research seems to be that low-income families have not migrated to high-payment areas in order to benefit from such programs;[27] hence individual government programs may well be effective in redistributing income. It is also worth noting that 60 percent of total state and local government spending is for health, education, and welfare—functions with a substantial redistributive potential. Whether these funds are spent to primarily benefit lower-income individuals is not known because of data limitations and because of problems with the estimation of expenditure benefits across income classes.[28]

There may be less potential for redistributive effects on the tax than on the expenditure side, in part because the federal government finances about one fifth of state and local government expenditures through grants. The burden distribution of state and local government taxes is probably not progressive, though there is more than a little debate over the incidence of the property tax.[29] Even if property taxes are less regressive than has been traditionally assumed, however, the tax system is overall probably no better than proportional. Sales taxes are proportional to slightly regressive, depending on the treatment of food, and the federal tax deduction provision tends to make the whole system more regressive. The net result, according to Okner and Pechman, is a heavy tax burden on the very low income and an approximately proportional distribution of tax burdens over most of the rest of the income distribution.[30]

What one would like from research in this area is an estimate of "net fiscal incidence," i.e., an estimate that takes both expenditure benefits and revenue burdens into account. Is the postbudget distribution of income more equal than the pre-budget distribution? Hard research may not give a clear answer to this distribution question, but one might offer the hypothesis that the very poor do not fare so well. State and local governments tax housing, utilities, and sometimes food, imposing a heavy tax burden on low-income families. A potentially offsetting effect is that health, education, and welfare expenditures may make an inordinately heavy contribution to the real income of low-income families. Yet are these expenditures made in a way to primarily benefit the lowest-income? It is not just the amounts spent for these functions but the composition and spatial distribution of such expenditures—e.g., in poor or rich neighborhoods, in central cities or suburbs, for clinics or hospitals—that significantly affect the real-income position of low-income residents. At least the concerns of state courts in school finance cases suggest that the actual distribution of these expenditures is not pro-poor.

Whether or not state and local government budgetary actions actually have a significant effect on income distribution, it does seem clear that state and local governments consciously pursue distributional objectives. The concern with distribution effects in virtually every tax reform proposal must be taken as evidence that distribution is seen as a valid role. It is not important that the motives behind this concern are political, only that changes in the distribution of real income are sometimes a stated policy objective of state and local governments. Tangible evidence of this concern is the enactment of property tax relief measures, such as "circuit breakers" and sales tax exclusions for food and other necessities. There is parallel evidence on the expenditure side. State grants, particularly for education, are sometimes allocated among jurisdictions on an equalizing basis, and some states have moved toward programs of "overburden aid" for hard-pressed central cities. State courts have shown a concern with the distributional role of state and local government in the celebrated school finance cases, where the property tax has come under attack as a financing mechanism that discriminates unfairly in favor of wealthier jurisdictions.[31]

It is also significant to note that the federal government has recognized the possibility for using state and local governments in national redistribution policies through public service employment programs. On balance, this evidence suggests that income redistribution cannot be thought of as exclusively or even primarily a federal government function. State and local government budgets, whether by design or not, have come to play an important distributional role.

Is the State and Local Government Sector Too Large?

The economic function left to state and local governments in the United States system is the allocation function, i.e., the determination of the amount and the mix of local public services to be offered. This determination cannot be separated totally from the growth question; it is possible that the fiscal choices made by state and local governments have contributed to a stunting of national economic growth. The issue is really that some analysts, politicians, and voters have come to believe that government is too big. Nondefense expenditures increased from 13.7 percent of GNP in 1954 to 26 percent in 1981. One question for the 1980s is whether the size of government—federal, state, and local—should be reduced and, if so, how and at what level?

Neither economic nor political theory provides guidelines for judging the optimal size of government. Because public goods cannot be bought for individual use as private goods can, consumers do not reveal their relative preferences for government services. Hence, they are unable to signal government decision makers that public goods are being oversupplied at their current prices.[32] Without a normative basis to establish whether government has become too large or is not large enough, the debate has become popularized, politicized, and more impressionistic than objective. Illustrative of the confusion are the postmortems on Proposition 13. By now it is not at all clear what revolted California's voters—low public sector productivity, high property taxes, or large state surpluses.

If one were looking for more objective guidelines to suggest whether the public sector is somehow too large, three possibilities might be raised: government is too small by comparison with other industrialized countries; government is too large because it interferes unduly with the market, lowers the return to investors, and retards economic growth; and government is too small because it has not succeeded in markedly correcting the unequal distribution of income.

Intercountry Comparisons. Intercountry comparisons of the size of government implicitly assume that average practice somehow constitutes a norm. Whether or not such a criterion is telling of anything, it is true that the size of government in the United States is small by comparison with that in other advanced economies (Table 2-5).

Even if intercountry comparison is a reasonable way to establish a norm for the size of the public sector, there are two

Table 2-5.   Intercountry Comparison of Government Size

	Ratio of Taxes to GDP	Per Capita GDP ($U.S.)
	1980	1979
Australia	27.7	8,836
Austria	41.2	9,107
Belgium	42.9	11,260
Canada	30.6	10,660
Denmark	45.5	12,925
Finland	34.2	8,701
France	41.0	10,720
West Germany	37.9	12,419
Italy	32.4	5,686
Japan	24.7[a]	8,627
Netherlands	44.8	10,624
Norway	46.4	11,486
Sweden	46.8	12,831
Switzerland	30.2	15,006
United Kingdom	34.9	7,192
United States	25.2	10,777
		Per Capita Personal Income
United States	26.7[b]	8,655
New York	42.5[b]	9,214

[a] 1979.
[b] Ratio of taxes to personal income.
Source: *United Nations Yearbook of National Accounts Statistics*, 1977, 1981, Tables 1 and 14a, International Monetary Fund, *Government Finance Statistics Yearbook*, Vol. 6, 1982; and *International Financial Statistics*, Vol. 35, 1982.

important problems with this kind of comparison. First, it does not compare the same package of public services, e.g., some countries have national health plans and more extensive welfare programs. It follows that it is not possible to use these data to show greater or lesser efficiency in government operations. Rather, the comparison shows differences in the scope, quality, cost, and efficiency of public service provision. To use the low government share in the United States to show that the public sector is too small implies a belief that services such as welfare, health, and higher education should be financed relatively more by general taxation, rather than partly through the private sector.

A potentially more serious problem with such a comparison is that it does not consider variations in the size of government within countries. Certainly the variation within the United States is great enough to where the overall federal, state, and local tax burden in some areas might compare favorably with those of some more highly centralized European countries. For example, if we add the federal, state, and local government tax share of personal income in New York State, the tax ratio rises to well above the United States average and the comparison with European countries is much more favorable.[33]

Investment Disincentives. An argument that has attracted much attention of late is that government has become too large and discourages economic growth through excessive taxes and unduly restrictive regulation. The most popular version of this argument is Arthur Laffer's "curve" (Figure 2-1) which shows that the tax rate may get so high that government revenues actually fall. Though Laffer saw tax rates as being within the "prohibitive range" in the late 1970s,[34] the little systematic testing that has been given his hypothesis does not support the claim that there is an inverse relationship between United States tax rates and government revenues.[35]

A stronger argument is that government taxes have gotten so high that they act as a disincentive to capital formation. The main culprits are said to be taxes on income and property, which have risen to 70 percent of total federal, state, and local government taxes and to approximately 15 percent of GNP. In-

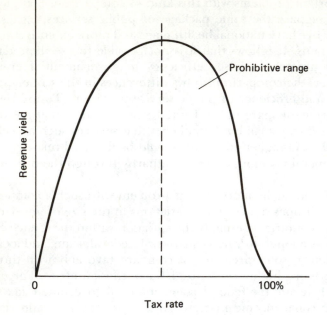

come taxes distort the choice between labor and leisure, particularly for the very young members of the labor force and for
lower-earning spouses, and may significantly reduce the overall
level of work effort in the economy. Income taxes also bias the
choices between savings and consumption since income saved
is taxed as current income and the returns from savings are
taxed again as current income. Corporate income taxes, property taxes, and personal income taxes all lower the rate of
return to capitalists. Boskin, among others, has argued that savings do respond to changes in the after-tax rate of return to
capital and hence higher taxes on capital reduce the future size
of the capital stock, labor productivity, wages, and income.[36]

If one accepts the argument that the current level of taxation of capital income does significantly retard capital formation, then two avenues of reform are open. The first calls for
structural changes in the tax system that would reduce the tax
burden on capital, such as integrating personal and corporate
income taxes, replacing the current income tax with an expen-

diture tax, or indexing the income tax for inflation.[37] The other reform possibility follows the line of argument that government has gotten too large and that a growing taxation of capital income has accompanied this government growth. A reduction in the size of government, if accompanied by a reduced rate of taxation on capital income, would result in increased investment and eventually increased real wages, income, and government revenue.

Though the capital formation argument is usually brought up in connection with federal tax reform, there are important state and local government fiscal implications. There are three good reasons why a realistic reform of the taxation of capital would also require reductions at the state and local government level. First, about one third of taxes on capital are levied by state and local governments, as compared to about one fifth as recently as ten years ago. Second, because of the deductibility provisions under the federal income tax, a tax rate reduction at the federal level would generate an automatic increase in effective tax rates paid at the state and local level, thereby offsetting a part of the federal reduction. Finally, reduced federal taxes would probably lead to reduced intergovernment transfers. This would require state and local governments to either cut expenditures or raise tax rates, and if they increased taxes in accordance with present tax structures, about half of the increase would come in the form of income and property taxes.

Income Redistribution.   It has long been argued that there is a direct relationship between the size of the public sector and the distribution of income.[38] From this argument one might make the point that the size of government in the United States is too small to generate an acceptable distribution of income.

The exact relationship between the growth in government size and changes in the income distribution is not known, but there is evidence to give an impression. Gillespie's work on the United States shows that the net fiscal impact of government taxing and spending is progressive,[39] but more recent work has shown little effect.[40] On the other hand, some comparative research against European countries, where the government sector is larger, indicates that (a) there is substantial redistribution through the public sector in most countries and (b) the United States has one of the least-equitable income distributions.[41]

One might weave these piecemeal findings into an argument that the larger governments in European countries reflect a greater government involvement in social insurance and social welfare activities. Such services are of immense importance to the real income position of the poor, and hence their provision through the public sector markedly reduces the degree of income inequality.[42] The implication for policy is that the size of government in the United States ought to be increased in the name of improving the distribution of income.

There are important flaws in this conclusion. Since the United States fiscal system is more decentralized than that in most advanced countries with a larger government sector, the direct relationship between growth in the government sector and reductions in the income inequality may not hold. Growing state and local government taxes would not likely improve the income distribution since sales and property taxes are not progressive and state income taxes tend to be less progressive than the federal income tax. Moreover, it is a question not simply of increased funding but rather of the effectiveness of this funding in providing benefits to the low income. Consider that the United States welfare payment system is badly flawed, the level of Social Security benefits is ever under fire, and federal and state education grants are as likely to land in suburbs as in cities. In light of this track record, can one say with any conviction that increasing the size of government in the United States will improve the income distribution? The track record in recent years would suggest not.

SUMMARY

The growth in the United States public sector during the past three decades was dominated by several important trends: (a) the share of GNP accounted for by state and local governments increased substantially; (b) the federal share of total public sector activity increased; (c) the expenditure increase was dominated by health, education, and welfare functions; (d) the state and local government sector became much more dependent on federal grants; and (e) state government became increasingly dominant in the state and local government financial system. There seems to have been a turnaround, or at least a long pause, in the first four of these trends since 1976.

Nevertheless, the importance of the state and local government sector in the economy has increased in the past three decades, and with this increasing importance has come new economic roles, particularly in the areas of macroeconomic policy and income distribution. The relationship as concerns federal stabilization policy attracted a good bit of attention in the mid and late 1970s when state and local governments were used as administrative agents of federal fiscal policy. The fiscal behavior of the state and local government sector was mildly counter cyclical through most of the 1970s as financial assets were accumulated during recoveries and drawn down during recessions. This explains the lack of success of Antirecession Fiscal Assistance, CETA, and Local Public Works grants as a stimulus package during the 1975–78 period. During the 1981–83 recession, however, procyclical actions became increasingly apparent as state and local governments raised taxes and cut spending to meet anticipated deficits.

The potential role of state and local government in income redistribution is becoming more important as their tax and expenditure levels increase, and as their responsibility for social service delivery grows. The net effect of state and local government budgets on the distribution of income has not been adequately measured. However, based on the best available evidence, we might guess that the distribution of tax burdens is proportional and that the distribution of expenditure benefits is mildly progressive.

The future growth of the state and local government sector and changes in its structure are uncertain. Recent trends suggest a slowing of the growth in the state and local government share of GNP. The late 1970s seemed to bring a feeling that government at all levels had gotten too big, that it was producing too little, and in particular that too much government was largely responsible for the weak economic performance of the

U.S. economy. This has led to the limitation movement. Though there does not seem to be a clear logic supporting the argument that government has become too big, the mood in the nation seems to be in the direction of slowing the growth in the public sector.

CHAPTER 3

THE FISCAL HEALTH OF THE STATE
AND LOCAL GOVERNMENT SECTOR

Is the state and local government sector fiscally healthy? In the
1960s, the answer would have been a resounding no. General
revenue sharing was being touted as a needed fiscal dividend
for hard-pressed state and local governments, and urban poverty and the quality of life in central cities were seen as major
national problems. Many would still hold to this view. Urban
poverty is even more concentrated in central cities, real per
capita income and population in many cities have declined ab-
solutely and relative to suburbs, and city-suburb disparities in
public service levels, tax effort, and unemployment rates are
more pronounced than ever. In many ways, urban governments are as poor and as dependent as their constituencies and
their outlook is almost as bleak. Though generally agreed upon
norms do not exist, the quality of public services provided in
many of these cities seems badly deficient. This situation, one
could argue, is part of a long-run deterioration that will make
short-run financial problems of the New York City, Cleveland,
and Detroit (Wayne County) variety an increasingly common
occurrence.

Others would argue that while there may be pockets of distress, the state and local government sector is fiscally sound,
maybe even flush. The 1975–79 economic recovery and in-

creased federal assistance stimulated state and local government revenues, generated cash reserves, and enabled widespread tax cuts. For some states, this prosperity has continued
into the 1981–83 recession. Even for central cities, distressed
conditions do not hold in many metropolitan areas and in any
case may be as much a result of bad management and con-
scious fiscal choices as an indication of true financial distress.
On these grounds, some have written off New York City,
Cleveland, and Detroit as special or unique cases that tell us
little about central cities in general. The most Pollyannaish of
all see a comparative advantage of central cities in recapturing
growth through a revitalization process referred to as
gentrification[1] and in benefiting from high gasoline prices,
which may return middle-income families from the suburbs.

The stakes in this debate are the allocation of federal resources—the amount of federal grants allocated to the state and
local government sector and the distribution of that amount
among governments and regions. Those who argue that many
cities are distressed and that many states have reached their
taxable capacity limits call for an expansion of the major aid
programs and for a "targeting" in the distribution of these aids
on distressed governments rather than a spreading among a
larger number of jurisdictions.[2] Those who argue that the fiscal
distress issue has been overstated call for a smaller federal aid
share in the total federal budget. Federal expenditure reductions to combat inflation, the need to fund other federal activities, and the political pressures to limit the growth of government are the major supporting arguments for this position.
Quite apart from the question of how much federal aid is necessary, there is considerable debate about how it should be distributed. Nearly everyone believes it ought to be targeted on
the most needy governments, but there is little agreement as to
what constitutes need.

This chapter is about the concept of fiscal stress, what it
means and how it may be measured. While it is preferred that
public policy actions—especially the distribution of federal aid
among cities—be based on hard analysis, it is clear that much
subjective judgment underlies the generation of indicators of
need. Analysts would do well to understand and flag these
judgments before passing them on to policy users. The pur-

pose here, then, is not only to survey the measurement possibilities but also to raise the caveats. The chapter concludes with a brief discussion of the fiscal performance of state and local governments in the early 1980s and the strengths and weaknesses suggested by this performance.

ALTERNATIVE METHODS OF MEASURING FISCAL HEALTH

How does one go about measuring and ranking the fiscal health of state and local governments? One approach involves determining the overall balance between revenues and expenditures for the state and local government sector in aggregate. This tack, which relies on the National Income Accounts (NIA), leads one toward questions about whether there is too much or too little federal aid flowing to state and local governments.

A second approach involves comparative analysis of the fiscal and economic condition of individual communities. This analysis is more normative in that it suggests the conditions that ought to be associated with fiscal health or distress and sets out to identify appropriate indicators. Distressed city studies, the development of formula allocators for federal assistance, and municipal bond ratings are results of this approach. The third possibility is to study the actual financial performance of state and local governments and to look for indications of financial strength or weakness. This approach is more in an accounting vein in that it involves measuring liquidity, using financial ratio analysis, and attempting to measure the actual margin of coverage of fixed obligations (e.g., debt service, pensions).

None of these approaches are flawless, and all are subject to serious conceptual and statistical problems. They are based on different sets of data and are used to answer different questions. This chapter uses these techniques to survey the evidence about the fiscal health of state and local governments but does so in a context of explaining the strengths and weaknesses of each approach.

THE STATE AND LOCAL SECTOR SURPLUS

The surplus or deficit position of the state and local government sector is regularly reported in the NIA[3] and is sometimes used as a measure of fiscal health. An NIA surplus, an excess of annual revenues over expenditures, would appear to mean an addition to cash reserves or an amount available to subsidize future tax reduction. As can be seen from column 1 of Table 3-1, this surplus averaged more than $30 billion during 1981. In the same year, federal aid to state and local governments was above $87 billion. The sentiment on the part of some federal officials and members of Congress is easily understood. If state and local governments have more revenue than they can spend, why should federal assistance to states continue at such a high level? More to the point, why should the federal government—whose 1983 budget deficit promises to be more than $100 billion—continue to subsidize this accumulation?[4] Indeed, if federal assistance were reduced by the amount of the state and local surplus, the federal budget could take a needed step toward balance. The question on the table is whether the NIA data can be properly used to make this point.

While there may be some validity to the argument that the state and local government sector is overaided, the argument does not easily rest on the NIA statistics. The use of the NIA surplus information to argue such policy changes is based on a set of premises that may not be valid: (a) that a surplus for any government may be interpreted as describing fiscal health (b) that the NIA surplus measure is a good indicator of excess financial capacity and (c) that these surpluses are sufficient evidence to warrent *permanent* changes in the federal aid system. None of these premises, in fact, are unquestionably valid, and none would seem to be the proper basis to call for major reductions in federal assistance to the state and local government sector. In the next section we consider measurement problems with the NIA surplus, and then turn to a questioning of these three premises.

Redefining the NIA Surplus [5]

One is tempted to interpret any surplus as an excess of revenues over expenditures, i.e., as cash that may be saved for some future use. This would be an incorrect interpretation of the NIA surplus measure. There are two important caveats to taking this view. First, the NIA measure overstates the actual surplus or level of "free reserves" because it includes net additions to the assets of state and local government pension funds. Because pension funds are owned by individuals, the excess of contributions and earnings over beneficiary payments does not represent a surplus for general government operations. If pension fund surpluses are subtracted from the NIA surplus, the remainder can be viewed as the "general" government surplus or deficit.[6] The results of this adjustment still may show a surplus, though of a much smaller magnitude and with a much less steady growth (see column 2 of Table 3-1). This general government surplus fell to 3 percent of total general expenditures by the end of 1978 and was in a deficit position by the end of 1981.

The general government surplus, though a better measure of fiscal health in the state and local government sector, is still flawed as a measure of free reserves available. It includes both current and capital expenditures but only a portion of capital financing (capital grants are included but net borrowing is not). The general government surplus, then, may be interpreted as the excess of current revenues and grants over all current *and* capital expenditures. A positive surplus indicates a net year-end savings and an amount available for debt retirement or for adding to cash balances. A negative surplus, or deficit, indicates that net borrowing must be undertaken to cover capital expenditures.

An alternative measure of the unrestricted amount available is the "operating surplus," i.e., the surplus exclusive of capital spending and financing. This measure represents the amount which governments have available to finance capital expenditures, reduce taxes, raise current expenditures, or accumulate reserves to use for any one of these purposes in the future. One would expect the operating surplus to always be positive, i.e., it is not conceivable that the state and local government sector in aggregate would be unable to cover its recurrent expenditures.

Computation of the operating surplus is no straightforward matter, but estimates by Gramlich[7] have been extended here through 1981 (see Appendix A for a description of the estimation method). As may be seen from the data in Table 3-2,

Table 3-1. Growth in State and Local Government General Surplus, Federal Aid, and Federal Budget Deficit

Year	Quarter	Total NIA Surplus of State and Local Sector	General Surplus of State and Local Governments	General Surplus as Percent of Total State and Local Government Expenditures [a]	Total Federal Aid	Annual Increase in Federal Aid	Federal Government Budget Deficit
1974	1	9.5 [b]	-0.3				
	2	8.8	-1.5				
	3	7.7	-3.0	-1.4	43.3	1.5 [c]	
	4	4.2	-6.8				
1975	1	3.7	-7.6				
	2	4.5	-7.2				
	3	6.6	-5.8	-2.7	54.6	11.3	-70.6
	4	8.9	-4.2				
1976	1	10.1	-4.5				
	2	13.8	-1.6				
	3	17.4	1.4	0.4	61.1	6.5	-53.1
	4	25.0	8.4				
1977	1	23.7	6.6				
	2	26.1	8.4				
	3	32.0	13.7	3.7	67.5	6.4	-45.9
	4	30.4	11.6				
1978	1	31.6	12.4				
	2	34.0	14.3				
	3	25.7	5.1	3.4	77.3	9.8	-29.5
	4	29.8	8.2				
1979	1	32.3	9.9				
	2	26.8	3.5				
	3	30.9	6.7	2.1	80.5	4.1	-16.1
	4	31.6	6.4				

Year	Quarter						
1980	1	29.1	3.3				
	2	23.3	-2.8				
	3	27.1	-1.0	0.2	88.7	88.7	-61.4
	4	33.0	3.9				
1981	1	31.3	1.1				
	2	32.9	1.7				
	3	33.5	1.2	0.0	87.7	-1.1	-60.0
	4	29.1[d]	-4.2[d]				
1982	1	27.7	-6.8				
	2	32.1	-3.6				
	3	32.3	-4.5	-1.1[e]	82.0[e]	-5.0[f]	-119.6[e]

[a] Numerator is average general surplus over four quarters.
[b] All values are current dollars in billions.
[c] 1973–74 increase.
[d] Estimate.
[e] Third quarter estimates.
[f] Third quarter 1982 vs. third quarter, 1981.
Source: U.S. Department of Commerce, Bureau of Economic Analysis, *National Income and Product Accounts, 1976–79*, July 1981; *Survey of Current Business*, various issues.

39

Table 3-2. Components of Growth in the State and Local Government Surplus

Year	NIA Surplus	Surplus Excluding Pension Funds	Operating Surplus	Operating Surplus as Percent of			
				Federal Grants[a]	Federal Budget Deficit	State and Local Government Revenues Raised from Own Source	State and Local Government Total General Expenditures
1970	1.8	-4.8	8.8	44.2	73.9	8.0	6.6
1971	3.4	-3.9	9.8	40.7	44.7	8.0	6.6
1972	13.7	5.6	19.1	58.1	110.4	13.7	11.7
1973	13.0	4.1	18.4	52.0	274.6	12.0	10.2
1974	7.6	-2.9	14.2	38.2	132.7	8.5	7.0
1975	6.2	-6.2	9.4	20.3	13.3	5.2	4.1
1976	16.6	.9	12.1	19.8	22.8	4.9	4.7
1977	28.0	10.1	18.8	27.9	41.0	6.8	6.9
1978	30.3	10.0	22.3	28.9	75.7	7.4	7.5
1979	30.4	6.6	11.7	14.5	72.7	3.5	3.6
1980	28.2	0.9	18.2	20.5	29.6	4.9	4.9
1981	31.7	-0.1	19.5	22.2	32.5	4.7	4.8

[a] Excluding construction grants for highways, water, and sewerage.
[b] All values are current dollars in billions.

Source: U.S. Department of Commerce, Bureau of Economic Analysis, *Survey of Current Business*, July 1974, July 1976, July 1977, July 1978, July 1979, July 1981, Tables 3.1, 3.2, 3.4, 3.7, and 3.14; Department of Commerce, Bureau of the Census, *Governmental Finances* in 1978–79, 1977–78, 1976–77, 1975–76, 1974–75, 1973–74, 1972–73, Table 3.

the amounts are positive and indicate a small fiscal latitude available to local governments, e.g., the operating surplus was equivalent to 4.7 percent of state and local government own source revenue in 1981.

Trends in the Surplus

Given these measurement and definition problems, we may examine the trend in the size of the general government surplus as a rough indicator of changes in the financial condition of the state and local government sector. It should not be surprising that we find the general surplus to behave in a cyclical fashion, i.e., deficits in the 1975 recession, in the mild 1980 downturn and in the 1981–83 recession; and surpluses in expansionary periods (see Table 3-1). To better describe this pattern, three periods of expansion and four of contraction, as defined by the Bureau of Economic Analysis, are shown in Table 3-3.[8] Using quarterly, seasonally-adjusted averages as the benchmark, these results show average deficits during recessions and surpluses during expansions.

We have indexed these changes in fiscal position by calculating a kind of "cyclical swing" in the general surplus. Cyclical swing has been defined as the absolute difference in the *average* quarterly general surplus between contractions and the following expansion.[9] The average quarterly surplus "swung" from a

Table 3-3. Surplus/Deficit Position of State and Local Governments During Business Cycles

Cycle	Cyclical Swing (in Billions of $)	Net Accumulation (in Billions of $)
1969:III–1973:IV	5.7	0.4
1973:IV–1980:I	8.4	20.1
1980:I–1981:III	1.7	1.6
1981:III–1982:III	−3.6	−17.5

Source: Robert Bretzfelder and Howard Friedenberg, "Sensitivity of Regional and State Nonfarm Wages and Salaries to the National Business Cycle, 1980:I–1981:II," *Survey of Current Business* (January 1982): 26–28; and Robert Bretzfelder and Howard Friedenberg, "Sensitivity of Regional and State Nonfarm Wages and Salaries to the National Business Cycles, 1948–1979," *Survey of Current Business* (May 1980): 15–27.

negative $3.6 billion to a positive $2.1 billion during the 1969–73 cycle. That is, state and local governments made up the average quarterly deficit of $3.6 billion and added another $2.1 billion for a swing of $5.7 billion during the cycle. Another way to read these data takes into account the average duration of the cycle and calculates "net accumulation," i.e., by how much did the state and local government sector recover its deficit and accumulate a surplus during the expansion? A larger net accumulation implies that the state and local government sector financial position was helped more by the recovery than it was hurt by the recession. This would appear to have been the case during the 1973–80 cycle. That is, state and local governments added $20 billion more to their surplus during nineteen quarters of expansion than they drew down during six quarters of recession.

These data also give some idea of the amount of pressure which the cycle places on state and local government financial position. During the relatively short 1980–81 cycle, $1.6 billion in general surplus was accumulated; but far more than this amount has been lost in the ensuing recession. The longer the 1981–83 recession lasts, the more the state and local government sector will give back the "gains" it made during 1975–80, i.e., the tax reductions, the capital expenditures financed from current savings, and the net debt reduction.

It is not possible to track the behavior of the operating surplus in the same way, because the data in Table 3-2 are presented on an annual basis. Still, if we take 1975 and 1981 to be indicative of contraction years, the same pattern would appear to hold. State and local governments have less left over to contribute to capital expenditures, debt reductions, and tax rate reduction in recessions than in periods of expansion.

Justifications for a Surplus

Irrespective of the business cycle, a year-end fiscal surplus for a state or local government is neither unusual or necessarily undesirable,[10] and it cannot be automatically interpreted as evidence of excess resources. In fact, most state and local governments are prohibited by law from budgeting for an operating fund deficit;[11] therefore, it is not surprising that the NIA show at least a small year-end cash surplus.[12] More to the point, governments, like people, save for precautionary reasons by building up cash reserves over a period of years. These balances are accumulated for contingencies such as a prolonged strike or a natural castastrophe (snow, flood), for cash flow problems stemming from the timing of revenue receipts and creditor payments, and for recessions. Practices among governments vary widely in terms of the size of reserves actually held, and there are only rules of thumb about the optimal size of general fund cash balances.[13]

Larger cash balances in some states and local areas may be justified as protection against severe business cycle fluctuations. States with a particular susceptibility to national economic fluctuations—Michigan, for example—could face severe fiscal fluctuations over the cycle. Even the more industrially diversified states face substantial increases in unemployment and welfare-related expenditures during a recession. Theoretically, governments could accumulate reserves during periods of economic expansion and draw these reserves down during contractions. Over the cycle, these reserves should approach the relatively small contingency amount described above. The experience with such a practice is limited. Michigan and Colorado have established budget stabilization reserves. New York and California established such funds after the Second World War, but the objectives of the funds were not achieved.[14] The lack of success, then and now, is not surprising.[15] The pronounced upward trend in state and local government expenditures over the past two decades has dwarfed cyclical fluctuations. If there were excess revenues in an expansionary period, they were quickly spent; if there were deficient revenues during a contraction, tax rates were increased or more was borrowed. As long as the national economy was growing rapidly, there was little need for such a fund.

The experience of the late 1970s and early 1980s has changed the growth orientation of fiscal planners. In the 1950s and 1960s, an overcommitment of expenditures or an overestimation of revenues or grants was an error that could be quickly covered by economic growth. There would always be more revenue next year than this and more public employees to contribute to the pension fund, and discretionary tax rate increases—as long as they were not too large—would be accepted by the voters. All that has changed, at least for many state and local governments. The new concerns are that pension systems are underfunded and that in many cases the shortfall will have to be financed from a shrinking tax base and a smaller population; long-term debt burden is too high to be carried by future revenue growth, and there seems no possible way to finance normal expenditures in the event of another recession. State and local government financial planners, forecasters, and administrators—a conservative lot in the best of times—have become even more careful. This new wariness, together with uncertainties about the future performance of the national economy, inflation, and the energy crisis, may account for some of the building up of reserves by state and local governments observed in the past few years.[16]

Aggregation Problems

The existence of an operating surplus for the state and local government sector does not imply a healthy fiscal position for every state and local government. Who would argue that the large surplus in Texas makes the fiscal condition of New York State any better? Since the NIA surplus is a measure that offsets surpluses in some states by deficits in others, an aggregate sector surplus would be possible even if most state and local governments were in financial trouble. For example, *The Fiscal Survey of the States* reported that three states—Alaska, California, and Texas—accounted for more than half of the aggregate balances of reporting state governments in 1978.[17]

NIA statistics also aggregate the fiscal conditions of governments within states; e.g., California's large state surplus is treated as offsetting the deficits of some California local governments. It is important to note this aggregation problem before making inferences about the fiscal health of local governments. Distressed cities can be located in states where there is an aggregate state and local government surplus. The extent of urban fiscal distress may be less influenced by the size of the state government surplus than by the fiscal responsibility that the state government assumes toward its local units. That lesson was learned well during the California experience of the late 1970s.

The aggregation problem with the surplus measure has led to the airing of some important questions about who in the state and local government sector is fiscally healthy and who is not. Is the surplus largely concentrated at the state government level, and even there in only a very few states? To the extent that there are local government surpluses, are they in the large cities or the small, and, particularly, how have the budgets of the largest cities fared during the recovery? Unfortunately, there are no firm, reliable data to resolve these issues. The best that can be done is a piecing together of fragmentary evidence, oftentimes from data that are not strictly comparable.

State Versus Local Government Surpluses.   Intuitively, one would expect the surplus or deficit to be concentrated at the state government level. State income and sales tax revenues are more bouyant than local property taxes during an economic expansion or contraction, and state governments have greater freedom in undertaking discretionary tax actions. A Bureau of Economic Analysis breakout of the state versus local surplus for the 1960–76 period suggests that this intuition is incorrect, at least for the early and mid-1970s.[18] During the 1971 and 1975 recessions, state governments ran larger deficits mainly because of their more income-sensitive tax structures and greater responsibility for welfare-related expenditures. In the first year of the post-1975 recovery, they accumulated a much smaller surplus than did local governments. These results supported the strenuous arguments of representatives of state government associations and governors that the picture was not one of huge state surpluses and local deficits.[19] The National Governors Association (NGA) estimated the accumulated balance in "free" state accounts to be no more than $6 billion by the end of fiscal year 1978. Remaining balances held by states are said to be restricted to narrow uses (by constitutional provision or by statute).

These results may not be so counterintuitive. Between 1975 and 1978, direct federal aid to cities increased dramatically. Moreover, there has been a trend toward a greater share of direct expenditures at the state government level and an increasing state government share in total state and local government financing. In the immediate aftermath of the 1975 recession, expenditures and debt increased faster at the state than at the local government level.[20] The healthier look of local government budgets, then, is in part due to these subsidies and transfers of responsibility. Another explanation is that there was more fiscal retrenchment at the local government level and that these cutbacks show up in the form of a larger local government surplus.

Variations in State Surpluses.   The NIA do not provide details on the financial position of individual states. To develop such estimates, one must resort to the NGA *Fiscal Survey of the States*[21] or to the Census of Governments' *Governmental Finances.*[22] Unfortunately, these two data sources are not comparable with the NIA data[23] or even with each other.

The use of the *Fiscal Survey* data confirms the suspicion that there is a wide variation among state governments in the size of the fiscal surplus, and that the aggregate surplus grew after the 1975 recession. During fiscal year 1978, forty-eight states reported ending balances of over $8.9 billion, equivalent to 8.6 percent of expenditures. Most of this surplus was accumulated by a small number of states. California alone accounted for over 41 percent of the total, and California, Alaska, and Texas accounted for over 56 percent. The aggregate surplus for the remaining forty-five states was $3.9 billion, an amount equivalent to only 4.5 percent of operating expenditures. Besides Alaska, California, and Texas, two other states (Wyoming and Oregon) had surpluses in excess of 20 percent of their total operating expenditures. Surpluses of between 10 and 20 percent of total spending were reported by another eight states, and only Pennsylvania reported a deficit. Clearly the real and absolute magnitude of the state government surplus varies from state to state. Yet in fiscal year 1978, the peak of the recovery, twenty-eight of forty-eight states reported surpluses in excess of the benchmark of 5 percent of total operating expenditures.[24]

State finances also responded in an uneven way to downturns in the economy. In 1979, aggregate balances in state general operating funds were projected to decline to about $4.3 billion, a drop of $4.5 billion (or 52 percent) from their 1978 level. This reduction was projected largely because thirty-five of forty-eight reporting states projected a smaller surplus in 1979 than 1978. The NGA concluded that this drawdown was a result of changes in state tax policy, a flattening or even downturn in the economy, and inflationary pressures on expenditures.[25] According to the National Conference of State Legislatures (NCSL), the initial outlook for 1982 was for only eleven states to have year-end balances in excess of 5 percent of annual spending, by comparison with eighteen states in fiscal 1981.[26] Again, there is much variation. The energy rich states anticipated sizeable surpluses; seventeen states expected to conclude fiscal year 1982 with year-end balances equivalent to less than 1 percent of annual spending; and twelve states anticipated deficits. In fact, six states did finish fiscal year 1982 with deficits, and another seventeen ended the fiscal year with virtually no balance. The twelve states which reported balances in excess of 5 percent of annual spending were Florida, Hawaii, Kansas, Oklahoma, Louisiana, Delaware, Montana, Nevada, New Mexico, North Dakota, Texas, and Wyoming.

State government budgets are probably hurt worse by recession than these data suggest. The NCSL reports that twenty-six states made cutbacks in fiscal year 1982 budgets after those budgets were proposed or enacted, largely because revenues grew by even less than had been projected.[27] This result squares with Mikesell's finding that the income elasticity of state taxes is greater during expansions than contractions.[28]

Variations in the Local Surplus.   Gramlich has attempted to disaggregate the budgetary position of the local government sector with Census of Governments data. Though not comparable with the NIA amounts or procedures, his estimates suggest that the largest cities and, in general, all municipal governments with populations in excess of 25 000 have fared worst. According to his results, the local government surplus reported by the Bureau of Economic Analysis must lie with smaller local governments, counties, and special districts. Such deduction is dangerous because relatively little work has been done on smaller cities, but this inference is consistent with Muller's finding that smaller cities have experienced the largest increases in federal aid.[29]

The finding that local governments in aggregate are in a surplus position raises the interesting question of the relative fiscal health of large cities on the various distressed lists. Can a distressed city have a budget surplus? Gramlich's data give an affirmative answer, at least in the case of the operating surplus concept. Of the twenty large cities he studied—including Cleveland—only New York City (in 1975–76) showed an operating deficit. Gramlich's answer and analysis are probably correct but cannot give a detailed picture of the budgetary condition of individual local governments because of the limitations of Census of Governments data.

Some very interesting information on the financial condition of large city governments comes from Dearborn's continuing studies of audited financial statements.[30] Of the twenty-eight large cities in his sample, he finds twenty-one instances of revenue or expenditure imbalances in at least one year between 1976 and 1979. For the twenty-seven largest cities (excluding New York City), his results show an aggregate general fund revenue or expenditure deficit of $154.2 million in 1976, a surplus of $230.9 million in 1977, and a surplus of $73.6 million in 1978. Dearborn's work is not only informative in tracking the current financial condition of cities but also convincing in demonstrating that such conclusions are best drawn from careful case-by-case analysis of local financial statements.

The upshot of this work seems clear. All cities have not suffered major fiscal problems during recessions. Indeed, local governments as a whole seemed to fare better than state governments during the 1974–75 recession and during the following national expansion. On the other hand, some cities were hurt more than others during the recession and helped less than others during the recovery. The evidence would seem to point to the larger, older cities as having suffered most through the cycle.

The Surplus and Fiscal Health

Even when measured for individual government units, a budget surplus is not a good comparative measure of long-term fiscal health. The annual operating surplus describes the excess of current revenues over current expenditures, an amount available for additional capital or current spending, tax reduction, funding for the pension system, or accumulation of reserves. The excess could mean a bouyant revenue system and truly indicate fiscal health. On the other hand, the excess could reflect no more than a temporary embarrassment of riches resulting from service cutbacks, reductions in capital expenditures and employment, deferred compensation, and so on. In the case of both state and local governments, there is more than a passing amount of evidence to indicate that the recovery period surpluses described above are more likely a temporary situation than a sign of permanent fiscal health.

For these reasons, comparative measures of the surplus may be misleading. The problem is less what the surplus measures than what it does not measure. Cities, or states, may have the same financial surplus but vastly different fiscal and economic characteristics that taint the interpretation. For example, two governments may have the same surplus but one may have a more dilapidated infrastructure, a greater debt service and retirement expenditure claim on future revenues, and a much higher level of taxation.

The use of budget deficits as an indicator of fiscal health or distress raises a broader issue: whether the financial condition of state governments can be assessed independent of any consideration of the financial condition of its constituent local government units. That is to say, can a state government be graded as having a healthy surplus position while certain of its local government units are fiscally distressed? The answer seems to be that most analysts and policy makers do not believe that local governments have a ranking claim on state government surpluses. Bond analysts often rate state government credit strength better than that of their constituent local government units. Massive amounts of direct federal aid to cities located in "surplus" states suggest that federal policy makers also see a distinction between the financial position of states and that of their local governments.

One would not expect state government to subscribe to the notion that local fiscal problems are state responsibilities. Through direct federal aid, local governments have sought and obtained substantial autonomy with respect to budget decisions. Because of this, the state may argue that it need not assume responsibility for the effects of whatever may place a local unit in financial stress. It follows that a state government surplus could exist, logically and properly, alongside local government deficits.

The view from city hall will differ. Local governments are creations of the state, and their fiscal operations are to a large extent regulated by the state. Tax rates and debt levels are limited, taxing powers are prescribed, and some local government expenditures are mandated by the state. City governments could argue that state governments regulate their fiscal decisions and constrain their fiscal options; hence, state governments should automatically assume some responsibility for their deficits. This argument leads to a position that the fiscal health of a state should not be separated from that of its constituent local governments; i.e., distressed local governments should have some claim on state government surpluses.

The state government view has held sway, though California's Proposition 13 movement is evidence of what local voters can do about commandeering a state's surplus for local purposes. By and large, however, there is not a commonly accepted view that local governments have first claim on any state government surplus. Because this is the case, the interpretation of the aggregate sector surplus in terms of what it implies for fiscal health must always be qualified. That is, local governments cannot be viewed as somehow more healthy because the state government surplus has increased.

The situation may be changing. Large direct local aid programs have been abandoned, and states are again becoming the focal point in the distribution of federal assistance. Moreover, the state share of total state and local government financing is increasing, and state aid to local governments has remained steady at its longstanding share of about one third of total state government expenditures. Finally, the Reagan administration's new federalism proposals define a greater future role for state governments. Local government fiscal problems will become more of a state responsibility in the 1980s than in the 1960s and 1970s.

Conclusions

The NIA surplus reveals nothing about the fiscal health of individual government units and less than one would like to know about the fiscal health of the state and local government sector in aggregate. The surplus measure provides indirect evidence about fiscal health in giving some indication of the direction of state and local government sector budgetary movements. An increasing operating surplus does suggest that revenues are growing faster than expenditures, even though programs may have been cut back and capital maintenance expenditures deferred.

The state and local government sector surplus remained between 5 and 10 percent of own-source revenues during the 1975–78 recovery—not an unusually high level—but began to fall with the onset of the 1981 recession. One should conclude from this that there is nothing abnormal about the cyclical performance of the sector surplus, except that it may have been distributed so unequally that some governments built little if any budgetary strength during the recovery period. Still, the existence of this surplus alongside tax reductions throughout the late 1970s suggests that the state and local government sector has not been so fiscally pressed as many believed. State and local government poverty is apparently less general and more limited to particular types of jurisdictions.

This conclusion suggests that one must look to another measure of fiscal distress. The major concern should be identification of pockets of fiscal distress, i.e., those areas of relatively high need and low resources. However, as those responsible for formulating grant distribution policy have learned, admitting the existence of distressed cities is much easier than identifying them.

MEASURING FISCAL DISTRESS

Fiscal health or distress is a qualitative term, and so it is not surprising that it means different things to different people. Indeed, since measures of distress may be used to allocate federal and perhaps state grant funds, there is good incentive for this diversity in view. Members of Congress can agree that their own cities are distressed, mayors can collectively agree that all cities are distressed, the NGA can argue that state governments are not especially well off, and so it goes.

In fact, there is no best measure of the fiscal health of cities and states. In one sense, all governments are in trouble because the level of public services is never adequate and taxes are always too high. On the other hand, governments cannot be in too much trouble if they are able to maintain an unhealthy level of fat in their budgets and continue to expand public employee benefits. Such anecdotal views are not very helpful in guiding public policy, and one must turn to some form of statistical measure. Unfortunately, the more objective measures of fiscal health, or distress, are not without problems. Indeed, different analysts reach different conclusions from the same "objective" measures.

One approach to measuring fiscal health is comparative. Whether all cities are healthy or not, some are better off than others. The idea of comparative analysis is to identify the outliers without establishing any absolute norms. The analysis usually involves comparing indicators of need, economic health, and fiscal performance to develop an overall index which has alternatively been referred to as fiscal need, distress, strain, and hardship.

The comparative approach is focused on urban areas, usually large cities, and attempts to measure relative economic, social, and fiscal health. The comparison usually considers more than budgetary position in trying to get a fix on the balance between resources available to the local governments and service level "needs." The specific measurements used are sometimes flawed and always debatable, but the intent of most of these studies is to identify cities whose populations have heavy concentrations of high-cost, low-income families. The spirit of such research relates to the possibility of redistribution of real income through the government sector; hence, one major use of financial distress studies is to identify candidates for special federal assistance or special federal concern. The work of Nathan and various of his colleagues[31] on identifying hardship cities was used to monitor the actual distribution of federal assistance, as was a Treasury study of distressed cities.[32] Other studies have been more directly concerned with developing formulas to allocate federal grant funds among governments.

Another important use to which such comparative studies might be put is in measuring the riskiness in investing in municipal bonds. Bond ratings are measures of relative creditworthiness and therefore require cross-sectional analyses of government fiscal and economic condition. Ironically, this use works toward penalizing distressed cities since they must be inherently greater credit risks.

Since any comparison of cities leads to the finding of outliers in terms of social, economic, and fiscal health, it is not surprising that all studies of this type find some cities that can be labeled distressed. It is not clear, however, that being an outlier in such a comparison is evidence of fiscal distress. In the more careful studies there is some sense to the comparative argument, but in others it is ludicrous.

Most lists of cities in trouble—whether objectively or subjectively derived—include older cities of the Northeast and Midwest and relatively few of the newer cities in the South and West, but there is still disagreement over the specific cities that ought to be included on the critical list. The debate centers on differences in the conceptual approaches and measurement techniques used and on the interpretation given the results. More basically, the problem is that one analyst's version of distress may differ markedly from another's. Some see age of housing and infrastructure and slow population growth to be *prima facie* evidence of greater need in the cities of the North, whereas others see lower incomes and the pressures of population growth to be evidence of greater need in the South. Such differences will not be resolved here, or in Congress, but it is useful to review the results of the distress studies in this light.

In the next sections we consider methodological issues and examine the implications of the various approaches used. We then turn to a comparison of the results and address the question of whether there is any substantial consensus about which cities are in trouble.

Methodological Issues

While there is no "right" way to do a comparative study of the financial health of cities, it is important to interpret the results in light of the questions asked and the research approach taken. The most important question is, "What is meant by financial distress or strain?" In other words, "What is a fiscally troubled city?" A proper set of indicators of the fiscal viability of a local government has several characteristics: it permits comparison with other cities, it is derived from analysis of both the past and the current situation as well as that projected for the future, and it reflects consideration of the economic and social structure of the local area as well as the financial condition of its governments. Most important, such a set of indicators should be based on an underlying theoretical model that enables evaluation of fiscal health with respect to clearly defined criteria. Though a number of the techniques commonly used address one or more of these issues in some fashion, none incorporate the full range of considerations suggested here. In particular, none of these studies explicitly consider projections, though all seem to contain, however implicitly, some conclusion about future prospects.[33]

Comparative Quantitative Analysis

The absence of a normative theory of public output has led economists to concentrate their attention on the more positive question of what determines municipal expenditure, revenue, and debt levels. From this concern has grown a series of studies which attempt to find a statistical relationship between fiscal outcomes and the social, economic, and demographic characteristics of the community.[34]

The cross-sectional fiscal distress studies are a second cousin of the traditional expenditure determinants literature. They make some assumption, often implicit, about the determinants of high or rising expenditure requirements and low or falling revenue yields, e.g., large concentrations of poor families, low per capita incomes, and declining populations. The analysis then involves determining outliers in terms of each of these indicators and somehow combining these to derive an overall measure of fiscal strain or distress. The answer one gets, however, depends on the sample of cities chosen for the comparison, the variables included in the analysis, the method used to estimate an index, and the cutoff index selected for distress.[35]

The samples studied have varied widely depending on the purposes of the analysis. In analyzing relative economic strength of urban areas, Nathan and Adams[36] studied standard metropolitan statistical areas (SMSAs) with populations over 500000 and Nathan and Fossett[37] analyzed the fifty-five largest cities. Bradbury, Downs, and Small studied 153 cities and 121 SMSAs.[38] In research pointed more to analyzing fiscal stress, Clark *et al.* have been studying a sample of fifty-seven cities of varying sizes[39] while Touche-Ross analyzed a nonrandom sample of sixty-six cities.[40] The Institute for the Future studied a random sample of forty cities with populations over 100000 and 100 cities with populations between 25000 and 100000.[41] The most comprehensive study, carried out by HUD, included all United States cities with populations above 50000.[42] Since distress in each of these studies is measured by a deviation from some sample average, the findings are not strictly comparable; i.e., the results obtained depend in part on the sample studied. For example, the mean values, the variances, and therefore the findings of the Touche-Ross study might have been altered drastically if Pueblo, Colorado; Daly City, California; and St. Petersburg, Florida, which were included in their sample, had been replaced by New York City, Detroit, and Newark, cities not included in their sample.

Another comparability problem relates to the choice of variables included to measure hardship or distress. Particularly important is whether the indicators are of current condition (e.g., per capita income) or of changes in financial condition (percent increase in per capita income). For example, an index can show more distress in the older northeastern cities if it begins by assuming that age of housing is an important indicator of distress. A Congressional Budget Office (CBO) survey of these studies described a wide variation in the variable choices made and hence a substantial comparability problem.[43]

There is not much difference among studies in the methods used to calculate the index. Most studies have standardized each variable by expressing it as a percent of the mean or the minimum value and then derived the index as a mean of the standardized variables.[44] After ranking cities by these indexes, there remains the problem of determining which are the outliers that will be labeled "distressed." The choice is arbitrary: some infer that it is the top (or bottom) two quintiles,[45] others take the lowest (or highest) one third,[46] and yet others define it in terms of some number of standard deviations above or below the mean.[47]

Despite these very great differences in approach, there is some consistency in the findings of these studies. The comparison of outliers in seven studies in Table 3-4 shows seventeen cities as distressed in more than one of these studies.[48] All except Washington, D.C., and Atlanta are located in the Northeast and industrial Midwest. The most comprehensive of the fiscal needs studies, the HUD analysis, resulted in a higher needs index for northeastern cities than for cities in any other region. The highest needs index found in that study was for northeastern cities with populations greater than 400 000.[49] Similarly, Nathan's hardship index is higher for northeastern cities than for any other region. Bradbury *et al.* find the greatest distress in the case of declining cities in declining SMSAs: "The most distressed and declining cities are familiar names: Atlanta, Boston, Cleveland, Dayton, Hartford, Philadelphia, Newark, Trenton."[50]

Some studies, more limited in their coverage, reach different conclusions. Kaplan, *et al.* have noted that, using the Nathan indicators and sample, New Orleans, Louisville, Miami, and Atlanta can rank "worse" than New York, Boston, and Philadelphia under various definitions of distress.[51] Still, the thirteen large southern cities in their comparison showed an average "urban conditions index" that was more than three times "better" than that of the five northeastern cities in their comparison. Clark *et al.* have studied a smaller sample of fifty-seven cities with a broader population range. His findings are not inconsistent with the findings that the most distressed cities are in the Northeast.[52] The Touche-Ross study, though flawed in many ways, also reaches the conclusion that "the most important financially pressed cities are in the industrially mature

Northeast."[53] Bradbury *et al.* compute an average score of −1.04 for northeastern and midwestern cities, 0.48 for southern cities, and 0.87 for western cities on a scale from -5 (most distressed) to +5 (least distressed).[54]

The comparative approach may define a city's well-being not only in terms of other cities but also in terms of its own suburbs. Kasarda has made the case that city fiscal problems are closely tied to an employment sorting-out process where the city has been giving up blue collar and semiskilled jobs in exchange for fewer white collar jobs, but has not had a net in-migration of middle- and upper-income residents.[55] The resulting effect on the city fisc is more services for commuters, a dwindling tax base, and a higher-cost, lower-resource-base resident population.

Sacks has given an empirical dimension to the disparities issue by tracking city-suburb disparities for a number of years. He has found a consistently greater fiscal, social, and economic disparity in the Northeast and Midwest than in the South and West.[56] His most recent estimates show a continuation of this pattern of disparity for the 1970–77 period.[57] Cities in the Northeast continue to lose jobs, both in the absolute and relative to their suburbs, and many of those in the Midwest are losing relative to their suburbs. Nearly all southern and western cities in Sacks's sample were experiencing employment growth. If anything, city-suburb disparities in employment have been accelerating and the situation has grown relatively worse in the older northeastern and midwestern cities. Nathan and Fossett reach the same conclusion in their study of the changing social and economic conditions of cities.[58]

Nathan and Adams have considered these disparities more systematically in developing an index of intercity hardship.[59] They compare city-suburb disparities in unemployment, age distribution of the population, education level, income level, crowded housing, and poverty. The results are not different from those cited above; indeed, the older industrial cities compare even less favorably when city-suburb disparities are considered.

One should resist jumping too quickly to the conclusion that the consensus in these results allows us to clearly identify

Table 3-4. Comparisons of Distressed Cities in Selected Studies

City	Nathan and Adams: Top Two Deciles	Nathan and Fossett: Top Two Deciles	Cucitti: High Social, Economic, or Fiscal Need	Institute for the Future: Five Cities Scoring Highest Fiscal Need	HUD: Five Cities Scoring Highest on Needs Index	Dearborn: Cumulative Budget Deficits[a]	Bradbury et al.: City Distress Ranking of −4 or −5	Standard and Poor's Bond Rating
Newark	X	X	X	X			X	BBB
Cleveland	X	X	X				X	BBB
Hartford	X						X	AA
Baltimore	X		X	X				A
Chicago	X		X			X		A−
St. Louis	X	X	X	X			X	A−
Atlanta	X						X	AA
Rochester	X	X						NR
Gary	X		X					AAA[b]
Dayton	X						X	AA−
New York		X	X		X	X		BBB
Buffalo		X	X					BBB
Pittsburgh		X	X			X		A
Boston		X	X		X	X	X	BBB+
Detroit		X	X	X				BB
Philadelphia		X					X	BBB+
Minneapolis					X			AAA
Washington, D.C.			X					NR[c]

58

City						Bond rating
Jersey City	X	X				BBB+
Birmingham	X					AA
Miami	X					A
New Orleans	X		X			A+
Atlantic City[d]				X		AA
Cambridge, Mass.				X		BB+
Milwaukee		X		X		AA+
Columbus		X				AA
Seattle						AA
Tampa	X					NR[c]
Camden					X	NR[c]
Houston			X			AAA
San Antonio			X			AA
San Francisco			X			AA

[a] Three-year (1976–78) total excess of expenditures over revenues.
[b] Rating due to bond insurance.
[c] Not rated.
[d] Not included in study.

Sources: Richard Nathan and Charles Adams, "Understanding Central City Hardship," *Political Science Quarterly* 91(1):47 (1976). Nathan and James Fossett, "Urban Conditions: The Future of the Federal Role," *Proceedings of the National Tax Association*, 1978. Gregory Schnied, Hubert Lipinsky, and Michael Palmer, *An Alternative Approach to General Revenue Sharing: A Needs Based Allocation Formula*, Washington, D.C.: Institute for the Future, 1975. Harold Bunce, *An Evaluation of the Community Development Block Formula*, Washington, D.C.: U.S. Department of Housing and Urban Development, 1976. Philip Dearborn, *The Financial Health of Major U.S. Cities in 1978*. Standard and Poor's, *Bond Guide*, July 1982. Katherine L. Bradbury, Anthony Downs, and Kenneth A. Small, *Urban Decline and the Future of American Cities*, Washington, D.C.: Brookings Institution, 1982, Chapter 3. Subcommittee on the City of the House Committee on Banking, Finance, and Urban Affairs, *City Need and the Responsiveness of Federal Grants Programs* (Washington, D.C.: GPO, 1978).

distressed local governments and formulate remedial public policy. There are strong arguments that these measures are biased against certain types of cities with certain types of fiscal problems. Southern and western cities, which have been able to expand boundaries through annexation and consolidation, may seem less distressed because their suburbs are included in comparisons whereas the suburbs of northern cities are not.[60] For this reason, results from comparisons of cities are an incorrect basis for distributing federal assistance because those cities that have done something about their boundary problems would be penalized. The comparison of taxable capacity and population characteristics should be made among metropolitan areas. This would reduce the interregional disparity in economic well-being and expenditure needs; i.e., it would make the distressed cities of the Northeast look less distressed—relative to the rest of the country—than they do now. On a policy level, this would imply that some part of suburban wealth should be reallocated to central cities as a prerequisite to more federal help.

Even this adjustment, however, would leave the slower growing northern urban areas high on the distressed list, and the measure would still take a northern view of distress: that age is a proxy for need, that growth creates fewer problems than decline, and that the rate of income growth is more important than the level of income. The northern view is not totally incorrect, but it is flawed and self-serving. The age of housing is not a good proxy for quality; old housing is not always worse housing and there are not good statistics on the quality of housing. Likewise, declining population is not necessarily bad. It may lessen fiscal pressures on some jurisdictions; e.g., fewer school-aged children may provide some breathing space for property tax financing of education. Growth, on the other hand, may be a mixed fiscal blessing because of pressures to expand infrastructure and finance new services.[61]

An argument against the traditional measures of city distress is that there are pockets of poverty in the Houstons and Jacksonvilles that are every bit as bad as those in the North, and where wage rates and public service levels are at great disparity with the rest of the city, but these disparities are hidden because southern city boundaries often include their suburbs.

Once comparison among *areas* (rather than cities) is made, this bias is removed. The remaining disparities within the area represent local choices about how to distribute public services, whether to have labor unions, and so forth. The results of these choices may well be distressing, but they should not be taken into account in measuring distress.

What all of this amounts to is a conclusion that northern cities are relatively less distressed than these studies have shown. They may still be worse off and most in need of federal assistance during a transition period when they are losing jobs and population, but we have not yet captured this greater need in comparative measures of fiscal distress.

Case Studies

Case studies of local government fiscal viability offer an alternative approach to measuring fiscal distress. They may be detailed and take into account the factors important to a specific city, and they may consider both short-term cash flow and long-term economic factors.[62] The shortcoming of the case study approach is that it does not easily provide a comparative dimension. For example, we may be able to determine that Buffalo faces a revenue shortfall for the next three years, but we do not know if it will be worse than Scranton's. Comparative case studies[63] would seem to be the intuitive answer to this dilemma, but a closer look suggests the very great problems with carrying out comparative case studies.

A common framework and a clearly delineated model are easily enough formulated, but there are major problems with estimating such a model. The first is that there are substantial data incomparabilities among cities, e.g., financial reports are not uniform and their comparison can be a difficult and tedious job. Second, every city is in some ways unique and any general model would have to be adapted to particular circumstances. Third, and perhaps most important, is the high cost of good comparative case study work.

There can be little question but that a case study approach is necessary to accurately evaluate and project the behavior of the local government fisc. The problem is that most case studies lack a well-defined and comparable model. A notable exception is the work of Dearborn, who analyzes the financial reports of the thirty largest cities on an annual basis.[64] His analysis is pointed to the short-term financial position of cities—their general fund revenue and expenditure shortfalls and their liquidity. Looking at the balance between revenues and expenditures between 1976 and 1978 as an indicator of fiscal health, he points out that "nineteen cities had an imbalance in at least one of the three most recent years, and that over the three years, nine cities, including several considered relatively strong financially, had cumulative expenditures in excess of revenues."[65] His list of cities in financial trouble, or close to the edge, includes some of those identified in the analyses discussed above but also includes some cities in the growing states (Table 3-4).

Municipal Credit Analysis

Events of recent years have given rise to mounting concern with the ability of particular jurisdictions to service existing debt and to meet other fixed obligations. This concern has led rating agencies, banks and underwriters to attempt to measure and compare governments according to their probability of default. Through the 1960s this was essentially an academic exercise. There had been little experience with actual default since the Great Depression, and an analyst could but use some combination of *a priori* reasoning and judgment to identify governments that were most default prone. The 1974–75 recession and its aftermath changed all that. The ability of the bond rating agencies and others in the municipals market to sort out the good credits from the bad received its first significant test in several decades. Though some would argue that it was found wanting,[66] fairness would require laying the blame on the failure of policy analysts of all colors to develop acceptable measures of fiscal stress and on governments for not providing adequate data for such purposes. Important strides have been made, but credit analysis is not yet a fully proven analytic method for identifying fiscal distress.

   The bond rating process is a comparative analysis[67] but requires much more analyst judgment than do the statistical studies described above. This is in part because many of the necessary comparative data (e.g., measures of overlapping debt) are not available on a comparable and timely basis, and careful scrutiny of individual financial reports is required. The general approach, however, is much the same as in the statistical studies. Governments are compared and ranked by various measures, and outliers are identified. Instead of being labeled "distressed" as in a scholarly study, they are given a lower credit grade and face a higher borrowing cost in the market. Ironically, when a definitive distress measure is developed, it will likely be used by the federal government to reward distressed governments with larger grants and by the rating agencies to penalize them with higher interest costs.[68]

Until very recently, the analytic techniques used by the major rating agencies and other municipal analysts had not been fully articulated.[69] Historical analyses suggested that the most important determinant of credit rating differences was the level of debt burden relative to taxable capacity.[70] The more recent view seems considerably more enlightened. For example, Standard & Poor's notes in its *Rating Guide* that "we consider an issuer's economic base the most critical element in the determination of a municipal bond rating."[71] Indeed, of the thirty-three cities on distressed lists reported in Table 3-4, Standard & Poor's rates two BB, seven BBB, six A, eight AA, two AAA and does not rate three. The nine cities rated BBB or below are common to more than one of the lists of cities in trouble. It is noteworthy that all nine cities are in the declining Northeast and Midwest.

It is interesting to note that the debt burden variable, which is still a major consideration in determining credit risk, does not generally lead to the conclusion that northeastern cities are any more troubled than other cities. Indeed, southern and midwestern cities show the highest levels of debt outstanding relative to general revenues.[72] Even in the case of New York City, debt burden does not appear to be the major factor distinguishing New York from other cities. Using time series of various indicators of debt burden, Aronson and King have argued that, although the New York City fiscal crisis was predictable, "when these same ratios and their standard deviations are calculated for the aggregate of state and local governments excluding New York State and its local governmental units, no dangerous trends are apparent."[73] Aronson and Marsden, in a study of 1977 data, were able to predict the distribution of cities among Moody's five credit rating categories with 83 percent accuracy and found "that the single variable with the most predictive power is the percent of the city's population that is black."[74]

THE RECENT FISCAL PERFORMANCE OF LARGE CITIES

Comparative analysis always produces outliers that may be labeled distressed. Notwithstanding the debate about which are the "proper" variables in such comparisons, it is a fact that some cities are fiscally better off than others and that some are at the edge of financial insolvency. A third approach to evaluating fiscal health is to examine the financial condition and current performance of state and local governments. Can one find reasons for optimism in the recent taxing, spending, and borrowing decisions of state and local governments?

Looking out from 1975, nearly any observer of municipal finances would have offered a gloomy prognosis. New York was by no means the only city facing deep-seated economic problems and a taxable capacity growth too slow to accommodate the growth in expenditure requirements. Various analysts saw a real possibility for default in Buffalo, Detroit, Boston, Yonkers, Cleveland, and even New York State.

In fact, however, there have been relatively few cases of financial collapse since 1975. Cleveland, Wayne County (Detroit), and the Chicago schools are notable exceptions, but there have not been many more New Yorks. Some have seen this absence of crisis as a sign of renewed fiscal and economic health in cities,[75] and others are more convinced that it reflects a postponement of crises yet to come.[76] Which is the correct view? Have overly pessimistic analysts overstated the case? After all, the central city infrastructure, which is obsolete and crumbling, has not yet crumbled, ten more years of woefully deficient central city services have not produced more urban ghetto riots, "underpaid" public employees have not brought city operations to a standstill with a series of major strikes, public employee layoffs have been accomplished without noticeably severe declines in public services, and city governments have indeed been able to pay their bills. In light of this, is there still a fiscal crisis? If one is to argue a crisis outlook for United States cities, then she must explain the absence of severe financial distress since 1975.

There are reasonable explanations. New York City's financial collapse in 1975 changed nearly everyone's view of urban fiscal problems. The focus of interest shifted from a concern with social problems and inadequate public services in inner cities to a preoccupation with financial strength and susceptibility to default. Public employee unions, local politicians and bureaucrats, federal and state government policy makers, the financial community, and even citizen groups seem to accept the new priority. More than any other single factor, this change in public attitude may be responsible for maintaining the financial solvency of northeastern cities. In effect, it made possible the kinds of sacrifices from public employees and public service beneficiaries that were necessary.

Beyond this change in attitude, one might offer three hypotheses to explain why there have been no more New Yorks:

The improving economy thesis. The post-1975 economic recovery benefited even distressed cities, the 1981–83 recession has not harmed them as disproportionately as did the 1975 recession, a revitalization of central cities is occurring, and the demographic makeup of cities is changing in a way that lessens the pressure for increased public expenditures.

The increasing resources thesis. Federal and state grants were substantial enough to prop up the slow growth in state and local taxes in the immediate aftermath of the 1975 recession. Thereafter, inflation also bid up local tax revenues. The result was that resources were adequate to cover expenditure requirements.

The deferral and cutbacks thesis. Because of the New York City scare, city governments were able to reduce employment rolls, dramatically slow the rate of increase in public employee wage rates, cut public service levels, and defer maintenance and additions to the capital stock.

As will be shown below, the evidence bears out some parts of each of these explanations of city financial health since 1975. The key question then is whether these favorable events will continue to buoy up the finances of distressed cities in the 1980s.

The Improving Economy Thesis

A major factor that brought some central cities and even one state government to the brink of financial disaster in 1975 was the decline in their economic base. The job and income loss shrunk available revenues, and increased unemployment pressured social service expenditures. Some have hypothesized that the situation has improved since 1975, that even distressed city economies have "come back," thereby holding up revenue growth.

While the post-1975 recovery helped state and local governments everywhere, some regions of the country benefited far more than others. The northern tier of states experienced a slower rate of income and employment growth than the southern tier and a corresponding slower rate of growth in aggregate state and local government revenues. Everyone got a little well during the recovery, but some regions got a lot better than others. A similar picture emerges when the economic and fiscal performance of large cities is examined. Even with the strong recovery, many central cities have not regained their former level of economic activity as rapidly as have suburban areas, and cities in the Northeast and industrial Midwest recovered from the 1975 recession more slowly than cities in other parts of the country.

There are a number of *a priori* reasons why core areas do not share equally in national growth during periods of recovery. During a recession, firms tend to reduce activities relatively more where operating costs are highest and where physical plant is oldest (i.e., in declining regions generally and in central cities specifically). The process does not reverse itself during the recovery. Plant and employment expansions tend to occur where comparative costs are lowest—in the growing regions, suburbs, and nonmetropolitan areas. The same pattern appears true with respect to the birth and death of firms.[77] Firms die as rapidly in suburbs as in cities during recession, but new firms open more rapidly in suburbs during recovery. As a result, one would expect central city areas to suffer greater employment losses during a recession and make fewer employment gains during a recovery than suburban areas. The problem of central city failure to recover is exacerbated by a location in the Northeast or industrial Midwest, where plant is oldest, energy is more costly, and labor costs and taxes tend to be high.

The available evidence would seem to bear out a hypothesis that core areas are hit hardest by recession and gain least in recovery. An Oak Ridge Laboratory study estimated that, on average, only core counties lost employment during the 1969–71 recession, and that core counties recovered during 1971–72 at less than one-half the rate of other counties.[78] A similar analysis is not available for the 1975 recession, but we have constructed a sample of the ten largest city-counties and examined the pattern of private sector employment growth.[79] The results of this analysis (Table 3-5) show that these large core counties were, on average, harder hit by the 1975 recession than was the rest of the nation and that they recovered more slowly. There are not yet available data to fully understand the impact of the 1981–83 recession, but the preliminary evidence suggests that industrial areas in the midwest have been especially hard hit.

The point here is that both theory and data tell us that core counties in the declining region do not share proportionately in national growth. However, it is true that an improved national economic performance during 1975–79 was a major factor in helping to forestall more serious financial problems. It seems reasonable to expect a continuation of this pattern in the 1980s and to look for an even more cautious fiscal behavior by core area governments. Perhaps an even more serious expectation is for central areas to continue losing economic ground to their suburbs. On the latter point, Sacks's estimates for city employment (by place of employment) paint a dismal picture. Of fifteen large northeastern cities that he has studied, four-

Table 3-5. Employment Growth in Ten Metropolitan Central Cities, 1965–77[a]

City/County				Percent Change				
	1965–72	1972–73	1973–74	1974–75	1975–76	1976–77	1977–78	1978–79	1979–80
Baltimore	4.0	1.7	-9.5	-6.7	-3.8	-1.2	2.2	1.8	0.8
Denver	37.4	8.2	-7.4	-4.8	2.3	2.8	12.2	6.4	2.6
Indianapolis (Marion County)	15.9	6.4	2.1	-4.8	3.7	2.9	5.6	5.7	-2.7
Jacksonville (Duval County)	37.6	8.0	5.8	-6.4	-0.9	-1.5	9.5	4.0	1.4
Nashville (Davidson County)	32.3	8.1	4.4	-4.4	4.2	3.8	8.6	6.0	-2.1
New Orleans	10.8	2.0	-10.2	-4.0	1.2	1.0	9.1	4.2	-1.9
New York City[b]	0.2	-3.0	-1.4	-6.2	-1.0	-2.7	3.1	4.3	-0.6
Philadelphia	-0.6	1.0	-3.2	-8.0	-1.3	-4.4	3.8	2.5	-2.8
St. Louis	-1.9	1.7	-7.4	-11.5	-0.2	-3.9	4.8	2.5	-4.8
San Francisco	10.3	2.2	15.2	-2.8	0.4	-5.3	10.9	2.3	2.3
United States	21.5	7.0	2.3	-4.7	3.4	3.9	8.1	7.3	-0.8

[a] Includes only covered employment.
[b] Includes New York, Bronx, Queens, Kings, and Richmond counties.
Source: U.S. Bureau of the Census, *County Business Patterns*, Washington, D.C.: Government Printing Office, various years.

teen had employment declines between 1970 and 1977. This may be compared with eight of twenty midwestern cities, twelve of twenty-five southern cities, and four of twenty western cities.[80]

The Increasing Resources Thesis

State and local government budgetary position improved markedly during the post-1975 recovery. Tax revenues increased in real terms between 1975 and 1977 while expenditures were held at austerity levels. As the recovery continued, the real expenditure reductions continued but real revenue growth began to decline. The quite large real reductions in state and local government taxes occurring at the end of the decade reflect a combination of (a) the drawing down of these "gains" in the form of reduced tax rates (b) the first effects of a slowdown in the national economy, and (c) the limitation movement. One can conclude from these trends that the combined effects of economic recovery and inflation (which stimulated local revenue growth) and the New York City scare (which kept expenditure budgets lean) all worked to the benefit of local government fiscal health after 1975.

Another important reason for the strong financial performance of large central cities after 1975 was the massive influx of direct federal aid. Coming on top of expenditure cutbacks, it gave many of the hardest-pressed local governments some fiscal breathing room. By 1978, direct federal grants in some cities accounted for one third to one half as much of the financing of total current expenditures as did revenues raised from own sources (Table 3-6). Much of this increase in direct aid was the Carter Administration's Economic Stimulus Package, the key elements of which were Antirecession Fiscal Assistance, Local Public Works, and Public Service Employment (CETA).

Can one count on a continuation of this pattern? The answer is probably no. The slowdown in federal aid to state and local governments—which began with Carter and has been warmly embraced by Reagan—will likely continue into the 1980s. The Economic Stimulus Package was an early casualty—reduced from more than $9 billion in fiscal 1979 to less than

Table 3-6. Direct Federal Aid as a Percent of Own-Source General Revenue for Selected Cities in FY, 1957–81

City	FY					Per Capita Federal Aid		
	1957	1967	1976	1978	1981	1976	1978	1981
St. Louis	0.6%	1.0%	23.6%	34.0%	40.6%	$ 86	$146	$239
Newark	0.2	1.7	11.4	30.4	17.9	47	137	67
Buffalo	1.3	2.1	55.6	77.5	54.6	163	259	218
Cleveland	2.0	8.3	22.8	57.9	25.3	65	165	121
Boston	a	10.0	31.5	20.9	14.5	204	173	160
unweighted average	0.8	4.6	29.0	44.1	30.6	113	176	161
Baltimore	1.7	3.8	38.9	53.7	45.1	167	264	279
Philadelphia	0.4	8.8	37.7	29.7	16.1	129	146	103
Detroit	1.3	13.1	50.2	44.2	85.6	161	170	379
Chicago	1.4	10.9	19.2b	46.7	44.8	47	126	157
Atlanta	4.3	2.0	15.1	19.7	20.7	52	80	133
unweighted average	1.8	7.7	32.2	38.8	42.4	111	157	210
Denver	0.6	1.2	21.2	26.2	16.8	90	142	130
Los Angeles	0.7	0.7	19.3	31.2	21.1	54	110	90
Dallas	0.0	a	20.0	13.2	15.5	51	41	59
Houston	0.2	3.1	19.4	15.3	16.9	44	40	67
Phoenix	1.1	10.6	35.0	51.9	33.6	57	111	101
unweighted average	0.5	3.1	23.0	27.6	20.8	61	89	90
Unweighted average of 15 cities	1.1	5.2	28.1	36.8	31.3	95	141	154

a Less than 0.5 percent.

b Percentage based on federal aid excluding general revenue sharing. Funds withheld pending judicial determination.

Source: The 1957, 1967, and 1976 estimates are ACIR staff computations based on U.S. Bureau of the Census, *City Government Finances in 1957, 1967 and 1976.* Estimated city own-source general revenue for 1978 based on annual average increase between 1971 and 1976. Direct federal grants to each city for fiscal 1978 based on (a) ACIR staff estimates of federal stimulus programs for 1978 and (b) Richard Nathan's estimates for all other federal aid in fiscal 1978 as set forth in his testimony before the Joint Economic Committee on July 28, 1977. (As reported in *Intergovernmental Perspective,* Winter 1976.) Computations for 1978 and 1981 were made by the author from *City Government Finances in 1978 and 1981.*

$3 billion in fiscal 1980. Already, many large cities have had to make painful adjustments to this withdrawal of federal aid, for example, the federal government "matched" every locally raised dollar in Newark with thirty cents in 1978 but with only eighteen cents in 1981 (Table 3-6). As for the longer sum, Peterson provides a startling extrapolation of where the Reagan administration's proposals will take the 1980 dependence on federal aid—25 percent of total state and local government expenditures. "If all the Administration's proposals were to come to fruition by 1991—a scant decade and a year later—the federal aid share in state and local budgets would be reduced to 3 to 4 percent."[81]

The outlook—for continued cutbacks in federal assistance—does not auger well for cities, particularly those that might be labeled distressed. They stand to lose in at least two ways. First, reductions in the flow of direct grants seriously compromise their revenue position. Second, reductions in the overall flow of grants to state and local governments will increase pressures on state government resources, which will in turn compromise their ability to finance services provided in urban areas. One result could be a reduction in real levels of state aid to local governments. In any case, the prospects are for fewer resources to flow to cities from higher level governments and certainly for less reliance on federal aid relative to all other revenue sources. The longer-term effect will be a slower growth in per capita real local government spending and likely an increasing reliance on state government financing.

The Deferrals and Cutbacks Thesis

The fiscal health of cities since 1975 may have been as much illusion as real, if they hid their fiscal deficits in lower public service levels and poorly maintained facilities. One might reasonably offer the following hypothesis: In the aftermath of the recession and with the New York City debacle still front page news, fiscal decision makers took a very conservative approach in formulating budgets. Public employment rolls were reduced either through layoffs or through attrition, expenditure increases for new services and pay raises were minimal, and capital maintenance and construction expenditures were deferred.

State and local governments may take discretionary action in three areas to slow the growth in public expenditures. They may (a) reduce the level of public employment, or slow its growth; (b) hold public employee compensation increases below the inflation rate; and (c) defer capital projects and/or maintenance. The issues here are whether such deferrals do explain some of the fiscal health of cities since 1975, and whether such deferrals can be continued into the 1980s.

Public Employment Growth.   As may be seen from Table 3-7, the rate of public employment increase has fluctuated since 1975 but has not returned to the growth rates of the 1969–74 period. Within the state and local government sector, state governments expanded public employment at the greater rate after 1975. This may reflect a stronger fiscal position of state governments in general, or it may simply show that public sector growth is occurring in the South, which is state-government dominated.

Among local governments, municipalities cut back the most, and among that group, large cities seem especially pressed. Public employment retrenchment appears to have been the rule rather than the exception among the nation's twenty largest cities. Between 1975 and 1977, there were absolute declines in city government employment in ten of the twenty largest cities and increases of less than 1 percent in three of the remaining ten (Table 3-8). Since 1977, sixteen large cities have reduced employment. These reductions may signal a cutback in services offered—to the extent that public service and public employment levels vary proportionately. At the same time, this may also be a salvation to city budgets; i.e., downward adjustments in employment may cushion the public employee wage increases that surely lie ahead.

Can these employment reductions be viewed as temporary measures that cannot be sustained? Will public service level reductions and the passage of time lead to a calling back of the lost employees of the late 1970s? The answer is probably not—for many governments—for a couple of reasons. First, voters seem unconvinced about the relationship between public service levels and public employment levels, as evidenced by the

Table 3-7. Comparisons of State and Local Government Fiscal Activity, 1969–81

Average Annual Percent Increase in	1969–74	1974–75	1975–76	1976–77	1977–78	1978–79	1979–80	1980–81
Real per capita total expenditures[a]								
State governments	4.6	7.1	9.2	-2.3	-2.0	-2.1	0.2	2.6
Local governments	3.6	4.8	5.0	-0.4	-0.3	-1.8	-2.4	0.6
Municipalities	3.9	4.7	4.9	-3.4	0.7	-3.9	-2.1	-0.5
Real per capita current expenditures								
State governments	5.7	8.5	5.1	3.4	4.5	-2.6	-0.1	2.7
Local governments	4.3	4.5	6.5	1.4	1.0	-2.2	-3.0	-0.3
Municipalities	4.7	3.8	5.6	0.1	1.2	-3.3	-3.4	-1.3
Real long-term debt outstanding								
State governments	4.4	0.3	9.7	4.5	6.2	-1.5	-3.5	0.3
Local governments	2.0	-4.3	0.9	3.2	0.3	-3.1	-2.3	-3.4
Municipalities	1.8	-4.3	5.3	1.2	4.1	-10.3	-3.2	-4.1
Employment								
State governments	4.0	3.4	2.0	3.7	2.2	3.6	1.1	-0.6
Local governments	3.8	2.2	0.7	3.8	0.9	1.5	0.9	-1.4
Municipalities	2.7	0.7	-1.6	2.9	-0.2	1.2	-1.2	-2.6
Real per employee compensation								
State governments	0.6	-2.5	1.1	0	-0.8	-3.8	-3.5	-0.6
Local governments	0.6	-1.8	0.3	-0.3	-3.1	-3.2	-3.7	-0.6
Municipalities	1.5	-2.4	0.9	-1.5	-2.1	-4.6	-3.5	2.0
Real per capita tax revenues								
State governments	4.4	-2.1	4.4	5.3	3.0	-2.1	-4.2	-0.9
Local governments	2.7	-1.6	3.3	3.0	-1.2	-10.9	-6.4	-0.5
Municipalities	2.0	-1.4	3.5	3.9	-1.8	-8.2	-5.1	-1.0

[a]Amounts deflated by the consumer price index.

Source: U.S. Department of Commerce, Bureau of the Census, *Governmental Finances in 1968–69, 1973–74, 1975–76, 1977–78, 1978–79, 1979–80, 1980–81;* U.S. Department of Commerce, Bureau of the Census, *Public Employment in 1980, 1981;* U.S. Department of Commerce, Bureau of the Census, *City Government Finances in 1968–69, 1973–74, 1974–75, 1975–76, 1976–77, 1977–78, 1978–79, 1979–80, 1980–81.*

73

Table 3—8. Average Annual Percent Change in Indicators of Financial Performance for Twenty Cities in 1975–81

	Current Expenditures		General Obligation Debt Outstanding		Employment		Payroll Per Employee		Taxes	
	1975–77	1977–81	1975–77	1977–81	1975–77	1977–81	1975–77	1977–81	1975–77	1977–81
Baltimore	7.1	0.1	0.2	9.2	-4.9	-2.2	-1.0	9.7	4.2	4.7
Boston	11.9	3.8	10.6	3.8	0.1	0.1	12.6	0.1	15.3	3.2
Cleveland	4.3	8.0	18.5	3.7	-7.6	-4.0	-1.9	5.3	3.0	12.9
Chicago	10.7	9.0	3.3	-2.0	-3.5	-1.7	5.8	6.7	4.9	4.9
Dallas	12.0	13.5	-1.4	7.7	2.5	-0.1	7.0	10.8	8.9	8.3
Detroit	5.2	12.3	-3.7	6.8	8.0	-3.9	12.8	14.1	7.0	2.3
Honolulu	19.1	1.6	7.8	4.5	7.3	-4.9	17.9	7.4	8.1	10.3
Houston	22.5	15.7	9.9	15.5	5.1	3.7	12.4	11.3	15.9	13.5
Indianapolis	13.4	8.9	2.8	2.4	-0.1	1.1	6.3	8.8	7.2	5.8
Los Angeles	8.8	9.5	8.0	1.6	-1.6	-2.8	2.3	10.9	10.9	6.4
Memphis	11.9	8.7	20.3	8.5	-13.8	-3.8	-6.1	9.5	8.9	8.7
Milwaukee	9.0	8.3	3.2	9.0	-1.9	-1.1	5.1	5.9	2.0	-1.1
New Orleans	12.2	13.4	-0.4	18.0	9.0	-6.6	26.0	8.1	7.3	13.1
New York	4.5	3.1	16.8	-8.9	-5.5	1.2	-0.7	7.5	11.5	5.4
Philadelphia	8.3	8.3	12.3	6.4	-0.3	-2.9	4.9	6.9	20.3	6.6
Phoenix	11.8	13.0	11.8	8.1	8.4	-0.1	15.2	10.3	12.6	9.6
San Antonio	19.6	10.9	25.6	20.3	1.7	-3.2	8.6	6.3	9.5	8.5
San Diego	8.5	10.3	-4.2	-2.0	1.4	-1.9	6.7	8.5	14.4	8.2
San Francisco	5.1	6.2	18.8	10.9	0.3	-1.1	3.2	10.9	15.6	1.2
Washington, D.C.	8.9	6.4	17.0	4.9	0.8	-3.8	7.1	8.1	16.6	11.2

Source: U.S. Department of Commerce, Bureau of Census, *City Government Finances in 1974–75, 1976–77, 1980–81; City Employment in 1975; 1977, 1981.*

74

limitation movement. Second, public employment levels have not fallen much faster than population levels, at least in cities and in some declining states.

Employee Compensation Growth.   There clearly were public employee compensation deferrals in the aftermath of the 1975 recession. There were no real increases at any level of state or local government between 1976 and 1980 (Table 3-7). The situation is somewhat different for the largest cities. The comparison in Table 3-8 shows that payroll per employee grew at or above the inflation rate for many of the largest cities during the 1975–77 period.[82] Since 1977, few of these cities—and none in the declining regions—have granted salary increases that approach the 1977–81 CPI average increase of nearly 11 percent.

Other evidence for compensation increases for the entire state and local government sector suggests a pattern of deferral relative to private sector wages and inflation.[83] Wage increases in the public sector have lagged behind those in the private sector since 1974 (Table 3-9). Moreover, average state and local government salaries have kept pace with the CPI in only two years since 1973. State and local government employee wages had caught up with private sector wages before the 1975 recession, but by the end of the decade they were falling behind again.

The picture is reversed for supplements to wages and salaries. State and local government employees have enjoyed increases well above those in the private sector and above the rate of inflation since 1973 (Table 3-10). Since a large portion of supplements is retirement cost, this may also constitute a form of deferral from the point of view of the current city budget.

The data would seem to make it clear that public employees played a major role in maintaining the financial solvency of state and local governments since 1975. The question for the 1980s is whether this practice can continue, i.e., will public employees continue to agree to no real increments and an increasing disparity with private sector wages. Again, the answer is likely negative. As the memory of the financial solvency issues of the late seventies fades, and as the unemployment rate falls, the

Table 3-9. Average Annual Wages and Salaries per Full Time
Equivalent Employee by Industry, 1962–81

Year[a]	All Industry	Private Industry	Federal Civilian	State and Local Government
1962	$ 5,162	$ 5,203	$ 6,644	$ 5,017
1972	8,760	8,588	12,679	8,916
1973	9,290	9,104	13,497	9,505
1974	9,991	9,830	14,112	10,063
1975	10,835	10,673	15,194	10,865
1976	11,608	11,451	16,269	11,639
1977	12,403	12,256	17,501	12,397
1978	13,302	13,184	18,946	13,065
1979	14,399	14,334	19,936	13,923
1980	15,790	15,748	21,247	15,172
1981	17,221	17,173	23,049	16,485
Average Annual Growth Rate (%)				
1962–72	5.4	5.1	6.7	5.9
1972–73	6.1	6.0	6.5	6.6
1973–74	7.5	8.0	4.6	5.9
1974–75	8.4	8.6	7.7	7.8
1975–76	7.1	7.3	7.1	7.1
1976–77	6.8	7.0	7.6	6.5
1977–78	7.2	7.6	8.2	5.4
1978–79	8.2	8.7	5.2	6.6
1979–80	9.7	9.9	6.6	9.0
1980–81	9.1	9.0	8.5	8.6
Average Growth per 1% Increase in CPI (%)				
1962–72	1.6	1.5	2.0	1.8
1972–73	0.98	0.97	1.05	1.06
1973–74	0.68	0.73	0.42	0.54
1974–75	0.92	0.95	0.85	0.86
1975–76	1.22	1.26	1.23	1.22
1976–77	1.08	1.11	1.21	1.03
1977–78	0.93	1.00	1.06	0.71
1978–79	0.71	0.76	0.45	0.57
1979–80	0.72	0.73	0.49	0.67
1980–81	0.89	0.88	0.83	0.84

[a] Calendar years.
Sources: U.S. Department of Commerce, Bureau of Economic Analysis, *The National Income and Product Accounts of the United States, 1929–74*, Tables 6.6 and 6.9; *National Income and Product Accounts, 1976–79*, July 1981, Tables 6.5B to 6.9B; and *Survey of Current Business*, July 1982, Table 6.9B.

call for a new public employee wage "catch-up" will reappear.
A reasonable hypothesis is that the wage rate concessions made
by public employees in the late 1970s and early 1980s were
really deferrals and sooner or later will have to be paid.

Table 3-10. Average Annual Supplements to Wages and Salaries per Full Time Equivalent Employee by Industry, 1962–81

Year[a]	All Industry	Private Industry	Federal Civilian	State and Local Government
1962	$ 469	$ 491	$ 554	$ 464
1972	1,125	1,151	1,497	1,110
1973	1,298	1,331	1,689	1,248
1974	1,460	1,485	2,007	1,437
1975	1,683	1,706	2,440	1,656
1976	1,910	1,917	2,811	1,960
1977	2,131	2,140	3,088	2,200
1978	2,339	2,351	3,296	2,419
1979	2,568	2,571	3,590	2,706
1980	2,824	2,824	3,945	3,003
1981	3,154	3,131	4,570	3,464
Average Annual Growth Rate (%)				
1962–72	9.1	8.9	10.5	8.7
1972–73	15.5	15.6	12.8	12.4
1973–74	12.5	11.6	18.8	15.1
1974–75	15.3	14.9	21.6	15.2
1975–76	13.5	12.4	15.2	18.4
1976–77	11.6	11.6	9.9	12.2
1977–78	9.8	9.9	6.7	10.0
1978–79	9.8	9.4	8.9	11.9
1979–80	10.0	9.8	9.9	11.0
1980–81	11.7	10.9	15.8	15.3
Average Growth per 1% Increase in CPI (%)				
1962–72	2.8	2.8	3.2	3.0
1972–73	2.5	2.5	2.1	2.0
1973–74	1.1	1.1	1.7	1.4
1974–75	1.7	1.6	2.4	1.7
1975–76	2.3	2.1	2.6	3.2
1976–77	1.8	1.8	1.6	1.9
1977–78	1.3	1.3	0.9	1.3
1978–79	0.9	0.8	0.8	1.0
1979–80	0.7	0.7	0.7	0.8
1980–81	1.1	1.1	1.5	1.5

[a] Calendar years.

Source: U.S. Department of Commerce, Office of Business Economics, *The National Income and Product Accounts of the United States, 1929–74*, Tables 6.4 and 6.7, *National Income and Product Accounts, 1976–79*, July 1981, Tables 6.5B to 6.9B; and *Survey of Current Business*, July 1982, Tables 6.5B–6.9B.

Deferred Capital Investment.   A politically convenient and administratively expedient way to pare expenditure programs is to postpone capital project investments or to defer maintenance on the existing capital stock. Capital spending cutbacks require no bargaining with unions and (sometimes) no major hassle with public interest groups and can be carried out quickly and without major layoffs. Hence, when the budget situation becomes tight and cutbacks are necessary, capital project postponement usually stands somewhere higher in the pecking order than employee layoffs and lower wage rate increases. During the last decade, with inflation driving up public sector costs and creating uncertainties about future revenue growth, the budget position and outlook were tight enough to prompt such deferrals. Peterson, *et al.*, report this to be exactly the Boston response to the appearance of serious revenue shortfalls in the 1970s[84] and Oakland's response to Proposition 13.[85]

In fact, capital expenditures of state and local governments have declined in real terms and as a share of the total budget. Peterson reported that gross capital investment fell from 27 percent of total state and local spending in 1965 to a low of 14 percent in 1977.[86] As might be expected from this pattern, there were real declines in state and local government debt outstanding through the late 1970s (Table 3-7).

While some of this decline might be attributed to the completion of the interstate highway system and to higher interest costs, much of it appears to be due to the postponement of capital project investments and the deferral of maintenance and renovation. Such deferrals have made the financial position of state and local governments appear stronger than it is. What is the meaning of an annual budget surplus where necessary capital expenditures have been put off? We can not answer this question other than by relying on impressionistic evidence about the inadequacies of the existing capital stock.

Unfortunately, few state or local governments do any kind of accounting that would enable a tracking of the quality of the local infrastructure, and therefore serious capital obsolescence problems are not easily identified. Nevertheless, some idea of the magnitude of the problem might be gained from a series of recent case studies. Two studies of the condition of the New York City infrastructure indicate a substantial deficit, one that is far beyond the city's financial capacity.[87] The city has established a ten-year, $12 billion capital improvement program, but even this would appear modest in that it is based on assumptions that the city will reenter the securities market on a "regular" basis after 1982, that current levels of federal capital aid will continue during the decade, and that costs will escalate at no more than 5 percent per year. The real price tag on New York City's capital improvement plan is likely to be far larger than the $12 billion. Infrastructure deficits of this size do not appear overnight, but there seems little question that deferrals during the 1970s accentuated the problem. Grossman points out the extent to which capital investment and maintenance expenditures were cut in the aftermath of the fiscal crisis; between 1974 and 1978, New York City's annual capital appropriations fell by nearly 70 percent.[88]

The Urban Institute studies of Cleveland,[89] Cincinnati,[90] Dallas,[91] Oakland[92] and Boston[93] provide some further but mixed evidence on the deferral question. Cleveland certainly fits the pattern with its badly deteriorated capital stock and declining real capital spending since 1968. The estimated backlog in needed basic improvements to its infrastructure system is $700 million,[94] nearly twice the level of total current expenditures. As in the case of New York City, Cleveland's infrastructure problems have been long in the making but have been helped along by recent deferrals. During the 1972–77 fiscal crisis period for the city, maintenance expenditures grew by 89 percent, as compared with 151 percent for total current expenditures and 162 percent for total spending.[95]

Dallas, Cincinnati and Oakland provide stories of more success with maintaining capital stock. Dallas is fiscally strong, with a low tax rate and the ability to finance capital projects with a substantially greater federal assistance share. There was a slowdown in real capital spending after the recession, but it could be accommodated because the capital stock was new. Cincinnati and Oakland present the opposite picture: old, declining cities that have managed capital assets carefully. The infrastructure backlog is moderate by comparison with other older cities and, at least in Cincinnati, does not appear to have been compromised by recent spending deferrals.

The future surely holds the possibility for more deferrals of capital investment and maintenance by state and local governments. A lack of good information on safety and operating standards is one reason. Sadly, the information choices seem to be acceptance of federally set standards—which inevitably would be so stringent and costly that they would have to be ignored—or "waiting until the bridge falls down." High interest rates and budget stringency are other reasons why state and local governments will do less than they need about the infrastructure problem during the next decade. Finally, there are political obstacles, especially to capital maintenance. Despite all that has been written, politicians will remain more enthusiastic about dedicating a new convention center than taking credit for repairing underground water mains.

On the other hand, capital projects—especially maintenance—cannot be so easily put off as in the past. For one thing, the public has been made more aware of the issue, and political advocacy has become more popular.[96] Moreover, some of the capital stock has truly reached a dilapidated condition. Indeed, capital replacements can be put off and renovation cycles extended, apparently without causing cities to crumble. However, the older the capital stock the more likely are these deferrals to cut into public service levels and economic development efforts. One would suspect that the slowdown in capital spending would create particularly severe capital obsolescence problems for older cities.

SUMMARY

The "fiscal health" of state and local governments is one of those elusive concepts that everyone talks about, but that few try to define and even fewer try to measure. Moreover, any proposed measure is likely to be controversial, at least because fiscal health depends on whose view is being taken: the year-end surplus which makes the municipal bond investor smile may well cost city residents a road resurfacing or city employees a wage rate increment.

The NIA general surplus of state and local governments gives some idea of movements in the financial condition of the aggregate state and local government sector. The trend in this general surplus has been cyclical, as surpluses were built up during expansions and drawn down during contractions. As long as the recoveries are as long and as strong as the recession, "fiscal condition" is not a major worry for the aggregate state and local government sector; however, there are wide variations in this condition. Some of the older, declining cities (most but not all in the North) have few reserves on which to draw, heavy fixed expenditure commitments, a disadvantaged and high-cost population, and a tax base that is not growing. Such cities and some states have for a long while been balancing budgets by deferring compensation increases and capital spending and by cutting back services.

Many studies of fiscal distress have attempted to identify cities that are somehow "worse off": in terms of age and dilapidation, economic performance, concentration of the poor or budgetary position. Again, common to most lists are the older cities of the North. Not all northern cities are distressed and not all distressed cities are in the North, but there seems no getting around the fact that older cities in the declining region have generally had a tougher time of it during the past decade.

How serious is the distressed-city problem, how close are the hardest-pressed state and local governments to financial disaster, and what are the prospects? With a few exceptions, cities have been able to avoid the New York City type of financial disaster. This is due in part to the strong economic rcovery, in part to the effects of inflation on tax bases, and in part to large increases in federal aid. As much as to any other factor, however, city fiscal health has been due to the scare of the 1975 recession. The New York City experience shifted virtually everyone's concern from the need to deal with the social problems of central cities to the need to remain financially solvent. As a result, there has been no increase in real spending by local governments in five years and a surprisingly general acceptance of this scenario.

This situation is not likely to continue. National economic growth promises to be slow, lower rates of inflation will not provide the stimulation of the 1970s to state sales and income taxes, and federal aid increases are surely not in the cards. The "easy" revenue increases of the late 1970s will not reappear. Expenditure control will also be tougher. Deferral of capital investment and maintenance cannot be so easily accomplished as in the past, especially in older urban areas; and real wage increments for public employees cannot be pushed indefinitely to the future. Sooner or later, public employees will renew their interest in catching up with private sector wages, the capital stock will have to be repaired, and urban unrest will refocus attention on living conditions and public service levels in central cities. When that day of reckoning comes, a new round of state and local government fiscal crises will not be far behind.

APPENDIX 3A

The NIA surplus (S) (exclusive of social insurance funds) is defined by the identity

$$R + G - CE - KE = S \qquad (3\text{-}1)$$

where

R = revenues from own sources

G = total federal grants (for current and capital purposes)

CE = current expenditures excluding debt retirement but including interest expenditures

KE = construction expenditures excluding purchases of land

We might view this surplus as having a current or operating (OS) and a capital (KS) component:

$$S = OS + KS \qquad (3\text{-}2)$$

The capital surplus might be expressed as

$$KG - IE - KE = KS \qquad (3\text{-}3)$$

where

KG = capital grants received from the federal government

IE = interest expenditures

Now if

$$CE = OCE + IE \tag{3-4}$$

where

OCE = "other" current expenditures

then we may subtract Equation 3-3 from Equation 3-1 to get a measure of the operating surplus:

$$OS = R + (G - KG) - OCE \tag{3-5}$$

Following Gramlich, we might view debt retirement (DR) as a proxy for capital consumption and deduct it from the operating surplus in

$$OS = R + (G - KG) - (OCE + DR) \tag{3-6}$$

CHAPTER 4

THE EFFECTS OF BUSINESS CYCLES AND INFLATION

More than any other single factor, the performance of the national economy shapes the financial health of state and local governments. Slower economic growth, inflation, and recessions or the expectation of recessions all affect the structure and growth of state and local government budgets. In some cases, inflation and recession increase budget deficits and push governments a step closer to insolvency, in others the unfavorable budgetary effects are cushioned by revenue systems that are buoyant with respect to rising prices, and in still others the revenue-dampening effects of slow national growth and recession are more than offset by the gains from inflation and from regional shifts in economic activity.

In this chapter, we try to explain how inflation and business cycles effect state and local government budgets. As is the case with most applications of economic theory, we are left with the unsatisfying answer that "it depends" . . . on various price and income elasticities, on the kinds of discretionary responses that governments make, on the kind of recession and inflation being faced, and on the type of government being discussed. The few studies that have attempted to estimate inflation and recession impacts are reviewed here to search for some consensus about the actual effects. Although the answers one gets from such a review are tentative and qualified, the overall picture that emerges gives some evidence about how inflation and recession compromise or enhance the fiscal health of state and local governments.

INFLATION

After a relatively long period of price stability, consumer prices began to rise sharply in 1973, increasing by 11 percent in 1974 and 9.2 percent in 1975. After falling off to about 6 percent for two years, prices again increased at double-digit rates for three years before softening during the 1981–83 recession. This general inflation had a marked effect on the growth of state and local government revenues, expenditures and borrowing, and possibly on the composition of budgets and on tax burden. These effects, however, are very complicated, to a point where it is not completely clear whether higher rates of inflation are a fiscal blessing or a fiscal problem.

Microeconomic theory suggests what we might expect from price inflation. If the increase in prices of all goods is uniform, i.e., there is no change in relative prices, and if the state and local government tax system is fully responsive to inflation, there will be no real effects on budgets and no induced fiscal responses. Taxes will be higher, but tax burdens will not,[1] public employees will earn more but not relative to the private sector, and so forth. The real position of the state and local government sector will not change.

In reality, price increases have not been uniform and state and local government revenue systems have varied widely in their response to inflation. The cost of state and local government purchases has increased faster than the general price level and some tax systems have come closer than others to fully capturing inflation-induced increases in income, consumption, and property values. So while it is intuitively obvious that inflated prices raise the cost of providing government services and stimulate tax bases, it is less obvious whether the revenue or the expenditure effects dominate.

We begin this inquiry about these very complicated fiscal impacts of inflation by first tracing out a set of *a priori* expectations and then looking for confirmation in the empirical work on the subject.

Inflationary Impacts on Public Expenditures: Theory

Inflation exerts an *absolute* and a *relative* price effect on government expenditures.[2] The absolute price effect is the one most often discussed. As the general price level in the economy rises, the price that state and local governments pay for their police officers, fire trucks, utilities, typewriters, and so on, also rises. There is an upward pressure on expenditures that may or may not be as great as the overall rate of inflation and that may or may not be offset by an inflation-induced increase in revenues. If revenues and expenditures both rise by the general inflation rate, then, *ceteris paribus,* budgets will increase in proportion to the increase in prices and there will be no change in the quantity of inputs employed.

However, revenues may not increase in proportion to inflation; e.g., inflation may bid up property values by more than local officials are willing to raise property assessments. This results in a reduction in the real income of the government, i.e., inflation raises the price of government goods by more than it raises revenues, hence the purchasing power of each dollar of revenue declines. In such a case, the government may react by reducing the quantity of inputs purchased and expenditures will not increase by the full rate of inflation. Call this the real income effect and note that its potential dampening influence on state and local government expenditures varies directly with the income elasticity of demand for state and local government produced goods. In the extreme case, where the demand for government goods is perfectly income-inelastic, tax rates will be increased to fully compensate for the loss in purchasing power.

There is also a relative price effect of inflation on expenditures. If all prices in the economy increase at the same rate, there is no inducement to cut back consumption of any one good at the expense of another. However, if the price of some goods increases faster than the price of others, substitution takes place, with the degree of substitution depending on the price elasticities of demand for the products. Suppose that the price of inputs purchased by state and local governments increased faster than the prices of all other goods and services. If all else were held constant, one would expect rational consumer-voters to respond by choosing a smaller state and local government sector. For example, if the price of schoolteachers increased relative to all else, it is likely that, *ceteris paribus,* fewer teachers would be hired than under a lesser change in relative prices. How many fewer teachers and the effects on the total wage bill will depend on the wage elasticity of demand for teachers.

One must distinguish between the expenditure effects of inflation that are automatic and those which result from induced policy actions. For example, an increase in the general rate of inflation will automatically increase state and local government expenditures on purchases of materials, whereas rising relative prices of these materials may set in motion discretionary quantity reductions that will offset some of this increase. On the other hand, if relative prices of state and local government inputs fall, then the upward pressure on expenditures will be reinforced as consumer-voters (and bureaucrats) demand more of the now-cheaper government goods. It is important to note that general inflation effects tend to be more "automatic" (the city simply pays the higher price of gasoline for its police cars), but relative price effects require discretionary actions (the city must take some policy action to reduce its fleet of cars).

The relative price effect may also change the mix of state and local government services provided, or even the methods of providing services. For example, a higher price of garbage collectors can lead to fewer collectors and more expensive and efficient equipment or to privatization of the service. The first option will depend on whether the technology will permit the substitution of capital for labor and the second on whether the relative price of private provision is lower. The answers vary from function to function, and from city to city.

The upshot of this discussion is that the expenditure impacts of inflation are a complicated matter involving direct, automatic effects and indirect, discretionary effects. These effects depend on input price movements, which are difficult to measure; on the impact of institutional arrangements, such as public employee unions; on technology, whether there are alternative production possibilities; and on the political will of state and local governments to undertake discretionary actions. We may never be able to sort out the pure effects of inflation, but we may begin to examine the empirical evidence on this question by considering the evidence for the major components of state and local government expenditures: labor costs; the cost of materials, equipment, and supplies; capital outlays; and transfer payments.

Price increases have not been uniform: Changes in the relative prices of energy, capital and food were at the heart of the high inflation rates of the mid-1970s and the softening of prices in the early 1980s. One of the few available choices for measuring the increase in prices faced by state and local governments is the implicit deflator for state and local government purchases, as reported in the NIA. As may be seen in Table 4-1, this index increased faster than the implicit price index for GNP, a comparable measure of the overall inflation rate in the economy.

Labor Costs

Since about 37 percent of state and local government expenditures is for wages and salaries, an understanding of how inflation has stimulated labor costs is important. The same scenario as above holds: labor costs are pushed up by inflation, *ceteris paribus*, to the extent that each of the following is true:

Community income increases in proportion to inflation

The local revenue structure is inflation responsive

The relative price of labor decreases and the demand for labor is price elastic

The demand for labor is income elastic

The inflationary impacts on labor expenditures are dampened, *ceteris paribus*, to the extent that

Community income increases less than in proportion to inflation

The local revenue structure is not inflation responsive

Table 4—1. Alternative Measures of Price Level Increase

| Year | Labor | | | | Labor and Materials | Capital Outlays | | Energy | |
| | BLS Middle Level of Living[a] | | CPI | GNP Implicit Deflator | GDP Deflator for SLG Purchases | Interest Rates on Long-Term Treasury Bonds (%) | Construction Costs[b] | Gas and Electricity | Fuel Oil and Coal |
	Amount	Index[e]							
1982	na	na	288.6	207.2	222.3	12.23	222.9	393.8	667.9
1981	25,407	222.0	272.3c	195.5	207.9	12.87c	204.2c	345.9c	675.9c
1980	23,134	202.1	247.0	177.4	184.7	10.81	186.0	301.8	556.0
1979	20,509	179.1	217.7	162.8	169.8	8.74	170.5	257.8	403.1
1978	18,622	162.7	195.3	152.1	156.5	7.89	158.2	232.6	298.3
1977	17,106	149.4	181.5	141.7	146.1	7.06	148.6	213.4	283.4
1976	16,236	141.8	170.5	133.9	137.7	6.78	137.3	189.0	250.8
1975	15,318	133.8	161.2	127.2	129.7	6.98	127.2	169.6	235.3
1974	14,333	125.2	147.7	116.0	118.4	6.99	115.8	145.8	214.6
1973	12,626	110.3	133.1	105.8	107.3	6.30	105.9	126.4	136.0
1972	11,446	100.0	125.3	100.0	100.0	5.63	100.0	120.5	118.5
1971	10,971	95.8	121.3	96.0	94.5	5.74	92.8	114.7	117.5
1970	10,664	93.2	116.3	91.4	88.3	6.59	85.6	107.3	110.1
1965	9,076	79.3	94.5	74.3	65.1	4.21	62.4	99.5	94.6

[a] Urban U.S. Intermediate Budget.
[b] Boeckh index for apartments, hotels, and office buildings.
[c] Preliminary 1981.
[d] Relative to 1965.

Source: U.S. Department of Commerce, Bureau of Economic Analysis, *Business Statistics, 1979; Survey of Current Business*, various issues; U.S. Department of Labor, Bureau of Labor Statistics, *Autumn Urban Family Budgets and Comparative Indexes for Selected Urban Areas*, annual; *Handbook of Labor Statistics, 1978*.

na = not available

The relative price of labor rises and the demand for labor is price elastic

The demand for labor is income inelastic

Actual inflationary impacts on labor costs cannot be read from available data in a straightforward way. Some method of estimation is necessary. When labor costs increase faster than the rate of inflation, the empirical problem is how much of the increase should be assigned to inflation. One approach is to assume that the full rate of inflation is captured in labor cost increases, e.g., if labor costs increase by 20 percent and prices by 10 percent, then half of the cost increase is due to inflation. This implies an assumption that state and local government labor expenditures are indexed to cost-of-living increases and that the demand for public employees is perfectly inelastic with respect to price. In the 1960s and early 1970s this may have been an appropriate assumption for estimation-average public employee wages increased by more than the full CPI increase, public employees were not being laid off, and revenues were more than keeping pace with inflation.

This approach will not work, however, when the CPI is increasing faster than average public employee wages. Indeed, with the increasing rates of inflation beginning in about 1973, average compensation[3] of state and local government workers increased at a rate less than the CPI[4] (Tables 3-9 and 3-10). Moreover, there has been a marked decrease in the rate of growth in public employment rolls (Table 3-7).

The story these data tell is that sometime after 1973 state and local governments began to use discretionary actions to offset some of the expenditure impacts of inflation. This response was possible because wage rate increments are a negotiated, discretionary action of state and local governments, i.e., governments are not required to pay full cost-of-living increments in the same way that they are required to pay a higher price for a gallon of gasoline. This feature has been used to keep the growth in the price of state and local government labor inputs low relative to the general price level.

This state of affairs leaves a complicated set of effects to sort out:

Inflation has increased the wage rate paid in the state and local government sector, thereby increasing expenditures. Some of this increase has been offset, however, because revenue growth has not kept pace with inflation, and the ensuing income effect has dampened public employment growth.

State and local governments negotiated lower wage increments for public employees, after 1973, than the rate of inflation. This has kept some of the inflationary pressure off state and local government expenditures.

The combination of higher labor costs due to general inflation and revenue increases below the general inflation rate may have dampened public employment growth, but the lower relative price of labor after 1973 may have increased it.

Increased federal grants in the mid-1970s made up for some of the real revenue loss due to inflation and thereby stimulated public employment growth.

To belabor a point, the public employment effects of inflation are not easily deduced. As was described above, state and local government employment has increased throughout most of the past decade. This increase has come about for a myriad of reasons, including increasing incomes, changing voter tastes, and urbanization, just to name a few. More recently, public employment has declined, in part as a response to slower growing income, voter resistance, and fears of budget insolvency. The question here is whether the rate of increase in public employment would have been higher or lower if the rate of inflation had been lower.

To sort out this net impact, an income effect and a substitution (relative price) effect have to be identified. First, the income effect. If the purchasing power of state and local government revenue delines during inflationary periods, layoffs or a lower rate of employment growth might be expected. Governments, like any consumer, purchase fewer inputs when real income falls. If the local revenue structure were responsive to inflation or had there been a very low inflation rate, real revenues would have been higher and a higher level of state and local government employment would have resulted. While this real income effect probably dominates, there may be an offsetting or reinforcing substitution effect due to the changing relative price of labor. The substitution effect is likely to be small because the demand for public employees is quite price inelastic; i.e., as wage rates go down (relative to other prices), state and local governments increase their employment rolls (or at least let them grow faster than they would have otherwise) but not by very much. For example, Ehrenberg's estimates suggest that a 10 percent wage rate increment would reduce public sector employment by only 3 to 4 percent.[5]

In fact, through most of the 1970s inflation outran the increase in state and local government labor costs. One might conclude that the size of the *real* public employment budget, *ceteris paribus,* was smaller than it would have been under a lower rate of inflation. This, in turn, suggests that a part of the cost of inflation is borne directly by public employees (in the form of lower real wages) and a part by residents (in the form of the lower public service levels attributable to having fewer public employees).

A number of qualifiers have to be offered to this speculation. There is simply too much variation in functional responsibility, labor practices, revenue structures, and economic conditions to permit such a generalization about the effect of inflation on labor costs for all state and local governments. Where unions are strong, public employee compensation tends to be higher.[6] Hence, one might conclude that all other things being equal, labor costs better keep pace with inflation in the heavily unionized areas of the Northeast and industrial Midwest. Where public employee organization is weak, labor is much more vulnerable and bears a substantial share of the burden of inflation.

Another important difference is whether the local revenue structure is responsive to increasing prices. For state and some local governments which rely heavily on sales and income taxes, the purchasing power of local government revenues may be kept intact. That is, the inflation-induced increase in sales and income tax bases may generate revenues that are more than adequate to cover the inflation-induced increase in the cost of providing a constant level of services. This would increase real government revenues and imply a greater willingness on the part of government to grant cost-of-living increases and less propensity to cut employment rolls. The net impact of inflation in such a case is to increase the public employment budget. In this case, public employees and certain residents share in the benefits of inflation at the expense of taxpayers, who must foot the bill for the increased cost. If taxpayers instead force a discretionary tax reduction, the real income of the government declines and the process is as described above.

Still other factors would cause us to question generalizations about the impact of inflation. For examples, different governments have different functional responsibilities and hence different uniformed, blue collar, and white collar employment mixes; and the precarious financial position of a Cleveland or a Detroit may hold wage responses to inflation below what they otherwise might have been. All of these reasons suggest the substantial problems with defining an "average response." Labor costs may well have responded less than proportionately to inflation for the state and local government sector as a whole since 1973, but for some governments the response was quite different from this average.

Finally, there is the question of federal grants. An increase in federal assistance, particularly programs such as CETA, kept public employment levels higher than they otherwise would have been. Particularly between 1970 and 1978, the large increases in federal grants shored up the real income position of state and local government and held public employment at what might be termed artificially high levels.

Nonlabor Costs

Nonlabor expenditures respond to inflation more directly since governments have little control over prices paid for materials and supplies. The alternatives are either to pay the higher price or reduce the quality or quantity of the inputs used. The former is often the choice because the nature of the production process in the state and local sector leaves little room for substitution between labor and nonlabor inputs.[7]

To examine the direct effects of price increases on nonlabor costs, one might assume that the government makes no quality or quantity adjustments. The inflation impact will then depend on whether the unit cost of materials purchased by state and local governments has risen as fast as the general price level. This approach to measuring inflationary impacts is outlined in Appendix B.

A comparison of the indexes in Table 4-1 suggests an about equal growth in the CPI and the implicit deflator for state and local government purchases. Most case studies have indicated a slower growth in the price of materials and supply purchases of state and local governments.

The cost of materials and supplies to governments is a weighted average: the quantity of each type of purchase weighted by the increase in the appropriate price index. Greytak, Gustely, and Dinkelmeyer constructed such an index for New York City material input costs for the 1965–72 period, using over sixty categories of purchases and a separate price index for each.[8] Their findings showed the cost of supplies to be increasing at a lower rate than the CPI, but materials and equipment to be increasing at about the same rate. Using a similar method for the 1971–74 period, Greytak and Jump found about the same relationship between the increasing price of material inputs and the CPI—material input prices increased by about 90 percent of the rate of increase in CPI. For five other local government areas studied, they found the materials-price response to vary from about 60 percent of the CPI in Orange County, California, to about 93 percent in Atlanta.[9] Cupoli, Peek, and Zorn, studying Washington, D.C. expenditures for the 1972–75 period, estimated that inflation drove up material costs by 31.6 percent while the increase in the CPI was only 28.7 percent.[10] Jump's estimates for the more recent 1977–80 period show that inflation has driven up material input expenditures by 29 percent by comparison with an actual increase of 43 percent and an increase of 36 percent in the CPI.[11]

These estimates are of potential impact, and are overstate-ments if governments elect to make quantity adjustments. Examples are deferral of road maintenance, telephone use restrictions, reduced school busing service, restricted travel, deferral of office machine replacement, keeping the city swimming pool closed, and postponing the purchase of tools and repair parts. This is the same kind of real income effect as noted above; because real government revenues fall when the inflation rate rises, the quantity of inputs will be reduced, i.e., to a lower level than would have been the case with a lower inflation rate. Unfortunately, data limitations make it impossible to observe actual price and quantity adjustments; hence, one can only conclude that where inflation dampens real revenue growth, it probably has had the net effect of lowering the quantity of materials and supplies used. State and local government expenditures on these items have not likely risen in proportion to the price increase.

Capital Costs

The effect of inflation on capital expenditures is even more difficult to sort out. The question is whether capital expenditures would be higher or lower, *ceteris paribus,* under a lower rate of inflation. One might begin with a consideration of the potential impact, i.e., assume that governments would not alter their capital project plans and measure the increased cost of those projects due to inflation. When viewed this way, the issue is simply one of how much construction and financing costs have risen and what is the relative importance of each in the makeup of total capital costs. Between 1965 and 1980, construction costs increased by 130 percent and interest rates on Treasury bonds by 205 percent. Inflation clearly had an upward pressure on the amount spent.

Was there a displacement toward or away from capital expenditures because of an increase in the *relative* price of capital expenditures? Over most of the 1970s, capital construction costs increased at less than the general inflation rate and interest rates grew faster (Table 4-2). One can only speculate about the net impact of these relative price changes, but it is clear that state and local governments have many discretionary options for countering increased capital project costs. Governments may

Table 4-2. The Composition of State and Local Government
Expenditures, 1965–80

	Percent of Total Expenditures			
	1965	1970	1975	1981
Labor costs	41.6	42.5	39.7	37.0
Materials, equipment, and supplies[a]	20.6	23.6	28.4	33.5
Construction	18.9	16.4	13.7	11.3
Land and equipment	5.1	3.6	3.2	2.6
Interest	3.4	3.4	3.8	4.2
Transfer payments	4.7	5.5	4.2	3.5
Insurance benefits and repayments	5.7	4.9	7.0	7.5

[a] Total current expenditures minus total wages and salaries.
Source: U.S. Bureau of the Census, *Governmental Finances in 1980–81, 1979–80* (1974–75, 1969–70, 1964–65).

avoid inflationary effects by reducing the size or quality of a project, postponing construction, or even canceling it altogether. For example, the proposed highway construction may be two-lane instead of four-lane or it may not go as far, the sewer system may not be extended for another two years, or the municipal auditorium may never be built. These effects of inflation are not easily measurable and surely do not show up in budgets, but they may well be the most important. Again, we cannot observe the quality and quantity adjustments actually made, but the evidence of recent years shows that state and local governments have substantially lowered their rate of capital formation.[12]

Transfer Payments

Inflation also affects state and local government expenditures by raising expenditures on transfer payments—particularly public assistance and Medicaid payments. These effects are not easily measured, and yet we know that transfer payments respond to inflation in that income maintenance is related to the cost of living and medical assistance is related to medical costs. However, the long-term effects of inflation are especially difficult to estimate because state and local governments have some discretion over how much they will spend on these programs.

Again it is the problem of inflation exerting a direct and an indirect effect.

Jump attempts to estimate the direct effects by assuming no change in the number of recipients and assuming that per recipient payments will rise by the full rate of inflation (measured by the increase in the BLS family budget).[13] He finds the "potential" inflation-induced increase to be 25 percent higher than the actual increase during 1972–77 and 15 percent higher during 1977–80. The reasons for this overestimation are clear: the number of recipients did fall and governments did undertake discretionary adjustments.

Medicaid and the Aid to Families with Dependent Children program (AFDC) are the most important of the transfer payment programs in state and local government budgets. With respect to the former, states have three avenues open in adjusting the level of payments in the face of increasing prices. They may change eligibility rules, thereby undertaking a quantity adjustment; they may adjust benefit levels, e.g., number of hospital days insured, number of physician benefits, drug and dental allowances; and they may adjust fee schedules.

Following the Medicare reimbursement schedule, which is essentially indexed, gives the greatest inflationary response. Though states have attempted to slow the increase in Medicaid costs by reducing primary health care services, they have been heavily burdened by the rising cost of hospital and nursing home services. Davis and Schoen report that, between 1969 and 1977, real annual Medicaid payments per recipient rose by only $23, from $338 to $361, the number of recipients doubled, and the general price of medical care nearly doubled.[14] At least half of the state and local government expenditure increase for Medicaid might be attributed to inflation.

An even greater proportion of the recent increase in state and local government expenditures for public assistance may be attributed to inflation. Since 1970, there has been little real growth in state and local government expenditures for public assistance even though nominal expenditures by state and local governments increased by 90 percent. This pattern, however, masks a real expenditure increase due to an increased number of recipients between 1970 and 1975 and real expenditure cutbacks after 1975.[15]

Another major type of transfer payment is state aid to local government. It is interesting to raise the issue of whether inflation affects a state government's choice between direct spending and local assistance. That is, as inflation drives up state government costs, is there, *ceteris paribus,* a tendency to cut back on aid to local governments rather than reduce the scope or quality of direct state expenditures? A time series analysis of the 1957–80 period suggests that this may indeed be the case. A simple estimate of the determinants of long-term changes in the state aid share of total state government expenditures shows that

$$A/E = -1.97 + 0.36Y - 0.50C \qquad (4\text{-}1)$$
$$(7.7) \quad (6.1) \qquad \bar{R}^2 = .84$$

where

A/E = state aid share of total state government expenditures

Y = nominal personal income (in millions)

C = consumer price index

and all variables are in natural logarithms with t statistics in parentheses. These results indicate that for any given rate of income growth, the aid share is dampened by a higher rate of inflation. This is to say that the aid share will exhibit a stronger positive response to an increase in real income than to the same percent increase in nominal income.

Total Expenditure Impacts

From this discussion two issues should be clear: first, inflation will induce government expenditures to increase but probably not by the full rate by which prices increase and, second, the induced budgetary effects are far from the total impact of inflation. Many of the effects of inflation will be hidden adjustments that are difficult if even possible to measure. Whether these adjustments—postponements, deferrals, layoffs, cutbacks—are a cost or a benefit to the community is not at all clear. Moreover, state and local government may be spurred to make other adjustments to forestall this retrenchment: tax rates may be increased to keep the purchasing power of government revenues constant, the burden of maintaining current service levels may be shifted to another generation via borrowing, and so forth. It is important to remain cognizant of this broader range of possible expenditure impacts of inflation.

Impact of Inflation on Expenditures

As to estimates of the overall budgetary impacts of inflation on state and local governments, there are surprisingly few studies. The best and most careful research is a series of studies carried out in the Metropolitan Studies Program of Syracuse University's Maxwell School, under the leadership of Greytak and Jump.[16] Working with data for New York City for the 1965–72 period, for a sample of six local governments and for the entire state and local government sector during the 1971–74 period, they computed expenditure-inflation indexes. The Greytak and Jump series attempts to estimate how much expenditures would grow if they responded fully to price increases; i.e., they assume a zero price elasticity of the demand for public employees and estimate the *potential* for expenditure growth due to inflation (see Appendix B).

Their results for current expenditures indicate that the inflationary impact during the 1972–74 period was greater than that for the entire 1967–72 period. Moreover, they show that the impact of inflation on expenditures could have accounted for virtually all of the expenditure increase of state and local governments over the 1972–74 period. Actual state and local government expenditures increased by only about 19 percent during these two fiscal years, but if state and local governments had fully responded to the effects of inflation, expenditures would have increased by 25 percent. In other words, if state and local governments had maintained 1972 employment levels and real nonlabor expenditures and had compensated employees and transfer recipients for increases in the cost of living, expenditures would have increased by 25.3 percent by 1974 (Table 4-3).

An application of the Greytak and Jump method, still using the 1972 base, to 1977 expenditures shows an expenditure-

Table 4-3. Expenditure Inflation Indexes, 1972–80

	1972–74		1972–77		1977–80	
	Index	Percent of Actual Expenditure Increase	Index	Percent of Actual Expenditure Increase	Index	Percent of Actual Expenditure Increase
States	125.4	100.1	147.5	81.8	132.1	93.2
Counties	125.4	105.7	147.3	85.2	132.6	100.1
Municipalities	125.4	105.3	146.7	87.8	132.4	102.1
Townships	125.6	n.a.	148.5	86.0	n.a.	n.a.
School districts	125.0	n.a.	143.4	88.4	n.a.	n.a.
Special districts	125.7	n.a.	146.5	67.6	n.a.	n.a.
All state and local governments	125.3	104.4	146.3	84.8	132.5	97.9

Source: David Greytak and Bernard Jump, Jr., *The Effects of Inflation on State and Local Government Finances, 1967–1974,* occasional paper 25, Metropolitan Studies Program, The Maxwell School (Syracuse, N.Y.: Syracuse University, 1975); and Bernard Jump, Jr., "The Effects of Inflation on State and Local Government Finances, 1972–1980" (Unpublished, 1983).

inflation index of 146.3, suggesting that inflation potentially accounted for about 85 percent of actual total expenditure growth between 1972 and 1977.[17] Finally, Jump's most recent estimates show that the "potential" impact of inflation far exceeded the actual expenditure increase between 1977 and 1980. For the state and local government sector as a whole, one might conclude from these results that inflation potentially accounted for virtually all of the expenditure increase between 1972 and 1980.[18]

This conclusion may not be so readily accepted for all types of local government because expenditure mixes vary substantially. Greytak and Jump carried out case studies for six local governments during the 1972–74 period to show the wide variation in the effects of inflation on expenditures. The aggregate state and local government expenditure inflation index was 125.3, but the indexes for these governments over the same period ranged from 165.9 in Snowhomish County, Washington, to 123.0 in New York City.[19] The percent of expenditure increase attributed to inflation ranged from 93 and 88 percent in Atlanta and New York City, to 60 percent in Orange County, California.

Chaiken and Walker used a wage index to estimate that 75 percent of the expenditure increase in Los Angeles between 1973 and 1978 could be attributed to inflation.[20] Cupoli *et al.* used the Greytak and Jump method to estimate that nearly 76 percent of the Washington, D.C. expenditure increase (excluding transfers) between 1972 and 1975 was due to inflation. The City of Dallas has used its forecasting model to ask the interesting and related question of how much future expenditures will respond to *higher* rates of inflation.[21] Working with a low versus a high inflation rate scenario, they conclude that the deficit in the fifth year of the forecast period could be twelve times greater under the high versus low rate.[22]

Expected Revenue Impacts

Revenues also respond to inflation in that the nominal value of tax bases rises with increasing incomes, prices, and property values. Hence, there is a potential to capture increased revenues induced by inflation. For sales and income taxes, the revenue response is more or less automatic and estimation of the inflation effects is straightforward enough. In the case of the property tax, however, the problem is far more complicated. Land and improvement values have increased dramatically during recent inflationary periods, thereby providing dramatic increases in the *potential* for increased property tax revenues. Indeed, in terms of the potential revenue effects of inflation, the property tax may be the biggest prize of all; but who would argue that local governments may easily capture this potential? The major impediment is the revaluation of properties. Indeed, Proposition 13 was partly a result of property tax assessments that reflected skyrocketing property values. The California solution to hold taxable property value growth to an arbitrary percentage suggests that during times of inflation good assessment practices are even more objectionable to voters than bad assessment practices.

If the problem of estimating inflationary impacts is difficult for the property tax, it is next to impossible for most intergovernment grants. One might hypothesize that because the more elastic federal and state tax structures respond to inflation, federal and state aid will also respond proportionately—as if it were an income-elastic tax. We might offer a crude test of this hypothesis by examining the long-term (1965–80) responsiveness of the grant share of federal government expenditures (F/B) to change in nominal income (Y) and the CPI (C):

$$\ln F/B = -7.76 + 0.96 \ln Y - 0.61 \ln C \qquad (4\text{-}2)$$
$$ (7.7) \qquad (2.6)$$

$$R^2 = .97$$

These results show that for any given growth rate in income, inflation has a dampening effect on the grant share of the federal budget.

Approaches to Estimating the Impact of Inflation on Revenues

In attempting to determine the impact of inflation on state and local government revenues, three general approaches have been taken. All are similar in that they somehow try to separate automatic from discretionary increases in revenue growth.[23] The *elasticity* models try to estimate the percent change in revenues resulting automatically from a 1 percent change in income:

$$\eta = \frac{(\Delta R/\Delta Y)}{(R/Y)} \qquad (4\text{-}3)$$

where

Y = personal income

R = revenue

If, for example, $\eta = 1.1$, a 1 percent increase in personal income will automatically increase revenues by 1.1 percent. Then, one might argue, for every 1 percent increase in personal income that is due to inflation, a 1.1 percent inflation-induced growth in revenues will result. If this reasoning is sound, it would seem that an answer to our question could be had from a straightforward estimation of (η) from historical data. Many studies have taken this approach, and there are numerous estimates of revenue-income elasticities.[24]

As a method for picking up inflationary impacts, the elasticity approach raises a number of questions. It assumes that the effects of inflation can be adequately measured by the growth in nominal personal income; e.g., a 4 percent real and 4 percent inflationary growth in personal income or any other combination of an 8 percent growth in personal income would have an identical effect on revenues. There are reasons to believe otherwise. One is that price increases may change the structure of personal income and consumption and therefore the elasticity of the tax in the future. For examples, if the ratio of taxable to total consumption rose with increasing prices, so would the sales tax elasticity; there are "progressivity" effects under state income taxes (i.e., bracket creep) which will drive up the elasticity and inflation may affect the source distribution of income, particularly capital gains, and thereby the elasticity of the income tax.

An equally serious problem with the elasticity approach has to do with the difficulty of separating automatic from discretionary effects on revenue growth. Particularly in the case of the property tax, it is all but impossible to identify an automatic responsiveness of tax revenues to growth in either personal income or price levels. These caveats suggest that straightforward use of historical data to provide an estimate of the revenue-inflation impact will be problematic.

An alternative to the elasticity approach is that taken by Greytak and Jump. They have attempted to estimate the *potential* tax base response to price increase. They ask the question, "How much would revenues grow in response to inflation if tax bases increased at their full potential and if effective tax rates remained constant?" They begin with 1972 and inflate each tax and user charge base by an appropriate index taken from the CPI, WPI, or BLS family expenditure survey. For example, for the property tax, they used BLS price indexes for residential housing and residential rents and various Boeckh indexes for commercial and industrial properties.

The problem of estimating the revenue impact of inflation is analogous to that on the expenditure side: the *potential* effects are for a greater increase in revenues than most governments will be willing (or politically able) to accept. The response to this increased revenue potential by state and local governments has been to allow effective property tax rates to fall by failing to reassess or by reducing income tax rates. In sum, a part of the potential revenue stimulus of inflation has been foregone.

A third approach, taken by the ACIR, is a substantial improvement on the elasticity estimation method.[25] They have adapted Vogel's model of state and local government expenditure growth during the business cycle,[26] and have estimated

$$\Delta R = 1.15 - 0.12\Delta G + 236.42\Delta D \qquad (4\text{-}4)$$
$$(5.54) \qquad (11.28)$$

$$R^2 = .883 \qquad DW = 1.35$$

where

ΔR = change in own-source revenue

ΔG = change in nominal GNP gap

ΔD = change in IPD

The product of the actual change in the IPD between any two years (ΔD) and the regression coefficient (236.42) gives an estimate of the effects of inflation on own-source revenues, holding constant the change in the nominal GNP gap. The ACIR study, while carefully done, is limited by their assumption that revenue changes (automatic and discretionary) can be explained by movements in the business cycle and the price level. There is a voluminous literature arguing that expenditure, and therefore revenue and tax rate levels, are responsive to changes in population, federal grants, changing economic and demographic structure, and so on. The omission of these important variables leads to (an uncertain) bias in the results.

The differences in the elasticity, ACIR, and Greytak and Jump approaches lie in the question asked. The elasticity approach asks how revenues, net of any discretionary change, respond to changes in nominal personal income. The ACIR approach attempts to explain actual changes in revenue during inflationary periods, including the effects of discretionary actions. Greytak and Jump attempt to show by how much revenue potential would change in response to inflation, i.e., how much more taxable capacity would be available to governments simply because of inflation if the governments could and actually did permit the inflation to be reflected in the tax bases.

Estimated Revenue Impacts

The Greytak and Jump indexes in Table 4-4 show that state and local government revenue potential grew by 16.9 percent between 1972 and 1974. In other words, if the 1972–74 increase in the nominal values of tax bases had been taxed at 1972 effective rates, the revenues raised by state and local governments would have increased by 16.9 percent, solely because of inflation. Between 1972 and 1977, the hypothetical inflation-induced increase in revenue potential was 38.7 percent. These inflation impacts were the equivalent of 94 percent of the total actual revenue increase between 1972 and 1974 and 82 percent of the increase between 1972 and 1977.

The ACIR study also concludes that state and local government revenues are stimulated by inflation, that they are from 6 to 16 percent higher than they otherwise would have been.[27]

Table 4-4. Revenue Inflation Indexes, 1972–80

	1972–74		1972–77		1977–80	
	Index	Percent of Actual Expenditure Increase	Index	Percent of Actual Expenditure Increase	Index	Percent of Actual Expenditure Increase
States	116.6	94.0	137.1	79.9	130.8	95.1
Counties	116.7	91.7	139.6	79.5	134.7	99.9
Municipalities	115.4	91.4	136.8	78.9	132.9	85.0
Townships	114.8	n.a.	142.6	86.7	n.a.	n.a.
School districts	119.2	n.a.	145.0	90.7	n.a.	n.a.
Special districts	113.3	n.a.	129.4	59.6	n.a.	n.a.
All state and local governments	116.9	94.3	138.7	81.5	132.4	99.9

Source: David Greytak and Bernard Jump, Jr., *The Effects of Inflation on State and Local Government Finances, 1967–1974*, occasional paper 25, Metropolitan Studies Program, The Maxwell School (Syracuse, N.Y.: Syracuse University, 1975); and Bernard Jump, Jr., "The Effects of Inflation on State and Local Government Finances, 1972–1980" (Unpublished, 1983).

Their estimate of an aggregate inflation stimulus of about $77 billion in revenues between 1973 and 1976 is substantially greater than the $40 billion estimated for 1972–76 with the Greytak and Jump method.[28] The difference is easily explained. The ACIR method does not adjust for widespread tax rate increases during this period; i.e., the tax rate increases are viewed as part of the effects of inflation. This is perfectly correct if the objective is to show the direct and induced effects of inflation on local government revenues and if the effect of other factors that determine tax rates is removed.

The conclusion of this analyses would seem to be that inflation exerts a stimulative effect on revenues. The Greytak and Jump method implies a hypothetical increase slightly less than the growth in the CPI for the 1972–76 period; the ACIR method predicts an inflation effect greater than the CPI increase. There still remains the issue of great variations in this effect by type of jurisdiction.

The Budgetary Effects of Inflation

The really important question is the net effect of inflation on the budget, i.e., whether inflation drives up revenues by more than it drives up costs. The ACIR answer for the 1973–76 period is that it does; the Greytak and Jump approach yields a conclusion for the 1972–76 period that it does not. The ACIR estimates net revenue gains during the 1973–76 period as 0.6 percent of own-source revenues in 1973, 3.9 percent in 1974, 5.5 percent in 1975, and 2.9 percent in 1976.[29] However, discretionary rate changes are included in their estimates of revenue increase due to inflation, causing an overestimate of the pure inflation effects on the revenue side (because other factors may have caused the tax rate increase). Moreover, they do not consider price effects on any expenditure base—they adjust revenue purchasing power by the IPD for state and local government purchases—causing one to suspect an underestimate of the inflation effects on expenditures. Again, the ACIR estimates are of the total direct and indirect effects of inflation on budgets and take into account any discretionary tax and expenditure adjustments the government may have made.

The Greytak and Jump estimates, to the contrary, are of

how expenditures and revenues would respond to inflation if no discretionary adjustments were made, i.e., there are no changes in tax rate, all inflation-induced changes in the tax base are captured, the number of employees and quantities of goods purchased remain constant, and no programs are cut back.

The Greytak and Jump estimates show that expenditures were potentially more responsive to inflation than were own-source revenues, at both the state and the local level during most of the 1970s. Indeed, while inflation was driving up expenditures by about 25 percent between 1972 and 1974 (Table 4-3), it was increasing revenues by only about 17 percent (Table 4-4). A similar pattern held for 1972–77, but the "potential" inflation-induced increases in state and local revenue bases nearly kept pace during 1977–80.

Another way to describe the potential budgetary effects of inflation is to consider the implications for the purchasing power of state and local government revenues. Purchasing power indexes for the several levels of government, based on 1972 revenues bases, are shown in Table 4-5. For example, the purchasing power index of 93.3 for 1972–74 implies that, after accounting for the effects of inflation on revenues and expenditures, the revenue base would be 6.7 percent too small to finance a constant level of services. In other words, the 1974 revenue base bought 6.7 percent fewer "constant service units" of government services than it bought in 1972. By the end of

Table 4-5. Indexes of Purchasing Power of Revenue Bases, 1972–80

	1972–74	1972–77	1972–80
States	93.0	93.0	88.3
Counties	93.1	95.0	92.5
Municipalities	92.0	93.3	89.3
Townships	91.4	96.0	96.0
School districts	95.4	101.1	105.1
Special districts	90.1	88.3	88.4
All state and local governments	93.3	94.8	90.4

Source: David Greytak and Bernard Jump Jr., *The Effects of Inflation on State and Local Government Finances, 1967–1974*, occasional paper 25, Metropolitan Studies Program, The Maxwell School (Syracuse, N.Y.: Syracuse University, 1975); and Bernard Jump Jr., "The Effects of Inflation on State and Local Government Finances, 1972–1980" (Unpublished, 1983).

the decade, the 1972 revenue base had been deflated by about 10 percent. The actual effect of inflation almost certainly was more severe than indicated by these estimates. This is because the revenue and expenditure inflation indexes measure the *potential* impact of inflation on the budget; these estimates are not meant to imply that state and local governments actually realized these revenue base effects or made these expenditures. Assessment lags mean that actual property taxes would not grow as implied here and therefore the detrimental effect of price indexes on budgets would be understated.[30] Moreover, for declining cities it is altogether possible that property values did not keep pace with the general rates of increase in property values experienced in the rest of the nation.

The quite substantial effects of inflation on city budgets are also evidenced in their own forecasts. In a survey of econometric models used by cities, Schroeder reports that both Kansas City, Missouri and Vancouver, British Columbia project erosions in purchasing power as a result of higher rates of inflation.[31] In both cases, this is largely due to the insensitivity of the property tax to changes in the price level.

There is little doubt but that the potential effects of inflation on state and local government budgets are substantial. The expenditure impacts may not show up immediately because of lagged responses or directly because governments may compensate for price increases by cutting services, but it seems clear that inflation has important and substantial effects on the cost side of the budget. The effects on the revenue side may be much less pronounced, particularly for property taxes and particularly in times of taxpayer resistance. On the basis of this evidence, it is reasonable to conclude that inflation does reduce the purchasing power of state and local government revenues and may do so by a substantial amount. The 10 percent reductions suggested in the Greytak and Jump analysis for the 1970s may not be too far from the mark given the overall inflation rates experienced during that period. For local governments, which are more heavily dependent on the property tax, the effect may be much greater.

RECESSION

The fiscal impacts of recession seem intuitively obvious. As income growth slows and the unemployment rate rises, the growth in state and local government revenue slackens. The harder hit the area economy is, and the more reliant it is on "sensitive" sales and income taxes, the greater the revenue loss is. The only appreciable impacts on the expenditure side are on certain social service functions which are sensitive to movements in the unemployment rate. These direct effects of recession are clearly unfavorable to state and local budgets.

There is, of course, much more to the story. Revenue declines brought on by recession will induce governments to undertake discretionary actions to make up for some of the loss. For example, state and local governments may increase tax rates or lay off workers. Such discretionary actions are an important impact of the business cycle but should be separated from the "purer" effects noted above.

The Expected Impacts of Recession

Recession may be viewed as a reduction in real incomes (or a slowing growth in real income), and its impact on the state and local government sector depends in part on the income elasticity of demand for public goods. The more elastic this demand, the more sensitive will be the state and local government sector to recession. Although the demand for local public goods appears to be income-elastic, suggesting a substantial fiscal response to recession, there are reasons to expect that discretionary actions might be taken to cushion the expected budget-cutting response. A first reason is that governments may expect the recession to be short-lived and take temporary measures to fund existing programs, e.g., shoring up revenues through short-term borrowing or by drawing on reserves.

A second possibility is that expenditures may be rigid downward because many state and local government expenditures are in the nature of fixed commitments. These include debt, pensions, "safety net" expenditures, a large portion of wages and salaries, and much of the general overhead of the government. To maintain these, tax rates may be increased to compensate for the revenue loss due to the recession.

The fiscal impact of recession may also be cushioned by some built-in features of state and local government tax structures. In states with a progressive income tax, the revenue losses attributable to slow real income growth and increasing unemployment are partially recouped by the "bumping up" of higher-income families into higher marginal tax brackets. This effect is especially likely when the rate of inflation is high. The growth in the property tax base will be slower during periods of recession: the demand for housing and industrial and commercial space will be off from previous levels and there will be a slower increase in values of existing properties. Still, the growth rate in the assessed value of taxable property is not likely to be adjusted to capture year-to-year fluctuations in land and housing prices. The poor reassessment practices that characterize the United States property tax system thus appear to have at least one advantage.

Finally, the impact of recession on budgets may be softened by discretionary expenditure adjustments. The timing of these fiscal adjustments is an important if often overlooked issue. While it is interesting to learn how state and local governments alter their taxes and expenditures in the face of recession, it is as interesting to learn when they make these adjustments. On the expenditure side, there may well be a lag before reductions begin, with temporary shortfalls made up in any one of a number of ways: short-term borrowing, underfunded pension systems, selling off of financial and real assets, deferment of compensation increases, and so forth. It may be that the full effects of recession on the expenditure side are not felt for several years and even then occur over a period of time. The expenditure effects of recession may be much greater than is indicated in most surveys.

Studies of the Fiscal Impact of Recession

The answer to the question of how state and local government budgets have fared during recession is to be found in empirical analysis. Following the discussion above, it is reasonable separately to review the evidence from two kinds of studies: first the studies of fiscal performance during the recession and then those few studies which have addressed the more difficult question of the purely fiscal impact of the recession.

Studies of Fiscal Performance. A number of analysts have attempted to understand the fiscal effects of recession by studying the fiscal performance of state and local governments during periods of recession. Some of these are no more than surveys of perceptions, but others are careful statistical analyses of the 1974–75 and 1981–83 recessions. Two conclusions can be drawn from this work: (a) the budgets of state and local governments were squeezed during the recession so that compensating tax increases and expenditure reductions did take place and (b) the fiscal squeeze was more severe for central cities, particularly those in the older industrial region.

The evidence points to increasing fiscal stress during recession years. The financial collapse of New York City was long in the making but ultimately brought on by the recession.[32] The near collapse of Yonkers, Buffalo, and New York State can be traced to the effects of recession, though all were brought to the brink by the long-term decline in their economic base. In each case the response was some combination of increased taxes and expenditure cutbacks. Stanley's case studies of Detroit, St. Louis, Buffalo, Cleveland, and New York City (carried out in late 1975) indicated projected budget deficits that would require either, or both, sizable expenditure cutbacks or tax rate increases.[33] Congressional testimony from representatives of many different state and local governments tended to support the claim that the recession was forcing drastic fiscal adjustments at the state and local government levels.[34]

At least two surveys tried to more systematically ferret out the tax and expenditure adjustments made by state and local governments in response to the 1974–75 recession. A Joint Economic Committee survey, covering 48 states and 140 local governments, concluded that state and local governments did indeed raise taxes, cut expenditures, and postpone or cancel capital improvement investments because of the recession,[35] but the estimated deflationary adjustments were a relatively modest 3.5 percent of total state and local government own-source revenue. Indeed, the results of this survey do not indicate pressure of a magnitude that would bring on acute fiscal distress. The second survey, carried out by the Senate Subcommittee on Intergovernmental Relations, covered about 400 jurisdictions.[36] Though no estimates were made of the magnitude of fiscal adjustments, it was found that one third of these governments raised taxes, over half instituted personnel limitations, and about one fifth delayed or canceled capital projects. Again, the immediate impacts of the recession—as indicated in these surveys—are not as far reaching as might have been imagined.

Survey work indicates a similar response by state and local governments in the 1981–83 recession. A JEC mail questionnaire to forty-eight large cities revealed a pattern of service level cuts, capital project deferrals, and tax increases in fiscal 1982.[37] Tax rate increases were reported by twenty and user charge increases by thirty-one of the forty-eight cities in the survey. An ACIR survey underlines this finding on the increased use of user charges: 215 of 307 responding cities reported increases.[38] The National Conference of State Legislatures fiscal survey at the end of 1981 showed twenty-nine states with prospects for fiscal year deficits or thin budget margins and twenty-four states reporting employment reductions in the preceding year.[39] None of these surveys provided enough information to estimate the severity of cutbacks or tax increases in response to the 1981–83 recession. The Tax Foundation, in its very useful annual compendium of state tax actions, tells that tax action in thirty states in fiscal 1981 raised revenues by a net $2.5 billion a year.[40] While this is the highest annual statutory increase in ten years, it represents only about 1.5 percent of total state government tax revenues.

If the overall fiscal effects of recession are not so devastating on a nationwise basis, it may be asked whether there are substantial variations in these effects across regions or across levels of government. The answer is that there are, with metropolitan central cities in particular and governments in the declining regions in general feeling the most pressure. The 1974–75 recession hit the older central cities hardest; they went in earlier and more deeply and have come out more slowly than the rest of the country. This was true in the 1969–72 recession and recovery[41] and for the 1974–78 recession and recovery.[42] All of the surveys mentioned above concluded that fiscal adjustments were more drastic in the more distressed cities and regions. The JEC survey found that the most severe fiscal adjustments took place in areas where the unemployment rate was highest.[43] Other JEC surveys, of sixty-seven large cities in 1977[44] and of forty-eight large cities in 1981,[45] reached a similar conclusion. Most studies have concluded that city governments were hardest pressed, though the NGA has argued that state governments were also forced to budgetary adjustments by the 1974–75 recession.[46] A GAO study has concluded that states fared better than cities and counties better than either.[47]

If there is a general conclusion to be drawn from these studies, it is that there are great variations in the magnitude of budgetary adjustments resulting from recession. Though in aggregate the adjustments do not appear to have been all that great, for some governments they may have been substantial. It does seem clear, however, that there is a pattern to fiscal adjustment during periods of recession. State and local governments tend to slow down on spending increases and increase tax rates, but the tax hikes are undertaken later, after other available funding opportunities are exhausted.

These surveys are useful in helping analysts understand what governments do in response to national recessions. However, the studies cannot help us get at the pure effects of recession because they are unable to abstract from the fiscal influences of all other factors, e.g., population decline, tax limitations, inflation. In particular, the failure to separate inflation from recession effects is a major problem with this literature.

Econometric Studies.   Recession creates idle resources, i.e., a gap between actual and full employment levels of economic activity. This in turn creates a gap between actual and full employment levels of revenue and expenditure. It seems clear that a proper measure of the effects of recession on revenues centers on the estimation of such a gap.

The Council of Economic Advisors estimates full employment receipts for state and local governments by applying actual average tax rates to full employment tax bases.[48] They estimated the revenue loss due to the recession to be 4.3 percent of actual revenues in 1974, 9.1 percent in 1975, and 6.6 percent in 1976. Vogel adjusted these estimates to account for discretionary tax rate increases by state and local governments during recessions and, hence, for a CEA overestimate of full employment receipts.[49] His method shows the revenue shortfall to be about half that of the CEA for the 1971 recession. Crider used estimated elasticities by type of tax and computed revenue yield under a recession and a full employment scenario.[50] He found revenues to be below their potential by 4.8 percent in 1974 and 10 percent in 1975. His estimates include only own-source revenues. The ACIR estimated a model similar to Vogel's to find a revenue loss equivalent to 8.4 percent of revenues in 1975.[51] However, the ACIR considered only own-source revenues, whereas the CEA and Vogel considered total revenues.

These approaches share two problems. All explain changes in actual revenues and hence include the discretionary reaction of state and local governments to recession and inflation. Vogel attempts to adjust for this, but it is not likely that his adjustments account for the full amount of discretionary change. The other problem has to do with model specification, i.e., with the failure to account for other factors that influence revenue growth. All attempt to control for inflation, but none consider secular trends in regional income or interregional migration. In sum, none of these estimates are of the pure effects of recession.

The ACIR also used this recession method to estimate the recession-related revenue loss for 1976 on a state-by-state basis. As might be expected, the variation is wide, ranging from revenue losses of 20.5 percent in Maine and 16.3 percent in Connecticut to less than 5 percent in several other states. The greatest impact is in the industrial states of the Mid-Atlantic and the Northeast. When the recession effects are separately estimated for all state and for all local governments, the conclusions are that state own-source revenues are almost twice as sensitive to the business cycle as are local own-source revenues.

Little attention has been paid to the impact of recession on state and local expenditures. Here and elsewhere[52] it has been argued that a deferral effect operates, which causes state and local governments to postpone expenditure increases during a recession and in its immediate aftermath. The ACIR has estimated such a deferral effect. They find that a recessionary gap tends to increase expenditures immediately but results in a decrease in expenditures during the following fiscal year.[53] When both the current and the deferred effects are considered, the recession impact on expenditures is negligible. Again, it is important to note that these are estimates based on how much state and local governments actually spent and hence include far more than just the effects of recession.

Crider, assuming that real earnings of state and local government employees declined by 1.4 percent between 1973 and 1975 because of the recession, estimates a $3 billion decline in expenditures.[54] This was partially offset by a $1 billion increase in state and local government spending for welfare and related services and hence a $2 billion recession-related decline. As the ACIR do, he finds a minuscule expenditure effect of recession.

Schroeder has carried out the interesting experiment of simulating the revenue impact of recession from the fiscal forecasting models used by four city governments: Kansas City, Vancouver, New Orleans, and Cincinnati.[55] At least from the point of view of these governments, there is no significant revenue impact of recession, primarily because of reliance on the property tax. In the case of Cincinnati, however, the recession scenario does result in a substantial revenue loss because of that city's reliance on a local income tax. Again, the impact of recession depends on the circumstances of the government being studied.

CONCLUSIONS

The main finding of the ACIR study *State-Local Finances in Recession and Inflation* is that the combined fiscal effects of recession and inflation on aggregate state and local government finances are not "excessively severe."[56] Although this result correctly describes their findings, it may be misleading. Indeed, the conclusions one might draw from this chapter are that the effects of inflation and recession are quite severe for certain types of state and local governments and may be a substantial and increasing problem for the entire sector.

Studies of the 1973–76 period place the revenue loss due to recession at 5 to 10 percent of total state and local government revenues, depending on the government and the severity of the recession. For some governments, notably those located in the declining regions and state governments with highly elastic tax structures, the revenue loss was estimated as high as 20 percent. Little impact on state and local government expenditures could be found. Several conclusions might be drawn from these results. First, even a 5 to 10 percent loss in revenue potential is considerable, and a 15 to 20 percent loss is disastrous. Second, these estimates understate the fiscal impact of recession in that they show the loss in revenue potential but do not adjust for the discretionary actions taken by these governments in the face of revenue loss. Hence, for example, the actual revenue growth in Massachusetts in 1976 may be 20 percent less than its full employment, noninflationary amount, but the gap might have been 30 percent if the state and local governments had not increased tax rates to make up for some of the loss. Finally, although expenditure impacts have not been estimated as important, most surveys show that the recession resulted in important program cutbacks and deferrals.

The inflation studies are also subject to the problem of whether and how to count the fiscal adjustments resulting from rising prices. The best research seems to imply loss in purchasing power of state and local government revenue bases of about 10 percent during the 1970s. At least three important implications for the future might be drawn from this work: local governments that are more labor intensive and more reliant on property taxation are hurt most by higher inflation rates; when the inflation rate rises to high levels, the impact on expenditures outstrips that on revenues; inflation induces service level cutbacks that may have longer-run effects on the viability of local economies.

One cannot easily infer the future from these studies and there are no reliable models that allow forecasts, but these results do give some basis for judging the probable impact of inflation and business cycles on state and local government finances. We might consider a few scenarios. First, assume that the inflation rate remains high relative to GNP growth. This will harm local governments most because of their labor-intensive expenditure base and their reliance on the property tax. Especially if inflation and slow economic growth combine to keep real private earnings from growing, there will be heavy voter resistance to discretionary attempts to capture the inflation-induced growth in property values. Among local governments, those with already high property tax rates and little new construction, and those with stronger public employee unions—the older central cities—will be hurt most. A buffer against this inflation effect is the possibility of increased state aid since inflation could increase state revenues by more than it increases state expenditures. The states that stand to gain most are those with progressive income tax structures, broad-based sales taxes, and relatively less direct expenditure responsibility. This includes many of the older states in the north, but there is some question about the ability of these states to withstand further increases in the effective tax rate. Indeed, New York is a good example of a state whose progressive tax structure has captured inflation-induced revenue increases but where an already high average tax rate has forced discretionary tax reductions. Still, we are led once again to the conclusion that state government discretionary action will play a pivotal role in determining local government fiscal health.

Under a second scenario where higher rates of inflation occur in concert with recession, the situation is altered to the detriment of state governments because they lose some of the revenue increments captured by inflation. Those states with the less elastic revenue structures suffer less from recession, but on the other hand they gain less from inflation. The most important feature of recession, however, is that some state and local governments suffer more than others. Again, it is those governments in the declining regions whose economies suffer most during recession. Therefore, older central cities suffer disproportionately heavier revenue losses during recession. Also, such cities are located in states that are likely to be facing a similar situation, therefore reducing the chances for marked increases in state aid. If this comes at a time when inflation is driving up local costs but having little effect on property tax revenues, these central cities become doubly damned.

APPENDIX 4A

The Effects of Inflation on State and Local Government Finances

Assume a community indifference curve (I_1) that describes consumer-voter preferences for public (G) and private (X) goods, as in Figure 4-1. With a budget constraint $(\hat{X}, \hat{G})$ and total community income of $O\hat{X}$, consumers will choose an equilibrium at E_0 with OG_0 public goods and OX_0 private goods. The level of taxation in this case is $X_0\hat{X}$, and the tax rate is $X_0\hat{X}/O\hat{X}$.

The issue in question is how this solution is affected by different rates of inflation.

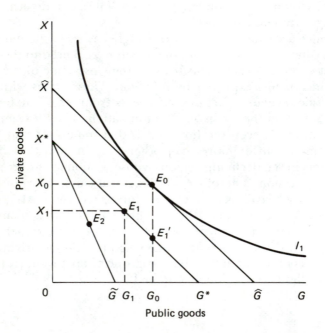

Case One. Assume that inflation does not affect relative prices (i.e., P_G/P_X does not change) and that community income increases in proportion to inflation. In this case, the equilibrium is restored to E_0 and there is no change in resource allocation or in the real public budget. Money expenditures and taxes of the government will have increased in proportion to inflation, but the tax rate will not change, the same number of employees as before will be on the rolls, and so forth.

Case Two. Assume that inflation does not affect relative prices but that community income is not restored to its previous level, i.e., real income falls. In this case the budget line shifts to X^*G^* and a new equilibrium along X^*G^*—at $E_1(G_1X_1)$. The greater the income elasticity of demand for public goods, the farther to the left of E_1 is the equilibrium. At E_1, there is a real income effect that reduces public and private expenditures in proportion to the reduction in real income. A solution at E'_1 means that taxes are increased to maintain the same level of G, i.e., there is a perfect income inelasticity of demand for public goods.

Case Three. Inflation reduces real community income by $X^*\hat{X}$ and causes the relative price of government goods to rise. The new budget line is $X^*\hat{G}$ and the new equilibrium may be at E_2. The move from E_1 to E_2 is caused by two effects: real income effect, which depends on the income elasticity of demand for public goods, and a substitution, or relative price, effect, which depends on the price elasticity of demand for public goods.

APPENDIX 4B

Measuring Expenditure-Inflation Impacts [1]

To measure the "potential" impact of inflation on expenditures requires price indexes for each class of state and local government expenditure. The problem can be defined more specifically as follows. The total actual expenditure change (ΔE) is

$$\Delta E = E_t - E_o \qquad (4B-1)$$

where

E_t = expenditures in year t

E_o = expenditures in some base year

and the change in expenditures due to inflation ($\Delta \hat{E}$) is

$$\Delta \hat{E} = pE_o \qquad (4B-2)$$

where

p = some percent increase in an appropriate price index

Hence, the share of the expenditure increase due to inflation is

$$\frac{\Delta \hat{E}}{\Delta E} = \frac{pE_o}{E_t - E_o} \qquad (4B-3)$$

As noted above, this result gives an estimate of the direct, probably maximum impact of inflation. It assumes no quantity adjustment.

122

The estimation of $\Delta\hat{E}/\Delta E$ is a simple exercise only if an appropriate price index is available. Unfortunately, the choice and the measurement of such an index are anything but simple. The problem is that an aggregate price index for state and local government expenditures would have to take into account the differential growth in prices for each component of the state and local government budget; i.e., a kind of market-basket survey of state and local government purchases is necessary. The implicit price deflator (IPD) for state and local government purchases (Table 4-1) provides such an estimate but is flawed for the purposes at hand in that it cannot reflect the wide variation in the package of services purchased by different state and local governments. It is not available on a regional basis. The only way around this problem would seem to be construction of a price index for each government, weighted to reflect the composition of purchases by that government.[2]

If labor costs are assumed to respond fully to the rate of inflation, the proper index would be a cost-of-living measure. This likely would play the strongest role in determining the wage rate increase necessary to compensate public employees for rising consumer prices. There are few choices of an index for this purpose. The Bureau of Labor Statistics estimates, for thirty-nine metropolitan areas, the cost of three levels of living.[3] This is a market-basket survey and is limited by its relatively narrow geographic coverage. On the other hand, it has the strengths of allowing for some regional variations in the cost of living and having been constructed explicitly for the purpose of measuring overtime changes in the cost of living. Some analysts have chosen to deflate labor cost increases by the national CPI, thereby assuming uniform price increases across the nation. Since it appears that prices are increasing faster in the growing regions, the index overestimates the effects of inflation on labor costs in the declining regions. On the other hand, if public sector labor unions bargain with national price index information (or if governments make wage agreements with national price level increases in mind), the national CPI is an appropriate index. Moreover, the CPI is available with relatively little time lag, whereas the BLS index is produced with a one-to-two-year lag.

The problem of choosing an appropriate index is even more difficult for nonlabor costs because of the wide range of goods and services involved. One possibility is to use the IPD for state and local government purchases. As noted above, however, this index has the disadvantages of including labor costs, and allowing for neither price level variations across regions nor variations in the type of materials purchased. The latter problem may be resolved by choosing a great number of specific price indexes, the very laborious procedure followed by Greytak and Jump[4] and by the City of Washington, D.C., in estimating inflation effects in conjunction with its long-term expenditure forecast.[5]

In sum, even if the inflation impact is defined only in terms of direct price effects, and even if we assume that state and local governments must pay the full price increases, measurement will be quite subjective. The answer we get for an inflation impact will vary considerably according to the index chosen. This is not to say that one cannot gain some idea about the impact of inflation from such estimation, but rather that the impacts should be interpreted with these conceptual and empirical flaws in mind.

CHAPTER 5

THE EFFECTS OF REGIONAL SHIFTS IN POPULATION AND ECONOMIC ACTIVITY

The shift in economic activity from the northeastern and midwestern industrial regions to the Southeast and Southwest has by now been thoroughly documented.[1] The accompanying financial impacts on state and local government are less well documented, but their presumed existence has dominated the formulation of federal grant policy for the last decade.[2] Surprisingly, the contribution of these regional shifts to the fiscal health of governments has been given little systematic attention. The result is that neither the linkage between changes in the economic base and fiscal health nor the effects of regional shifts on government fiscal choices are well understood. Nowhere has this shortfall in knowledge shown up so clearly as in the formulation of remedial public policy to deal with the fiscal problems of state and local governments in declining regions.

Perhaps it is because the relationship between the economy and the fisc is so difficult to untangle and because state and local governments have so little control over the performance of regional economies that policy analysts have turned in other directions to grapple with fiscal problems.[3] There probably is not a more glaring example of this misdirection than in the proposed solutions to the New York City fiscal problem. At least in the early stages much more attention was focused on financial management issues than on the fiscal implications of the economic decline that was taking place. As a result, it is no great surprise that management reforms did little to deal with the city's fundamental long-term fiscal problems.

Just as New York City's financial problems were so severe that the underlying economic causes were largely overlooked, the Sunbelt's economic bonanza has obscured what may be serious and growing state and local government fiscal problems. Industrial development and increasing per capita incomes are leading an infrastructure and human capital investment program, which in turn implies long-term debt and maintenance requirements and an increasingly expensive public sector. Will future economic growth in the region be adequate to sustain public sector operations at "competitive" tax levels? Again the answer depends on what one can say about the response of public budgets to economic growth and structural economic change.

The objective in this chapter is to describe and analyze the linkage between regional variations in economic and demographic change and state and local government finances.[4] For the declining regions, particularly the more heavily industrialized states, this analysis shows an imbalance between growth in public sector activities and growth in the capacity to finance activities. For some states this has resulted in what might be termed an "overdeveloped public sector," i.e., a level of government activity that cannot be sustained. Such overexpansion of public sector activities holds an important lesson for many southern and western states, which are now in a growth period and facing the same set of factors that drove up government costs in the North: inflation, rapid in-migration, growing public service demands, and increasing union strength.

Regional shifts in population and employment are not undesirable per se. Hence, their reversal should not be the object of remedial public policy at the national government level. A trend toward interregional income equality and a growing interstate homogeneity in the quality of public services are not detrimental to the nation's welfare. What is harmful about regional shifts and what ought to be at the center of concern about

public policy to deal with such shifts are the effects on unemployment, poverty, and the ability of state and local governments to finance and deliver adequate services. In a sense, all
three of these concerns have to do with the distribution of income—the concern for the share of purchasing power and
public services accruing to low-income families. Unfortunately,
these more fundamental issues have been all but forgotten in a
national policy debate about how the federal government should
divide its assistance among growing and declining states.

Regardless of one's view as to where problems are most serious or as to how they might be resolved, it is clear that an
understanding of the linkages between regional shifts in employment and population, the unemployment problems of large
cities, and the fiscal problems of state and local governments is
essential to formulating an intelligent public policy. This chapter is a modest attempt to deal with one dimension of this linkage: the relationship between regional economic shifts and state
and local government finances.

This analysis is concerned with regional variations in the
finances of jurisdictions in growing and declining regions. If
any regularities are to be ferreted out, some form of aggregation of the nearly 80000 United States jurisdictions must be
used. Since the major concern here is with how the fisc has
been compromised by regional movements in population, jobs,
and income, the choice has been made to aggregate by state
and by region. Clearly one could learn more by studying the
finances of every state and city, but such an approach is im-
practicable.

We use the following breakdown. "Northern tier" is the east
north central, middle Atlantic, and New England census regions; "southern tier" is the south Atlantic, east south central,
and west south regions; and "western tier" is the Pacific, Mountain, and Plains regions.[5] Our grouping is not the conventional
one, in that the Plains states are included in the western region
rather than with the midwestern states. This was done so as to
group the industrial midwestern and northeastern states into a
single nothern tier.[6]

There are major problems with making inferences from
analysis of aggregated regional data. One especially important

shortcoming is that there is much variation within regions. For example, growth in Florida and Texas swamps that in the rest of the South, California is quite different from the Rocky Mountain states, and New England's economy has performed better than that of the middle Atlantic subregion. Still, the three-region breakdown used here does pick up the essential regional difference: the southern and western tiers are growing and the northern states are not. In fact, most states in the three regions fit this pattern.

A second caveat in this approach is that there are state-to-state variations in institutional structure that do not fall neatly into regional groupings. These include differences in revenue structure and the assignment of functions and financing between the state and local government levels. Such differences lead to anomalies. For example, in terms of fiscal structure Texas is more like Ohio than like South Carolina, and in terms of jurisdictional boundaries Atlanta is more like Syracuse than like Houston. The reader should remain cognizant of such variations, especially when this analysis is overenthusiastic in identifying "clear" regional variations.[7]

THE EXISTING PATTERN OF REGIONAL VARIATIONS

A key to understanding how regional shifts might compromise state and local government budgets is a knowledge of regional differences in revenue structures, expenditure patterns, and intergovernmental arrangements. Specifically, the important considerations include:

1. The assignment of expenditure and financing responsibility between the state and its local governments

2. The structure of local government and the potential for regionwide service delivery or financing

3. The level and functional composition of expenditures

4. The level of public employee compensation, public employment and the importance of public employee unions

5. The level of taxation and its composition by major sources

6. The reliance on debt and federal grants as financing sources

7. Central city/outside central city disparities in local government revenues and expenditures

Revenue and Expenditure Assignment

There are two approaches to identifying regional variations in the relative importance of state and local governments. One is to study the characteristics of southern, western, and northern states and to present whatever pattern emerges. The other is to devise an objective classification of state fiscal systems and to search the results for a regional pattern. The latter approach, taken here, is borrowed from some research carried out by the Metropolitan Studies Program of Syracuse University for the ACIR.[8]

To develop a state fiscal classification scheme, expenditure and financing data were gathered for total state and local expenditures for 1980. From these data, four fiscal characteristics were measured. The first two—percent of taxes raised at the state and at the local level—represents the relative financing responsibilities of the two government levels. The second group of fiscal characteristics—state and local direct expenditure shares—describes final spending responsibilities (rather than original source of financing) of state versus local governments.

The fifty state fiscal systems described by these four characteristics exhibit many varied and distinctive combinations of intergovernmental relationships. That some general patterns emerge indicates that, although each state may be unique, certain common patterns of state and local fiscal relationships exist.

The fifty states were grouped into categories of high, moderate, and low state government financing responsibilities and expenditure shares. These groupings were used to cross-classify state and local fiscal systems as one of three major types: *state government dominated, local government dominated,* and *mixed systems.* These results are described in Table 5-1, which may be

Table 5-1. Classification of State Fiscal Systems, 1980

State Government Financing Responsibility	State Expenditure Responsibility[a]		
	High	Moderate	Low
High[b,c]	Alaska	Washington	California
	Delaware	Idaho	Minnesota
	Hawaii	Mississippi	
	Kentucky	North Carolina	
	New Mexico	Oklahoma	
	West Virginia		
	Alabama		
	Arkansas		
	Maine		
	South Carolina		
Moderate	Rhode Island	Maryland	Michigan
	North Dakota	Wyoming	Nevada
		Louisiana	Wisconsin
		Utah	Arizona
		Tennessee	Iowa
		Virginia	Pennsylvania
			Indiana
			Florida
			Georgia
			Texas
Low	South Dakota	Massachusetts	New York
	Vermont	Montana	Colorado
		Oregon	Illinois
		Connecticut	Nebraska
		Kansas	New Jersey
		Missouri	Ohio
		New Hampshire	

[a] State expenditure responsibility is the state share of total state and local direct expenditures.

[b] High, moderate, and low designations for each category relate to whether the state placed in the top fifteen, middle twenty, or bottom fifteen among states.

[c] State financial responsibility is the share of total state and local expenditures financed by the state.

Source: For the approach taken, see ACIR, *Federal Grants: Their Effects on State-Local Expenditures, Employment Levels, Wage Rates* (Washington, D.C.: GPO, 1977). Data used for this analysis are from *Governmental Finances in 1980.*

read as showing the greatest state government domination in
the top left corner and the least in the bottom right. For example, Alaska, Kentucky, and Arkansas have very high state
control over financing and spending whereas Ohio, New York,
and Illinois are relatively decentralized. States in the upper
right-hand corner are also relatively decentralized in terms of
expenditure discretion but finance local governments relatively
more through state grants than through local taxation.

It may be noted that nine of the sixteen southern tier states
exhibit a moderate to high state financing responsibility and a
moderate to high state expenditure responsibility. No southern
state is to be found in the locally dominated group. By contrast,
only two of the fourteen northern tier states—Maine and Min-
nesota—may be classified as state dominated on the financing
side. Eight of the fourteen northern tier states may be classified
as locally dominated in terms of financing responsibility, and
another five show a low state government expenditure responsibility. The western states are more of a mixture in their intergovernmental arrangements.[9]

Local Government Structure

A second important difference between northern and southern
tier states is the structure of local government in metropolitan
areas. Northern central cities are thought of as having heavy
concentrations of the poor, an antiquated, dilapidated infrastructure surrounded by more affluent suburbs, and little hope
for annexation, consolidation or regionwide financing. Many
northeastern metropolitan areas fit this stereotype all too well.
The southern tier cities might be painted as newer, subject to
less city and suburb wealth difference, and more successful at
annexation and consolidation. The examples of Jacksonville,
Miami, Nashville, Houston, and Baton Rouge come quickly to
mind.

There is more than impressionistic evidence to support this
stereotype. Sacks reports striking regional differences in the
percentage of metropolitan area populations residing within the
central city.[10] As may be seen in Table 5-2, he found an average of 51 percent of metropolitan population residing inside
central cities in the South, as compared to 39 and 44 percent,

Table 5-2. City-Suburb Disparities in Population for 85 Largest SMSAs

	Number of SMSAs	Central City as Proportion of Total SMSA Population		Percent Increase in Population, 1970–80		Percent Increase in Central City Acreage, 1970–80
		1970	1980	Central City	Suburbs	
East	18[a]	43	39	−12.1	2.9	0.0
Midwest	23	44	38	−12.0	13.0	4.0
South	27	57	51	10.2	38.9	18.8
West	18	42	39	10.5	26.7	10.2
Total	85	46	41	−3.3	16.2	11.8

[a] All values are unweighted averages.
Source: Department of Housing and Urban Development, *Changing Conditions in Metropolitan Areas, Urban Data Reports,* No. 1 (Washington, D.C.: Office of Policy Development and Research, June 1979) and updates provided by Sacks.

132

respectively, in the East and Midwest.[11] Moreover, he shows that between 1970 and 1980 this percentage declined in all regions. On the average, central cities in the East and Midwest were losing population while those in the South and West were gaining. The conclusion seems clear that central cities in the South and West are a more dominant force in their respective metropolitan areas.

Much of this advantaged position of southern central cities must be ascribed to the greater success of the South in consolidation attempts and/or in the use of more areawide financing mechanisms. Marando observes that consolidation is essentially a southern regional phenomenon and that annexation has occurred extensively throughout the United States with the exception of the northeastern region.[12] Sacks has studied acreage increases for central cities between 1970 and 1980 and finds virtually no evidence of annexation in the East (Table 5-2). Between 1970 and 1978, southern states accounted for more than half of all areas annexed and for about 40 percent of the total population annexed.[13]

Expenditure Level and Structure

There are important regional variations in the level and functional distribution of expenditures. The northern and western states spend more—about one fourth more on a per capita basis—than do the southern tier states (Table 5-3).[14] This pattern holds for most states within the three regions. Only two northern and western tier states (Indiana and Missouri) spend less than the southern mean, and only two southern tier states (Delaware and Maryland) spend above the northern and western mean. This relatively low expenditure level in the South, even in the midst of an increased flow of resources to that region, is important in understanding the possibilities for fiscal adjustment. It means, if expenditures are any indication of services provided, that southern states have very low public service levels. On the other hand, it also means that southern states may expand tax and spending levels by a significant amount before reaching "noncompetitive" levels.

In terms of expenditure distribution, the southern states allocate a relatively greater share of total public resources to ed-

Table 5-3. Expenditure and Employment Characteristics of State and Local Governments

State and Region	Per Capita Expenditures ($)	Percent of Current Expenditures			State and Local Government Employees	
		Education	Welfare	Health Hospitals	Per 10,000 Population	Average Wage ($)
NORTHERN TIER	1,864	39.2	17.1	9.4	462	1,533
East North Central	1,729	43.5	16.2	9.9	442	1,532
Illinois	1,761	40.9	16.7	7.5	439	1,587
Indiana	1,400	50.9	11.9	12.8	446	1,306
Michigan	1,962	42.5	17.3	10.2	442	1,780
Ohio	1,572	44.0	16.1	11.9	434	1,380
Wisconsin	1,929	44.2	16.7	8.2	466	1,522
Middle Atlantic	2,041	36.2	17.5	9.3	485	1,578
New Jersey	1,885	40.8	14.2	7.8	490	1,515
New York	2,419	33.3	18.1	10.5	543	1,667
Pennsylvania	1,594	39.6	18.6	7.6	397	1,445
New England	1,793	36.1	18.2	8.2	460	1,394
Connecticut	1,715	38.6	15.4	7.2	450	1,400
Maine	1,533	38.0	20.0	5.0	451	1,198
Massachusetts	1,941	33.4	19.6	9.6	471	1,433
New Hampshire	1,512	41.3	15.4	5.6	433	1,274
Rhode Island	1,941	36.1	19.3	8.5	463	1,557
Vermont	1,747	43.9	14.1	6.0	475	1,240
SOUTHERN TIER	1,501	45.5	11.7	12.8	485	1,258
South Atlantic	1,525	44.6	11.0	12.8	490	1,279
Delaware	2,060	42.8	10.0	5.6	530	1,378
Maryland	1,918	42.0	13.0	8.5	513	1,538
North Carolina	1,421	48.6	11.4	10.8	490	1,228
Virginia	1,601	46.3	11.9	10.0	498	1,311
South Carolina	1,435	49.1	11.6	16.5	499	1,189
Georgia	1,538	41.6	12.8	18.9	525	1,153
Florida	1,469	43.3	8.1	13.9	453	1,289
West Virginia	1,625	43.9	10.3	9.7	489	1,207

East South Central	1,179	467	14.0	13.3	43.1	1,445
Alabama	1,181	484	16.3	11.0	44.4	1,448
Kentucky	1,251	413	8.3	16.5	43.3	1,495
Mississippi	1,031	502	15.8	13.4	44.3	1,487
Tennessee	1,213	476	15.7	12.8	41.1	1,397
West South Central	1,272	487	12.1	11.7	48.4	1,500
Arkansas	1,077	452	11.6	14.3	47.0	1,303
Louisiana	1,238	509	13.3	12.5	41.6	1,808
Oklahoma	1,194	527	10.3	15.6	48.1	1,583
Texas	1,329	478	12.1	10.2	51.2	1,499
WESTERN TIER	1,606	483	9.4	14.8	41.1	1,946
Pacific	1,815	468	8.9	16.6	39.2	2,121
Alaska	2,392	803	3.8	6.7	33.4	7,210
California	1,862	458	9.3	18.3	37.8	2,100
Hawaii	1,535	496	7.5	15.6	34.2	2,181
Oregon	1,541	504	6.8	10.7	44.1	2,102
Washington	1,713	466	9.6	13.4	48.6	2,083
Mountain	1,465	508	9.7	9.1	49.1	1,774
Arizona	1,596	491	8.9	6.3	52.0	1,748
Colorado	1,540	507	9.8	10.8	48.7	1,787
Idaho	1,266	480	10.2	10.0	46.5	1,501
Montana	1,347	546	7.3	10.8	46.6	1,892
Nevada	1,557	497	12.6	8.0	36.2	2,074
New Mexico	1,288	578	10.1	9.5	50.2	1,893
Utah	1,360	439	8.2	11.5	54.6	1,704
Wyoming	1,511	653	12.4	5.0	48.8	2,783
Plains	1,332	495	10.5	14.2	44.3	1,734
Iowa	1,414	494	11.0	13.8	48.3	1,753
Kansas	1,247	540	10.1	12.7	46.3	1,775
Minnesota	1,493	488	10.2	17.4	39.9	2,102
Missouri	1,200	450	12.4	13.8	43.8	1,413
Nebraska	1,283	579	11.1	10.2	49.2	1,665
North Dakota	1,523	499	5.3	10.9	45.4	1,947
South Dakota	1,178	502	5.8	12.1	43.3	1,715

Source: U.S. Bureau of the Census, Government Finances in 1980–81; U.S. Department of Commerce, Current Population Reports, "Annual Estimates of States"; Resident Population and Public Employment in 1981, July 1982.

ucation and health whereas northern and western states spend more for welfare. It is interesting to note that no northern state allocates as little to public welfare as the southern mean of 11.7 percent. Indeed, if southern states were to make the same per capita welfare expenditures as northern states, the North-South gap in per capita expenditures would be cut to about 10 percent. This pattern suggests that the full federal assumption of welfare financing would hold especially important fiscal relief implications for the northern tier of states.[15] By contrast, the Reagan administration's proposal to turn AFDC and food stamp financing back to the states would likely reinforce the already heavier emphasis on public welfare spending in the northern region.

Public Employment and Wage Levels

It will be surprising to many to learn that there is a greater average level of state and local government employment, relative to population, in the South than in the North (Table 5-3). The variations in the northern states range from Pennsylvania's 397 state and local government employees per 10000 population to New York's 543 while in the South the spread is from Kentucky's 413 to Delaware's 530. Indeed, only Florida, Kentucky, and Arkansas among the southern states have a lower employment level than the northern mean.

The higher level of public employment in southern states, (about 5 percent above the northern level) is not easily explained, but a number of hypotheses might be offered. It would be consistent with an economies-of-scale hypothesis: the more populous, more highly urbanized states conceivably would need fewer employees to service a given number of people. (Note the very high employment levels in sparsely populated Nebraska, Wyoming, and New Mexico.) Likewise, lower density may leave much less room for capital-labor substitution, leaving the southern states with a more labor-intensive public sector.

The higher level of public employment in the South does not square with the hypothesis that public employment tends to be higher in slower growing or declining regions. Muller compared twelve growing cities and fourteen declining cities on the basis of per capita employment in functions common to city governments. In this admittedly small sample, he found the declining cities to have 12.1 workers per 1000 residents and the growing cities 8.7.[16] Perhaps even more interesting is his finding that the gap widened between 1967 and 1972. No such relationship between the level of state and local employment and population growth or decline can be found in the regions examined here.

A third explanation could be that the more centralized government structure that generally prevails in the southern states somehow leads to greater levels of public employment. This is not consistent with *a priori* reasoning, which would suggest that centralization would eliminate much duplication and, *ceteris paribus,* lead to lower employment levels. The problem here is that all other factors are not held constant.

Finally, the public employment level differences may reflect the downward sloping demand curve for public employees, i.e., lower employment levels in the northern and western states are a result of higher wage levels in those states. Average public employee wages are higher in the northern and western tiers than in the South by almost any standard (Table 5-3). While per capita income is 16 percent higher in the North and the West than in the South, the North-South gap in average public sector wages is 22 percent and the West-South gap is 28 percent. The pattern holds for most states. There are a number of possible reasons why public sector workers receive such low wages in the southern states: low productivity, the absence of strong unions, a lower opportunity wage in the private sector, the willingness of workers to trade climate for wages, or the possibility that governments in the southern states do not perform as wide a range of public functions and hence do not require as expensive a mix of labor skills. Muller has also studied wage variations among local governments using his growth-decline dichotomy and, for his sample, has determined that average wage levels tend to be higher in older and declining cities. His plausible explanation of this difference is the greater ability of municipal employee associations in older cities to press for more favorable contract terms, coupled with cost-of-living differences and perhaps a necessary premium for what is perceived as a lower quality of life in the older, more congested cities of the Northeast and industrial Midwest.

Even if payroll per full-time equivalent employee is a reasonable measure of interstate variations in the average wage,[17] there remains the problem of measuring interstate variations in the level of pensions and fringe benefits. Again, there are inadequate data to make proper cross-state comparisons, and one must be content with assuming that interstate variations in the average wage, as measured above, accurately reflect interstate variations in total compensation.[18] There is good reason to expect that it does not, since benefits are often tied to wage levels, e.g., pensions and Social Security contributions. Hence, it is likely that regional differences in total compensation are greater than those in the average wage.

Finally, there remains the problem of accounting for cost-of-living differentials, which may change this pattern of interstate differences. To estimate the influence of regional cost-of-living differences, we have deflated average wages in 1975 with the HUD estimated fair market rent index for that year.[19] When adjusted for living cost differentials in this manner, the 1975 advantage of northern tier average public sector wages over southern tier falls from about 20 percent to an almost negligible 2 percent. This does not demonstrate that North-South public employee wage differences are primarily due to cost-of-living differences.[20] However, this calculation does suggest that price level differences may explain a substantial proportion of regional public sector wage rate differences.

If all of these caveats are disregarded or if it can be assumed that the North-South bias created by the data problems somehow cancels out, the greater average wage in the northern tier suggests that a substantial part of the state and local expenditure difference in the northern and southern states is due to public employee compensation differences. If it is further accepted that differentials in average wages across regions are not the result of public employee productivity differentials, then we have further evidence that the higher level of per capita spending in the northern states substantially overstates the difference in the average quality of services provided in the two regions.

Sources of Finance

Three aspects of the financing of state and local government expenditures are important in describing regional variations in fiscal systems: reliance on debt financing, the structure of taxes raised, and the level of revenue effort exerted. With respect to borrowing, the level of per capita general obligation debt in the northern and western tiers is higher than in the South (Table 5-4). Much of this variation, however, is due to differences in the capacity to carry debt. Indeed, comparisons of the debt-income ratio, which measures the level of debt relative to fiscal capacity show that the disparity is very narrow though the highest levels of debt burden are still in the northern tier. In fact, a state-by-state analysis shows that very high debt burdens belong to those states thought to be facing serious fiscal problems, viz., New Jersey, New York, Pennsylvania, and Massachusetts (Appendix Table 5-A). By contrast, the level of debt in the east north central states is lower than that in *any* southern subregion, attesting again to the problems with inferences from regional averages.

Table 5-4. Regional Variations in State and Local Government Finances

	Northern Tier States	Southern Tier States	Western Tier States
Per capita debt outstanding	$1,578	$1,358	$1,538
Debt outstanding as percent of personal income	14.4	14.2	14.0
Percent of revenues derived from			
Property tax	27.8	17.8	19.6
Sales tax	14.4	18.5	18.3
Income tax	22.0	12.3	18.2
Per capita federal grants	$ 396	$ 352	$ 427
Federal grants as a percent of own-source revenues	26.0	28.7	26.4

Source: U.S. Bureau of the Census, *Governmental Finances in 1980–81*.

In terms of revenue structure, there are distinct and important differences between regions. Southern and western states are more heavily reliant on sales taxes, northern states are more dependent on property and income taxes, southern states make relatively little use of income taxation, and western states have the most diversified tax structures (Table 5-4). This difference is largely a reflection of the division of financial responsibility for services between the state and local levels. Where local government involvement in the delivery of services is strong, there tends to be much heavier use of the property tax. Since the southern states tend to be more state government dominated, there is less reliance on property taxation. This difference is of considerable importance to the potential response of the fisc to growth or decline in the economic base. In the South, where there is heavy reliance on sales taxation, a combination of real economic growth and inflation will automatically generate substantial new revenues for expansion of the public sector. In the northern tier, where reliance is greater on property taxation, even the tax base growth generated by inflationary increases in income will not be fully or easily captured.[21]

In terms of the controversial issue of the regional distribution of federal aid the northern states receive, on average, 12 percent more in per capita terms than do southern states, but about 15 percent less than western states. Dependence on federal aid as a revenue source is about the same in the North and the West, but somewhat higher in the South. It is interesting to note, however, that during the post-1975 recovery period, per capita federal aid increased by a greater amount in the northern tier and the revenue dependence on federal aid actually fell in the southern tier.

Local Fiscal Problems

State-to-state variations in fiscal structure and performance mask differences between regions in the problems facing the largest local governments within the regions. Indeed, the standard stereotype would have central cities in a substantially worse position than their suburbs in terms of income level, public service level, and concentration of the poor.

Nathan and Dommel's "hardship index" compares cities both

with their surrounding suburban areas and with each other.[22] Of the fourteen cities scoring poorest on this hardship index, eleven are in the northern tier of states and only two, Atlanta and Richmond, are in the South. Of the ten cities found better off, five were in the southern tier and none in the North. Sacks's compendium of metropolitan fiscal disparities, also supports the stereotype.[23] Southern cities are poorer than northern cities but much better off relative to their own suburbs (Table 5-5). However, in all regions, per capita income is higher in suburbs than in central cities and is growing faster.

Summary: Regional Variations in State and Local Finances

These data show certain clear differences in fiscal structure and performance of state and local governments in the three regions. While there certainly are exceptions to each of these patterns, several general observations appear to hold. First, fiscal systems in the southern tier states are more dominated by state government. This means heavier state government responsibility for both financing and direct expenditures, which in turn means that the growth and distribution of total state and local expenditures is more controllable and that the growth in expenditures is financed from a more elastic revenue source. In the southern tier states, the sales tax is relied upon to a much greater extent than in the North. In the northeastern and mid-

Table 5-5. City-Suburb Disparities in Per Capita Personal Income

Region	Central City Per Capita Income ($)		Ratio of City to Suburb Per Capita Income		Percent Increase in Per Capita Income, 1975–80	
	1970	1980	1970	1980	Central City	Suburb
East	3,131[a]	6,260	.84	.74	45.1	61.8
Midwest	3,192	6,954	.92	.83	52.3	64.6
South	2,929	6,982	1.05	.97	58.0	67.2
West	3,407	7,809	1.03	.95	56.6	66.8
United States	3,165	6,997	.96	.88	53.1	63.9

[a] All values are unweighted averages.

Source: Department of Housing and Urban Development, *Changing Conditions in Metropolitan Areas,* and updates provided by Seymour Sacks.

western states, on the other hand, fiscal systems tend to be dominated more by local governments. As a result, there is a potential for much greater disparity in public spending levels in jurisdictions within the state and there is much heavier reliance on the local property tax.

With respect to the level of spending, 1981 per capita expenditures were nearly 25 percent lower in the southern states than in the rest of the nation. However, a part of this difference is due to the higher level of welfare expenditure in the northern and western tier states. Moreover, since these differences are not adjusted for regional variations in prices and since average public employee wages are much higher in the North, the difference in public service levels may be considerably less than is suggested by the 25 percent gap in per capita expenditures. Public employment levels per 10000 population are greater in the southern states and do not appear to vary systematically with the rate of population growth of a state.

There is a major difference between the two regions with respect to the fiscal health of their largest local governments. The Northeast and industrial Midwest regions seem to fit the stereotype of declining and poor central cities surrounded by relatively wealthy and less fiscally pressed suburbs. This pattern does not hold so uniformly in the West and the South. This advantaged position of southern central cities can be attributed in part to the newness of the cities and to their local government structure, which often tends to encompass growing suburban areas. There appears to be much less jurisdictional fragmentation in the West and South, in part because of the greater potential for annexation and consolidation during the rapid growth period of the past two decades. To the contrary, northern cities, which are usually surrounded by older, incorporated jurisdictions, find it all but impossible to expand jurisdictional boundaries.

COMPARATIVE FISCAL AND ECONOMIC GROWTH

How have regional movements in people and jobs affected the budgets of state and local governments? Have governments in declining regions cut expenditures or have they increased taxes to maintain service levels? Have governments in growing regions increased taxes and services to satisfy the demands of inmigrants? To what extent has a changing capacity to finance influenced fiscal decisions in growing and stagnant regions? To begin to get at these questions, one needs to explore the evidence on regional variations in (a) the fiscal responsiveness to economic growth; (b) the extent to which public expenditure growth has been influenced by demand versus cost effects; and (c) the choice among increased tax effort, borrowing and property vs. nonproperty taxes.[24]

Five time periods have been defined to study the fiscal response to economic performance in the three regions. The 1962–67 period saw a Southward movement of population and economic activity that accelerated between 1967 and 1972. The 1972–75 period includes the recession that heightened the Sunbelt movement, the 1975–77 period accounts for some of the effects of the recovery period, and the years since 1978 have seen a slackening national economic growth and a new recession. Three indicators are considered here: personal income, population, and employment.

Economic and Population Base Changes

The shift in economic activity from the northern to the southern states has been widely if not thoroughly studied. Jusenius and Ledebur[25] and Jackson et al.[26] have described this shift in terms of population movement, Greenberg and Valente[27] and Garnick[28] have studied the trends in employment, and the Congressional Budget Office[29] has described the pattern of growth in earnings and personal income.

Personal Income. Per capita personal income is a composite measure that indicates the average level of well-being of citizens in a region. As may be seen in Table 5-6, the per capita income growth in the southern and western tiers was greater than in the North for most of the 1962–81 period. This pattern appears to hold for most states in the three regions and is part of the well-known regional convergence of average standards of living in the United States.[30]

The meaning of this trend is that state and local govern-

Table 5-6. Average Annual Percent Increase in Per Capita Personal Income

State and Region	1962–67	1967–72	1972–75	1975–77	1977–81	1981 Level
NORTHERN TIER	5.8	6.6	8.6	9.5	10.3	$10,950
East North Central	5.9	6.6	9.9	10.8	9.6	10,656
Illinois	5.6	6.4	9.7	9.4	9.7	11,576
Indiana	5.9	6.4	9.0	11.0	9.2	9,720
Michigan	6.7	6.9	7.6	12.4	9.3	10,790
Ohio	5.9	6.7	8.5	10.9	9.8	10,313
Wisconsin	5.5	6.8	9.6	10.7	9.9	10,035
Middle Atlantic	5.7	6.6	8.5	8.2	10.8	11,246
New Jersey	5.3	7.1	8.5	8.6	10.9	12,127
New York	5.7	6.3	8.0	7.4	11.0	11,466
Pennsylvania	6.0	6.7	9.4	9.4	10.4	10,370
New England	5.6	6.6	8.3	9.3	11.2	11,058
Connecticut	5.6	5.9	8.4	9.4	11.9	12,816
Maine	6.0	7.0	9.1	10.7	10.3	8,535
Massachusetts	5.2	7.0	8.2	8.0	11.1	11,128
New Hampshire	5.6	6.6	8.3	10.9	11.2	9,994
Rhode Island	6.4	5.9	8.5	9.4	10.9	10,153
Vermont	7.0	7.0	7.5	8.8	11.0	8,723
SOUTHERN TIER	7.1	8.1	9.4	10.2	11.3	9,582
South Atlantic	7.0	8.6	8.6	9.5	10.9	9,719
Delaware	4.9	6.2	8.4	7.9	10.3	11,095
Maryland	5.4	8.0	8.9	9.0	11.0	11,477
North Carolina	7.5	8.4	8.8	9.1	10.6	8,649
Virginia	7.2	8.5	9.4	10.0	11.0	10,349
South Carolina	8.2	8.7	9.2	9.9	10.3	8,039
Georgia	7.9	8.4	7.9	10.0	10.7	8,934
Florida	6.5	9.3	7.6	9.5	11.7	10,165
West Virginia	7.0	8.1	10.6	9.8	9.5	8,377
East South Central	7.3	8.4	9.5	10.5	10.2	8,201
Alabama	7.0	8.6	10.1	10.5	10.2	8,219
Kentucky	6.8	7.8	10.2	10.0	9.8	8,420
Mississippi	8.7	8.8	8.9	12.1	10.5	7,408
Tennessee	7.2	8.4	8.7	10.1	10.3	8,447
West South Central	7.1	7.0	10.7	11.2	12.4	10,203
Arkansas	7.6	8.1	10.4	10.5	10.4	8,044
Louisiana	7.5	6.4	10.7	12.3	12.6	9,518
Oklahoma	6.9	7.0	10.7	10.7	12.9	10,247
Texas	6.9	7.0	10.7	11.1	12.4	10,729
WESTERN TIER	5.5	6.9	9.5	9.9	10.8	10,948
Pacific	5.2	6.4	9.3	10.1	10.7	11,679
Alaska	6.1	7.2	22.2	7.4	5.8	13,763
California	5.0	6.5	8.8	10.2	11.0	11,923
Hawaii	6.9	8.0	9.4	8.7	9.7	11,036
Oregon	5.4	7.0	9.5	11.0	9.3	10,008
Washington	5.9	5.4	11.2	9.6	11.0	11,277

State and Region	1962–67	1967–72	1972–75	1975–77	1977–81	1981 Level
Mountain	4.4	8.3	8.9	9.7	11.2	9,920
Arizona	5.0	9.2	7.0	9.4	12.0	9,754
Colorado	4.5	8.5	9.3	9.7	12.1	11,215
Idaho	5.3	8.0	9.7	10.3	10.1	8,937
Montana	3.9	7.9	10.2	6.7	11.2	9,410
Nevada	2.0	7.7	7.6	11.2	10.3	11,576
New Mexico	4.4	8.0	9.8	9.9	10.4	8,529
Utah	3.9	7.1	9.0	10.3	9.3	8,313
Wyoming	4.1	8.2	11.7	11.4	11.5	11,665
Plains	6.4	7.2	10.1	9.5	10.7	10,270
Iowa	6.9	6.8	11.6	9.1	10.7	10,474
Kansas	6.4	7.6	10.0	9.4	10.9	10,813
Minnesota	6.3	7.5	9.8	11.4	10.7	10,768
Missouri	6.2	6.2	9.2	9.9	10.0	9,651
Nebraska	6.1	7.7	10.4	7.4	11.3	10,366
North Dakota	5.6	10.7	11.5	2.1	13.6	10,213
South Dakota	5.4	8.5	9.1	8.3	10.9	8,833

Source: Department of Commerce, *Survey of Current Business*, August 1976, August, 1978, August 1982; *Current Population Reports*, Series P-25, No. 727, July 1978, July 1982.

ments in different regions of the country are becoming much more alike in their capacity to finance public services; northern states can less afford to provide the better package of education services and income transfer payments and heretofore poorer states can now afford to catch up.

Changes in the composition of income can also be important to the fiscal health of state and local governments. In particular, if there were an increase in the share of transfer payments (Social Security, pensions, AFDC receipts) in total personal income, the taxpaying "power" of a given dollar in personal income might be reduced. In fact, the transfer payments share has remained about the same in all regions (13.9 percent in the North and South and 12.8 percent in the West in 1980). These data offer no evidence that changes in the composition of income have compromised the variation in taxable capacity from state to state. However, in the case of large central city governments, changes in the composition of personal income may well have had a dampening effect on potential revenue growth. In particular, the shift of income composition from manufacturing to government and services may have depressed the level of property tax revenues to below what they otherwise would have been.[31] Again, these effects will be less pronounced in southern states, where there is much less reliance on local property taxation.

Employment. Public and private sector employment has grown more rapidly in the southern and western tier states for past two decades. Perhaps even more important in the context of this analysis is that the relatively low rate of employment growth in the northern tier between 1967 and 1972 turned to literally no growth, and in some states decline, between 1972 and 1975. Employment growth in the North has been relatively slow since 1975. In the southern tier, on the other hand, although the growth rate decreased between 1972 and 1975, only one state (Delaware) showed an absolute job loss. Indeed, the southern and western regions participated to a much greater extent than northern states in the post-1975 recovery (Table 5-7). Some subregions performed differently from the rest of their region, but on the whole these regional disparities accurately describe the situation.

Garnick has argued that these regional shifts in national employment shares reflect substantial declines in large northern central cities, with central counties of the large SMSAs in particular having been subject to absolute declines in employment (especially manufacturing) after 1960.[32] The same pattern has been documented in studies of employment growth in the ten largest city-counties.[33] Declines were registered in New York City, Philadelphia, and St. Louis, with only a modest increment in Baltimore. The largest percentage increases in employment were in Denver, Indianapolis, Jacksonville, Nashville, and New Orleans.[34] Also in agreement are Sacks's estimates for 1970–77 which show employment declines in fourteen of sixteen northeastern cities studied, eight of twenty midwestern cities, three of twenty-eight southern cities, and four of twenty western cities. He estimates the average annual rate of employment growth to be −1.6 percent in the northeastern cities, −0.3 percent in the Midwest, 3.0 percent in the South, and 2.3 percent in the West.[35]

Table 5-7. Indicators of Fiscal Capacity and Need

	Average Annual Growth Rate				
	1962–67	1967–72	1972–75	1975–77	1977–81
Employment					
Northern tier	2.9	1.1	0.3	2.4	1.1
Southern tier	4.5	3.8	2.7	4.3	3.6
Western tier	3.7	2.8	2.8	4.9	3.3
Population					
Northern tier	1.10	0.69	0.02	0.06	0.09
Southern tier	1.16	1.65	1.90	1.65	2.26
Western tier	1.43	1.42	1.61	1.71	2.17
AFDC recipients					
Northern tier	7.32	17.19	2.36	−2.16	−0.36
Southern tier	4.12	15.97	−0.33	−4.99	−0.83
Western tier	11.59	13.64	0.57	−1.35	−0.85
Enrollments					
Northern tier	2.72	1.32	−1.28	−1.67	−3.96
Southern tier	1.88	0.74	−0.25	−0.95	−0.50
Western tier	2.84	0.76	−1.11	−1.05	−2.02
Per capita income					
Northern tier	5.79	6.58	8.61	9.51	10.3
Soutern tier	7.12	8.08	9.41	10.22	11.3
Western tier	5.52	6.93	9.48	9.86	10.8

Source: Employment data from U.S. Department of Labor, *Employment and Earnings, States and Areas, 1939–1978;* U.S. Department of Labor, *Supplement to Employment and Earnings, States, and Areas Data for 1977–81.* Population data from U.S. Bureau of Census, unpublished source; AFDC information from U.S. Bureau of the Census, *Statistical Abstract of the United States: 1963, 1968, 1973, 1977, 1978* and Department of Health and Human Services *1981 Social Security Bulletin Annual Statistical Supplement, 1977–79.* Enrollment data from U.S. Bureau of the Census, *Statistical Abstract of the United States: 1970,* and National Center for Education Statistics, *Digest of Educational Statistics,* 1977 and 1981. Per capita data from Department of Commerce, *Survey of Current Business,* August, 1976, August 1978, July 1981 and *Current Population Reports,* Series P-25, No. 727, July 1978, No. 911, April 1982.

Population. Yet a third way to measure the change in economic activity in the three regions is to examine the pattern and trend of population growth. On the revenue side, a declining population may mean a diminished capacity to finance public services if the population lost consists of higher-income families. The evidence indicates this to be the case; regional migrants tend to be younger and better educated than nonmigrants at the point of origin or destination.[36] Migrants into the faster growing regions, on the other hand, may raise expenditure demands as well as the revenue base. Because they are typically migrating from the northern states, where public service levels are higher, they may increase the pressure for increased public expenditures. The expenditure "determinants" literature provides some evidence that population growth and changing demographic makeup influence the level of public expenditures. Weinstein and Firestine, for example, have analyzed the relations between migration, demographic change, and state and local government budgets and find evidence of positive effects of in-migration on spending levels.[37] Other studies have identified population size and density and concentrations of the poor as being significant determinants of the level of public spending.[38]

The evidence suggests that migration has probably raised expenditure pressures in all regions but has had the most compromising effect on the fiscal position of northern states. Population growth in the northern tier has slowed markedly since 1962 and has been negligible since 1972 (Table 5-7) while the rate of population growth in the South and West has remained high. No state outside the northern tier showed a population decline between 1972 and 1980 (except Iowa during 1977–80), while four northern states—Massachusetts, New York, Pennsylvania, and Rhode Island—lost population. Though most of the population changes were due to migration, it is interesting to note that because of higher fertility rates the southern tier would have grown faster than the northern tier even in the absence of migration between the regions.[39] With respect to the composition of population change, little data are available on the income level and employment characteristics of migrants.[40]

There are other compositional changes in population that may effect the budgetary position of state and local governments. The number of AFDC recipients might be taken as a rough indicator of the change in concentration of poor families. Again, the data indicate a comparative disadvantage for northern tier states. The number of AFDC recipients increased at a generally higher rate in the North than in the other regions in the first three periods considered (Table 5-7), while the reverse was true for percentage increases in total population. During the post-1975 recovery, the number of AFDC recipients declined everywhere, but most rapidly in the southern tier. By 1977, AFDC recipients as a proportion of the population in the northern region were 5.7 percent, 50 percent above the proportion in the South. It may also be seen from Table 5-7 that the number of school-aged children declined at the highest rate in the northern region, perhaps suggesting some relief from the pressures for public expenditure increases. The deconcentration of population from northern metropolitan areas may also have provided some expenditure relief during the 1970s, but the reverse may have been true in the South and West, where metropolitan area populations increased.[41]

In terms of population change within metropolitan areas, some evidence is available on the changes by central city/outside central city and by race. These data show that all cities have tended to lose their share of metropolitan area population to suburbs, but the loss has been greatest in the North. The population decline in the major cities of the East between 1960 and 1970 was predominantly an exodus of white population—no major central city in the East showed a gain of white population between 1960 and 1970.[42]

Expenditure Growth Patterns

Given the slower economic and population growth in the northern states, a commensurately slower growth in fiscal activity might have been expected. In fact, per capita expenditure growth in the northern tier states was above that in the southern and western states through 1975 (Table 5-8). Indeed, expenditures grew proportionately more than personal income in all regions between 1962 and 1972, as indicated by the expenditure-revenue elasticities presented in Table 5-8.[43] Even in the 1972–75 period, when total employment increased by 2.7 percent in the South, 2.8 percent in the West, and only 0.3 percent in the North, relative per capita expenditure growth in the northern states did not fall off markedly. From this evidence, one might conclude that, during this period, there was not a strong relationship between the growth in public expenditures in the two regions and the capacity to finance that growth.[44] In particular state and local governments in the northern region, seemed unwilling or unable to recognize the increasingly strin-

Table 5-8.   Indicators of Expansion in Fiscal Activity

Indicator	Average Annual Percent Increase		
	Northern Tier	Southern Tier	Western Tier
Per capita state and local government expenditures			
1962–67	6.42	7.08	7.00
1967–72	13.22	9.78	9.14
1972–75	11.42	12.31	10.50
1975–77	7.54	9.27	9.16
1977–78	5.45	9.30	10.56
1978–79	9.51	11.94	6.23
1979–80	10.75	13.07	14.63
1980–81	8.94	7.83	10.69
Expenditure-income elasticity			
1962–67	1.11	0.99	1.27
1967–72	2.01	1.21	1.32
1972–75	1.33	1.31	1.11
1975–77	0.79	0.91	0.93
1977–78	0.54	0.82	0.91
1978–79	0.84	1.10	0.51
1979–80	1.05	1.08	1.43
1980–81	0.98	0.89	0.89
State and local government employment per 10,000 population			
1962–67	3.6	4.4	3.4
1967–72	2.6	2.8	2.4
1972–75	2.1	2.8	1.9
1975–77	0.4	1.9	1.6
1977–81	0.2	−0.5	−1.8
State and local government payroll per employee			
1962–67	5.2	4.9	4.4
1967–72	6.8	6.1	5.8
1972–75	6.8	8.2	8.6
1975–77	5.9	7.1	7.1
1977–81	7.7	8.5	8.8

Source: Government employment and payroll data from U.S. Bureau of the Census, *State Distribution of Public Employment, 1962.* Population data from *Current Population Reports,* Series P-25, No. 727, July 1978 and No. 911, July 1982. Government expenditure data from U.S. Department of Commerce, Bureau of the Census, Governmental Finances in 1980–81, 1979–80, 1976–77, 1973–74, 1970–71, 1967–68, 1964–65, 1963–64.

gent fiscal limitations imposed by their slow-growing economic bases. The jolt that finally drove home this new reality was the 1975 recession.

The first evidence of serious fiscal restraint in the state and local government sector shows up in the 1975–78 recovery period, when the growth in expenditures fell below the growth in income in all regions. In some states this lagged and long overdue response to slow-growing economic activity was spurred by the New York City financial collapse and the near disasters in several other cities. These crises finally made it clear that the public sector in many northern tier states could no longer sustain itself. Reduction, cutbacks, and deferrals became the centerpieces of state and local government fiscal policies. This austerity pattern has generally held since 1978.

Expenditure Growth Determinants

The recession turned around the pattern of state and local government expenditure growth, but, many other factors had important effects on regional variations in the fiscal response to regional economic shifts. These influences, which grew out of the economic and demographic changes outlined above, might be thought of as demand-side and supply-side factors. On the demand side, growing requirements for services resulted in increased numbers of public employees and thereby exerted an upward pressure on expenditures. On the supply side, increased public employee compensation resulted from union pressures and inflation and forced up expenditure levels.

Demand-Side Effects. There is a wealth of literature on expenditure determinants that attests to the difficulties of separating demand from supply influence in explaining expenditure growth and variations.[45] Those difficulties notwithstanding, one might proxy the growth in service demand with the three indicators examined above: population growth to indicate the general increase in public service requirements, increase in AFDC recipients to indicate the growth in the needs of the poor, and increase in primary and secondary school enrollments to indicate the potential increase in the education claim on state and local government budgets. To the extent that these factors increased over the time period studied, an increase in total state and local government expenditures might be expected.

Population grew faster in the South and West, indicating an increased need for public services in those regions. There was much less pressure from population growth in the northern region; indeed, several of the more industrialized states lost population. On the revenue side, the evidence suggests that regional migration probably transferred a substantial amount of taxable capacity from the losing to the gaining regions. There were also compositional effects: the northern states continued to have a heavier concentration of the poor but the relative number of school-aged children increased more in the growing southern and western regions.

One might hypothesize that the net effects of interregional migration were to disadvantage the northern states. Although there was some relaxation of expenditure pressures because of slower population growth, there was an increase in expenditure pressure due to an increasing concentration of the poor. Moreover, migration probably reduced taxable capacity to below what would have been the case under a no-migration scenario. Paradoxically, public expenditures were probably also bid up in states receiving migration because in-migrants came with expectations for higher levels of public services. On the other hand, they also brought a higher level of capacity to pay taxes, thereby ameliorating some of the budgetary pressures.

Public employment did increase rapidly in all regions between 1962 and 1975 in response to population and school enrollment growth and growing numbers of the poor. Indeed, the number of public employees grew considerably faster than population in all regions. From the employment growth patterns described in Table 5-8, there is no indication that northern tier states recognized the fiscal constraints to maintaining this growth.

Things began to change after the 1975 recession. There has been little increase in per capita public employment in the North—a direct response to the slow economic and population growth of the region. There has also been a marked slowdown in public employment growth in the West, in part a response to Proposition 13. Public employment growth in southern states has been erratic since 1975. The implication here is that after 1975, both growing and declining states began to adjust to their economic situation.

Supply-Side Effects. Pressures for increased public expenditures can also come from the supply side, in the form of increased compensation of public employees. As may be seen in Table 5-8, the percentage increase in payroll per employee was slightly higher in the northern than in the southern or western states over the 1962–72 period—this despite the fact that the relative capacity to finance such increases in northern states was declining. By the 1972–75 period, the rate of increase in average wages in the North had fallen below that in the South and West.[46] This pattern has continued since 1975.

Revenue Growth

The comparisons above might be summarized as showing that, relative to personal income growth, expenditures in the northern states expanded too fast during the 1960s and early 1970s. As a consequence, revenue effort in the northern tier states increased more rapidly than in other regions. The post-1975 retrenchment eased this pressure some but could not reverse the disadvantaged tax position that northern states had bought (Appendix Table 5-A). ACIR analyses of both the level and the direction of tax effort classified nine northern and only three southern states as having high and rising levels of tax effort.[47]

How did state and local governments adjust their tax systems as economic growth changed during the 1960s and early 1970s? A comparison of the growth in own-source revenues with the growth in personal income, revenue-income elasticities, are shown in Table 5-9.[48] For example, between 1972 and 1975, for every 1 percent increase in personal income, the "average" state and local government increased its revenues by 1.05 percent in the North, 1.06 percent in the South, and 0.95 percent in the West. Surprisingly, the income elasticities are highest for the northern region before 1972 and about the same as for the other regions through 1977. Despite its slower growth in income, population, and jobs, taxes have continued to rise at a roughly comparable rate in the northern region. There has been substantial revenue austerity in all regions since 1977—most states have kept their revenue growth at or below that in personal income.

Table 5-9.   Overall Responsiveness of Revenues to Economic Activity, 1962–81

	1962–67	1967–72	1972–75	1975–77	1977–81
Northern tier					
Average Annual Percent Change					
Own-source revenue	8.16	12.58	9.05	9.90	8.50
Personal income	6.96	7.31	8.63	9.57	10.40
Own-source revenue-income					
elasticity	1.17	1.72	1.05	1.03	0.25
Southern tier					
Average Annual Percent Change					
Own-source revenue	9.12	12.20	12.15	11.25	12.93
Personal income	8.37	9.86	11.50	12.03	13.28
Own-source revenue-income					
elasticity	1.09	1.24	1.06	0.94	0.97
Western tier					
Average Annual Percent Change					
Own-source revenue	8.96	11.42	10.71	12.54	11.34
Personal income	7.03	8.45	11.24	11.74	12.78
Own-source revenue-income					
elasticity	1.27	1.35	0.95	1.07	0.89

Source: U.S. Bureau of the Census, *Governmental Finances in 1962, 1966–67, 1971–72, 1974–75, 1976–77, 1980–81*, GF67; and Department of Commerce, *Survey of Current Business*, August 1976, 1978, 1982.

The presentation in Table 5-10 disaggregates increases in state and local government revenue by source of increase. The results are helpful in understanding the mechanics of the fiscal response over the period in question. Three patterns of change stand out. First, there was a growing use of sales and income taxes in all regions. Second, there continues to be a much lighter reliance on property taxes in the southern states. Third, the regional pattern of reliance on federal grant financing has changed. The southern and western states were more dependent on grants throughout this period, but this dependence has not increased substantially. The northern states, on the other hand, financed only 19 percent of their 1962–67 expenditure increases with grants as compared to 27 percent of their 1975–77 period increase, and 23 percent of their 1977–80 increase. The direct federal-to-local aid included in the stimulus package accounted for much of this increase; hence the increased reliance after 1975 may be a temporary change rather than a long-

Table 5-10. Sources of Increase in General Revenues of State and Local Governments

	Northern Tier	Southern Tier	Western Tier
Increase due to property tax (%)			
1962–67	21.9	16.3	25.8
1967–72	24.1	13.1	24.0
1972–75	18.6	12.1	18.0
1975–77	18.6	15.6	23.3
1977–81	15.4	11.0	−0.4
Increase due to sales and income taxes (%)			
1962–67	24.6	18.8	16.1
1967–72	26.8	25.7	24.6
1972–75	36.7	27.5	42.4
1975–77	35.7	25.3	28.2
1977–81	31.5	25.2	33.6
Increase due to federal aid (%)			
1962–67	19.0	25.1	26.0
1967–72	20.2	22.3	20.3
1972–75	25.7	27.5	22.3
1975–77	26.9	26.8	26.0
1977–81	21.4	19.8	19.3

Source: U.S. Department of Commerce, Bureau of the Census, *Governmental Finances in 1962, 66–67, 71–72, 74–75, 76–77, 80–81.*

term trend. Again, this pattern holds true for most states in the three regions.

IMPLICATIONS FOR PUBLIC POLICY

For purposes of public policy formulation, it is important to at least try and separate the general fiscal problems of state and local governments from those that have been exacerbated by regional shifts. The dilemma faced by the declining states in the Northeast is that their public sector has become overdeveloped relative to their financial capacity. As a result, tax burdens are high, there is little additional public money to be devoted to what are thought to be serious city fiscal problems, and fixed debt and pension commitments command an ever-increasing share of budgets. Because regional shifts in economic activity do not yet appear to have run their course, the prospects that this situation will ease are not good. To be sure, this fiscal di-

lemma does not fit all state and local governments in the northeastern and midwestern regions and likely describes some
southern and western metropolitan area governments as well,
but the pattern is true enough to be a reasonably accurate generalization. The southern fiscal problem is different, almost opposite. The public sector tends to be underdeveloped, facing
increasing pressures to spend more but remaining hesitant to
increase tax rates to northern levels.

Alternative Strategies

How should policy be adjusted to deal with the fiscal problems
resulting from regional shifts? One strategy would be to take
no direct action. The argument would be that market forces
will eventually correct regional disparities in real income, employment, and population and that a narrowing of regional disparities in public service levels will follow. Eventually, as growth
in the resource base continues to slow, growth in the public
sector in the North will also slow. The problem with this line
of reasoning is that shrinkage in the public sector in the North
will likely mean a cutting of service levels in those areas where
expenditures are greatest—health, education, and welfare. This
may imply that much of the painful burden of the transition to
a lower level of public services will be borne by lower income
residents in the declining regions.[49]

Others have proposed a more active strategy, ranging from
subsidies to bring about a reversal of northern economic decline to increased federal assistance to the declining region during the transition period. In practice, there are several policy
options available to deal with this issue: cut services, raise taxes,
increase productivity, increase federal assistance, or improve the
local economy. The first three are options for state and local
government action, and the last two require federal action.

Options for State and Local Governments.   Increased productivity
in the public sector is a favorite policy recommendation of politicians everywhere because it resolves fiscal problems without
requiring governments to either raise taxes or cut services. Better yet, since productivity in the public sector cannot be unam-
biguously measured there is no way to evaluate the success or

failure of a productivity improvement program.[50] From the point of view of a city manager or city council, productivity improvement may seem much less the panacea. While there is clearly room for improved management at the local government level, large savings (relative to projected deficits) from increased productivity in the public sector are not a realistic expectation.[51]

Revenues might be increased through further increase in the effective tax rate. The argument against this strategy is the possible retarding effect on economic development. State and local government revenue effort in the northeastern and midwestern regions is already high relative to that in the South, a difference that would reinforce the argument to lower rather than raise taxes for competitive reasons. Although this pattern certainly does not hold for all states in the declining regions— Connecticut and Ohio have revenue efforts among the lowest in the United States—it fits many of the large industrial states. Southern states, on the other hand, seem loathe to raise taxes to northern levels and possibly sacrifice what they have long believed to be an important comparative advantage. Over all this lies a general mood in the country to resist tax increases for any purpose.

Service level reductions are the most likely route to be followed by the declining northern tier state and local governments. While there will be some absolute cutbacks in the sense of reductions in the scope of services, expenditure retrenchment will mostly take the form of services not expanding to accommodate increasing needs or to fully match inflationary cost increases. However, this cutback in services does not mean that expenditures will decline. Increasing wages and benefits— even if outpaced by inflation—can drive up expenditures by a significant amount without raising service levels. The outlook in the South is more likely an increasing of service levels, both in the absolute and relative to the northern tier.

There is another type of state and local government reform, one that is highly desirable though politically difficult. If the tax base in the suburbs could be tapped more fully so as to balance the need for services with the capacity to finance, the fiscal situation in central cities could be markedly improved.

History has not shown this to be a viable alternative in the northern industrial states, but it has been accomplished in the South through consolidations and annexations.

Options for the Federal Government.   There is an endless number of proposals for federal action to deal with regional shifts. Most are politically motivated and involve arguments by interested parties that more federal money should be targeted to their region. No administration in the past two decades has been able to integrate these conflicting claims into a coherent national regional development policy. Though the responsibility for formulating such a policy is clearly on the shoulders of the national government, political constraints are so severe that a policy statement is not likely to emerge.

In tracing out the options for federal action, we might first consider those that directly address the fiscal problems of state and local government in the declining regions. A first and obvious federal approach would be to increase the flow of aid to the states in order to prop up their sagging public sectors. However, it is important to identify the objectives of this increased aid flow. A program of increased federal aid during a transition period in which a state was seeking to balance its long-term spending expectations with its likely future economic growth would be a sane program. The problem in the declining regions is that state and local governments must get their expectations for public service levels in line with their capacity to finance those service levels and their willingness to increase taxes. Neither perpetual federal grant subsidies nor across-the-board cuts in federal assistance are good long-term answers.

There are a number of compensatory federal policies that might be undertaken during the fiscal adjustment period—that period when the public sector in the North is moving to a lower level commensurate with its capacity to finance. One element of such a program would be a continuation and expansion of the countercyclical revenue-sharing program and the temporary public sector job-related programs. The most important ingredient of fiscal reform, however, would be an increased level of federal financing of public welfare, including Medicaid.

Such programs offer state and local governments the kind

of flexibility needed to cover some of the public service deficits and unemployment-related costs of decline and also fit the criterion of being compensatory. Yet within this program of compensatory grants, there must be stringent conditions. States will ultimately have to develop long-term fiscal plans for their state and local government sectors. These plans will have to show how the state's public sector intends to move its expenditure growth requirements into line with its projected increase in financial capacity. Compensatory grants would also have to carry the requirement that aid be more heavily targeted on those who 'suffer most from the transition period: the poor and the unemployed.

Another oft-suggested approach to shoring up the declining regions is to improve their comparative economic advantage through a program of regional development subsidies. One proposal for dealing with the problems of decline is the creation of a regional energy and development corporation that would finance regional development projects using federally guaranteed taxable bonds.[52] It is hoped that such an activity would accelerate development of eastern coal and result in substantial job generation. Other types of regional subsidies have been suggested for the same purpose, i.e., to improve the competitive position of the declining regions. These include proposals for a federal tax program of double-accelerated depreciation for firms making new investments in regions of economic stagnation, the establishment of federal tax credits and expanded energy entitlements to offset the energy premium that the Northeast pays, and a change in the emphasis of federal programs from new construction to reconstruction and rehabilitation.[53]

If regional subsidies work, they could have a strong positive effect on the finances of governments in the declining regions. There are two caveats, however, even to the potentially favorable government finance effects. One is that the fiscal problems in the declining regions are very much the fiscal problems of the central cities in those regions. Historically, these cities have not always shared in the economic growth of the region, and therefore it is not clear how much their fiscal positions would improve in the event regional shifts slowed. A second, and related, caveat is that state and local governments in the declining regions tend to be more heavily dependent on local property taxation, which may make it difficult to fully capture increases in regional income and employment for the public sector. The most important issue with respect to regional subsidies, however, remains whether or not they induce any net improvement in private sector economic activity.

What, then, should be federal policy toward the states in the southern region, growing but still poorer, having lower public service levels but taxing at lower rates, and facing the new pressures of rapid population growth? In a sense, many of the southern problems will be resolved by continued shifts of economic activity and continued growth. In the energy-intensive states, this growth will be supplemented by substantial energy revenues—depending on the price of oil. What this leaves is the need for a federal policy to adjust grant distributions to reflect (a) the very heavy concentration of the poor in the rural South and (b) proper changes in the share of federal grants allocated to southern states. It is reasonable to expect that, as relative income levels in the growing regions continue to climb, federal grant shares should begin to diminish.

Improved Fiscal Balance

The fiscal problem of many northern tier states is that their public sectors are overdeveloped. The resource bases of these states will no longer support the higher level of public services provided unless tax rates are continually increased. While shifts in population and economic activity are tending to equalize income levels across the country, the northern states have retained dominance in their relative national role in state and local fiscal activity. This can no longer be done. A downward transition must be recognized, and policy should center on selecting priorities in the adjustment of public service levels. With appropriate federal aid, this need not mean severe service cutbacks in all areas, but rather a slow growth in services provided while the rest of the nation catches up. A program of transition grants could ease the pain in this catch-up period.

Lessons for the Growing Regions

It is likely that the rapid fiscal expansion in the state and local sector in the South has yet to come. Investments in public infrastructure and human capital often lag behind growth in population and income level. It is noteworthy that this growth has been particularly rapid over the past five years.

If the southern tier of states is about to enter a fiscal growth period similar to that experienced in the northern tier in the 1960s and early 1970s, some of the painful fiscal lessons of that period might be well learned. Many of the problems facing the northern tier states are not of their own making. The very rapid fiscal expansion in the mid and late 1960s and early 1970s was to a large extent the result of union pressures for higher employee compensation—a demand that was abetted by a high rate of inflation—and a crowding of high-cost low-income citizens into the central cities. Much of this expenditure increase would have been difficult to avoid. Other aspects of the expansion, however, were more discretionary, for example, the adding of substantial numbers to the public employee rolls and the buying into federal programs to expand the scope of service offered.

The growing states with rapidly developing public sectors have much to learn from this experience. The lesson is not that public employee unionization should be resisted or that public service levels should be kept at modest levels but rather that the longer-term consequences of fiscal decisions should be continually and systematically monitored. Moreover, there are conditions in the growing regions that may make the growth experience much less painful than in the northern tier. A more favorable local government structure and a more elastic tax mix may allow bigger, newer cities in the growth regions to avoid the central city financial crises which are now so common in the northern tier.

Appendix Table 5-A. 1981 Levels of Revenue Effort and General
Obligation Debt

State and Region	Revenues from Own Sources per $1,000 of Personal Income	General Obligation Debt	
		Per Capita	As Percent of Personal Income
NORTHERN TIER	139.3	1,578	14.4
East North Central	130.8	1,120	10.5
Illinois	126.0	1,332	11.5
Indiana	119.0	769	7.9
Michigan	148.7	1,231	11.5
Ohio	116.7	917	8.9
Wisconsin	153.0	1,250	12.4
Middle Atlantic	150.7	2,051	18.2
New Jersey	127.7	1,709	14.0
New York	175.6	2,528	22.0
Pennsylvania	126.6	1,571	15.1
New England	132.7	1,711	15.5
Connecticut	114.3	1,897	14.7
Maine	137.4	1,246	14.5
Massachusetts	144.5	1,684	15.0
New Hampshire	105.5	1,488	14.6
Rhode Island	143.8	2,281	22.3
Vermont	149.8	1,564	17.8
SOUTHERN TIER	128.6	1,358	14.2
South Atlantic	126.3	1,258	13.0
Delaware	149.2	2,855	25.6
Maryland	137.5	1,910	16.5
North Carolina	122.9	795	9.1
Virginia	120.4	1,085	10.3
South Carolina	134.6	1,232	15.1
Georgia	137.6	1,210	13.3
Florida	115.0	1,264	11.9
West Virginia	138.9	1,884	22.5
East South Central	134.3	1,360	16.6
Alabama	149.5	1,129	13.6
Kentucky	125.7	2,032	24.1
Mississippi	142.1	839	11.3
Tennessee	124.9	1,322	15.6
West South Central	129.1	1,511	14.8
Arkansas	121.2	1,004	12.4
Louisiana	151.9	2,044	21.0
Oklahoma	135.3	1,259	12.0
Texas	122.8	1,565	14.0
WESTERN TIER	147.7	1,538	14.0
Pacific	152.7	1,679	14.4
Alaska	892.2	12,970	91.9
California	140.2	1,090	8.9
Hawaii	164.0	2,186	19.5

Oregon	165.9	3,136	31.1
Washington	130.6	3,176	27.6
Mountain	150.6	1,299	13.1
Arizona	139.5	1,884	18.8
Colorado	129.6	1,524	1.2
Idaho	127.3	761	8.4
Montana	164.4	1,508	15.9
Nevada	134.8	1,747	14.3
Utah	148.8	1,485	17.2
Wyoming	239.9	3,233	26.4
New Mexico	217.9	2,051	23.6
Plains	135.0	1,437	14.0
Iowa	137.2	805	7.7
Kansas	130.1	1,605	14.7
Minnesota	156.1	1,909	17.6
Missouri	109.5	901	9.3
Nebraska	138.4	2,849	27.4
North Dakota	173.6	1,239	12.0
South Dakota	140.6	1,633	18.6

Source: U.S. Bureau of the Census, *Governmental Finances in 1980–81, Current Population Report*, July 1982; Department of Commerce, *Survey of Current Business*, August 1982.

CHAPTER 6

THE NEXT DECADE IN STATE AND LOCAL GOVERNMENT FINANCE: A PERIOD OF ADJUSTMENT

The 1980s will be a period of fiscal adjustment for state and local governments. The formerly rich states will be struggling to hold their public service package at a level they can afford, the formerly poor states will be struggling to raise service levels in response to the demands of their new populations, and all will have to adjust to a slower-growing United States economy and more uncertainty about inflation, recession, and the interest rate. The lessons on how to get along with less will be painfully learned by more than a few state and local governments.

How will changes in the United States economy affect state and local government finances in the 1980s, and what government policy responses will be necessary? Will state and local governments increase their expenditures as a share of GNP and will they be more or less concerned with income redistribution? Will newer federalisms and the infrastructure backlog push up state and local government taxes and borrowing or will voters continue pressure to limit the size of government at all levels? Will the chronic fiscal problems of the declining cities still be with us in 1990? In trying to answer such important questions, we first consider those national economic and demographic factors that will shape the outlook and then turn to a discussion of the essentials of a national urban policy and of possible policy adjustments by state and local governments. The chapter concludes with a judgment about what the next few years hold in store for state and local government finances.

FACTORS SHAPING THE OUTLOOK

That state and local governments everywhere are facing problems of adjustment is a reflection of the performance of the United States economy and of the changing structure of its population. A slowing national income growth and a shift in its regional distribution, a changing population structure, changes in federal budget and federal grant policy, and a new voter resistance to big government and regulation all exert important pressures on the condition of state and local government finances, and all will call for policy responses.

In truth, the changes are less recent than some policy analysts and government officials should be willing to admit. The lower rate of income and population growth has been recognized for several years now, as has the ongoing pattern of regional shifts in population and economic activity. Old fiscal habits die slowly, however, and adjustments take time. Moreover, such adjustments are difficult to make because some state and local government costs are not controllable (pensions, debt), some are not easily adjustable (AFDC payments), and every administration seems to complicate matters with its own brand of new federalism.

National Economic Performance

The performance of the United States economy is the major determinant of the fiscal health of state and local governments. The nature of the effects, however, are complicated and are not uniform across all local governments. In the following sections, we offer three hypotheses:

> That the slower growth of the United States economy in the 1980s (versus the 1970s) will lead to a declining GNP share of the state and local government sector.

That the lower rate of inflation expected for the 1980s will lead to a higher level of real state and local government expenditures than would a higher rate of inflation.

That more uncertainty about inflation and recession will dampen the growth in state and local government expenditures.

Slower Growth.   The prospect for the 1980s is for real GNP to grow more slowly than in the 1960s and 1970s. Between 1970 and 1980, the real GNP growth rate was positive in seven years and averaged 4.8 percent in those years. For the ten years of positive growth rates in the 1960s, the average was 4.2 percent. Many analysts see the 1980s as holding lower rates of real growth.

The Reagan administration's forecast of future economic conditions—projections that are consistent with the economic policy objectives of the administration and *assume* steady progress in reducing unemployment, inflation, and interest rates—is one corner of optimism about the future. In its 1983 Report, the President's Council of Economic Advisers projected a 6.5 percent unemployment rate, a 4.4 percent inflation rate and a 4.0 percent real GNP growth rate by 1988.[1] To the extent that these long-term inflation and unemployment targets are not attainable, slower real income growth will result.

The Bureau of Labor Statistics is less optimistic and has made baseline projections of a 3.2 to 3.6 annual real growth rate in GNP for the 1980s. These projections require that inflation slow from 5.5 percent in the early 1980s to 4.4 percent by the end of the decade and that the unemployment rate gradually fall to 4.5 percent by 1990.[2] The Congressional Budget Office "baseline" projections to 1988 see a 3.5 percent GNP growth rate to be attainable, with a 7.5 percent unemployment rate and a 3.7 percent rate of inflation.[3] Their "low path" projections are for a real GNP growth rate of 3.0 percent. The Joint Economic Committee reports Data Resources' (DRI) 1986 forecasts of a real GNP growth in the 3.7 percent range with unemployment at 6.6 percent and inflation at 7.6 percent.[4] The Bureau of Economic Analysis of the United States Department of Commerce projects a real growth rate in personal income of 3.3 percent between 1978 and 2000.[5] From almost every vantage, the conclusion seems to be the same. For at least a few years, the United States economy is going to grow more slowly than it did during the past two decades.

In light of these prospects for slower national economic growth, one might ask about the possibilities for growth in the state and local government sector. Will state and local government finances shrink in proportion to the general economy, or can this sector capture an increasing share of a smaller pie? Under their baseline employment expansion assumptions, the BLS projected the state and local government sector to decline between 1980 and 1985 in terms of employment (12 percent of total employment to 11.6 percent), purchases of goods and services (12.6 percent of GNP to 11.1 percent), and personal taxes (3.2 to 2.9 percent of GNP).[6] The DRI stagflation forecast is for a decline in real purchases by state and local governments after 1982.[7] Hence in at least two models the consensus seems to be a smaller share for the state and local government sector.

Another approach to assessing the outlook is to extrapolate state and local government revenues under a lower national growth rate in GNP. If the growth rate remained at 3.5 percent in the 1980s—about 1.0 percent below the average increase in the 1970s—state and local governments would face a difficult choice. A first possibility is that they could hold tax burdens constant at 8.3 percent of GNP, but would lose about 7 percent of tax revenues annually. This would lead, necessarily, to substantial expenditure retrenchment and a smaller state and local government sector. A different choice would be to keep the real level of tax revenues constant by allowing the tax burden to rise from 8.3 to 8.9 percent of GNP. This alternative would allow the state and local government sector to maintain its share of national economic activity, but eliminates any possibilities for tax reduction. A third choice would be to resume the growth patterns of the 1960s and early 1970s and allow the tax burden to rise above the 8.9 percent level.

All else being held constant, one might guess at an outcome somewhere between these first two choices and, consequently, a state and local government sector that would be smaller in 1990 than it was in 1980. All else, however, is not constant. In particular, the growth in federal grants will surely be well below its 6.9 percent annual real increase of the 1970–80 period. Even if we make the unlikely assumption that the federal grant share of GNP remained constant (at its 1981 level) throughout the 1980s, a 3.5 percent growth rate in real GNP would imply an annual revenue shortfall equivalent to 2.6 percent of state and local government taxes.

To summarize, the slowing of real growth—for example, the downward shift to a 3.5 percent real economic growth rate— will depress the growth in tax bases and federal grants and leave state and local governments with a revenue gap equivalent to about 9.6 percent of taxes. They may fill this gap by increasing the tax burden from 8.3 to 9.1 percent of GNP or cutting general expenditures by 5.4 percent. The most likely solution, some combination of these choices, suggests that the state and local government sector will decline relative to the rest of the economy.

What complicates any statement about the fiscal implications of this economic scenario is that some areas of the country will be hit harder than others by slow growth and by cutbacks in the real amount of federal aid. The industrialized states in the Northeast and Midwest will probably experience very little real growth, and central cities in those regions will be the hardest pressed. Some governments could well face revenue growth rates lower than the national rate of inflation; i.e., little if any real revenue growth may occur. Indeed, there was no real growth in revenues raised from own sources by state and local governments in New York, New Jersey, or Indiana between 1977 and 1980. Six other states (Connecticut, Delaware, Maine, Massachusetts, Pennsylvania, and Vermont) joined these three with no real growth between 1978 and 1980.

Many of the growing states will not escape the revenue effects of the national slowdown. Those without substantial energy resources could face a larger *reduction* in their rate of revenue increase than many of the northern states, who have already entered a period of fiscal austerity.[8] Still, the growing states will experience positive real revenue growth, and, because their tax rates are relatively low, they have latitude for discretionary increases.

Inflation. Most projections for the 1980s do not see the inflation rate approaching the double-digit levels of the middle and late 1970s. The Administration projects a 4.4 percent rate by 1988 and the CBO an even lower rate. A lower rate of inflation, *ceteris paribus,* should remove some of the budetary pressure from state and local governments and could lead to a larger state and local government share of GNP than would occur under a higher rate.

As was argued in Chapter 4, inflation stimulates "potential" expenditures by more than it stimulates the revenue base, hence the purchasing power of state and local government tax bases declines. In general the higher the inflation rate, the less able is the government to capture the increased tax potential and the greater is the purchasing power loss. This income effect dampens total expenditure growth, even though it sets discretionary tax rate increases in motion to recoup some of the loss. A lower inflation rate, on the other hand, allows governments to tap a greater proportion of the inflated tax bases. As a result real state and local government budgets will be larger than under a higher inflation rate.

Again, this scenario will not hold for every state and local government. Local governments would seem hardest hit by high inflation in that their property tax revenues are not so inflation-sensitive as is their labor intensive input mix. Thus large city governments could gain most from a lower inflation rate. The biggest losers stand to be state governments with progressive tax structures. For example, Governor Hugh Carey of New York State probably could not have carried out his income tax cutting program of the late 1970s without an assist from inflation. Inflation and bracket creep kept income and sales tax revenues rising even while statutory income tax rate reductions were taking place, and money wage increases to state employees hid the real declines that were actually being given.

Of course, the economic framework that can lead to lower inflation in the 1980s is fragile. High federal deficits, the military buildup, the failure of real interest rates to drop, and another oil crisis could all lead to a higher rate of price inflation. Should this happen, local governments would be hardest pressed and the aggregate level of state and local government sector activity would be lower.

Uncertainty.   Finally, there is the issue of uncertainty, i.e., how will the prospects of unstable economic growth affect fiscal decisions of state and local governments? As uncertainty about recession and inflation increases, do state and local governments view their expenditure and revenue requirements in a different light? The answer is that they do and the likely response is larger precautionary balances, i.e., fewer expenditures and higher tax rates than in a more stable environment. State and local governments will likely avoid commitments to long-term programs, shy away from new activities and attempt to reduce the proportion of uncontrollable expenditures—those mandated by law—in their budgets.[9] Cutbacks and threatened cutbacks in federal grants will further accentuate the uncertain fiscal environment.

Regional Shifts in Economic Activity

Many analysts see the movement of people and jobs to the South and West continuing through the end of the century. Estimates of regional population and income growth by the Department of Commerce[10] and regional population and employment growth by the Oak Ridge Laboratory[11] are in agrreement on this outlook. Census[12] and Joint Center for Urban Studies[13] population projections offer a similar prognosis. However, no matter how sophisticated the model, such projections are in some sense an extrapolation of past trends and do not adequately account for major turning points. In this respect, there have been important changes in the early 1980s that may or may not carry through the decade. Most notable here are the lower rates of inflation and the softening of oil prices, both of which could improve the comparative position of northeast cities.

Evidence of a New Equilibrium?   Many observers of the conditions of life in the United States have taken note of the problems in the sunbelt.[14] Their argument is that some limits to growth have been reached in this region, that the quality of life which attracted so many northerners has begun to deteriorate, and that a continuation of the regional shifts of the 1970s may not be in the cards. There is some evidence and logic to support an argument that the growing and declining regions are approaching a new economic equilibrium. The evidence, however, is not as convincing as the impressions reported by casual observers.

If one is to argue that a more balanced regional growth will characterize the 1980s, he must argue that the forces which have promoted regional shifts are no longer so strong. More specifically,

> That the relative costs of doing business are shifting in favor of northern states.

> That people's preferences are shifting away from a desire for more sun and warm weather.

> That many states in the growing region have reached "bottlenecks" in natural resource availability or public services and that these bottlenecks will constrain further growth.

The evidence does not make it clear that recent years have seen major improvements in the relative competitiveness of the declining regions in attracting industry, i.e., in the relative costs of energy and labor, the level of taxation, and nearness to markets. There are no clear signs of a permanent new comparative advantage in energy cost and availability in northern states. Energy costs are higher and availability more uncertain where reliance on imported oil is greater, i.e., in the North. The cost of fuels is highest in the northern states,[15] and some students of the energy sector see an increasing regional divergence in energy prices.[16] Yet the early 1980s has seen a softening in this trend with a worldwide oil glut and a drop in oil prices. Energy prices still may be relatively higher in the North in the 1980s than in the 1970s, but the disparity may not grow so much as had been expected.

A somewhat more encouraging story may be told for labor costs. A comparison of average weekly earnings in the manu-

Table 6-1. Average Weekly Earnings in the Manufacturing Sector

	1972	1977	1981	Average Annual Percent Increase	
				1972–77	1977–81
North	$154.16[a]	$224.35[a]	$312.83[a]	7.80	8.67
	—	231.63[b]	320.93[b]	—	8.49
South	132.85[c]	197.72[c]	282.52[c]	8.28	9.33
	—	202.13[d]	290.36[d]	—	9.48
West	157.46[e]	236.94[e]	328.29[c]	8.52	8.49
	—	237.03[f]	331.39[f]	—	8.74

[a] Does not include Michigan.
[b] Includes Michigan.
[c] Does not include Louisiana or Texas.
[d] Includes Louisiana and Texas.
[e] Does not include Kansas, Colorado, Montana, Iowa, or South Dakota
[f] Does not include Kansas.
Source: U.S. Bureau of Labor Statistics, *Employment and Earnings, States and Areas, 1939–78* (1979); *Employment and Earnings,* May 1981; and *Supplement to Employment and Earnings, States and Areas, 1977–81.*

facturing sector shows that northern wages were 16 percent higher than southern wages in 1972, 13 percent higher in 1977, and 12 percent higher in 1981 (Table 6-1). Despite some short-comings in these BLS data, the evidence suggests a regional convergence in labor costs. The prospects for further convergence may be evaluated in terms of the increasing pressures on low-wage regions caused by (a) increasing cost of living and (b) increasing unionization. It is generally believed that the cost of living is rising faster in the South and that this will bid up wages faster. Weinstein reports that between 1972 and 1978, the BLS level-of-living index rose by 66.4 percent in southern cities but only by 56.6 percent in cities in the Northeast region.[17] If one performs the same analysis for the 1972–79 period, however, this conclusion does not hold. The BLS intermediate-level-of-living cost rose by 78.9 percent in the Northeast, 78.1 percent in the north central states, 80.8 percent in the South and 80.7 percent in the West. If Washington, D.C., is excluded from the South, the average increase in that region was only 78.7 percent, less than the increase in the Northeast.

Wage rates in the growing regions could also be pressured by the spread of unions—perhaps a natural consequence of the movement of manufacturing from the industrialized Northeast and Midwest. Interestingly, regional changes in union membership do not conform to this suspicion. Unionization has decreased throughout the nation, from 27 percent of the nonagricultural work force in 1972 to 23 percent in 1978. The most heavily unionized area of the country, the north central region, saw the biggest decrease, from 44 to 28 percent. However, the South, which was the least unionized region in 1972, saw as great a decline as did the heavily unionized Northeast: southern union membership dropped from 16 to 14 percent of the work force while northeastern membership fell from 33 to 31 percent.

Although these data do offer some evidence that the South is losing its comparative labor cost advantage, the story is complicated and generalizations about convergence are very difficult to make. Birch probably has matters about right in his conclusion that there is evidence of wage rate convergence in some sectors (wholesale trade and services) but not in others.[18] To borrow his observation on regional cost disparities in the mid-1970s, "by and large, the extent of the differences is much greater than the degree of convergence."[19] The increasing cost of Sunbelt labor may be improving the relative attractiveness of northern plant locations, but the process of convergence is painfully slow.

One might also speculate that the rate of taxation is becoming more similar from region to region and therefore will slow regional job shifts. Relative tax levels (measured as the ratio of taxes to personal income) have been converging since the early 1970s (Table 6-2). Does this imply that the declining states are gaining a comparative advantage? The answer is maybe, but very slowly. The maybe is because severance tax collections in some energy rich states, included in Table 6-2, result in an overstatement of effort since much of the burden of these taxes is exported. In any case, the process of convergence is a very slow one. Note that none of the southern subregions show a tax effort index as high as the national average in 1981.[20]

Finally, there are the nonquantifiables, e.g., the preference for warm weather and less congested living that may have driven many workers away from the northern region. One can look only to indirect evidence to suggest that these preferences have

Table 6-2. Index of State and Local Government Tax Burden

Census Region	1962	1972	1977	1980	1981
New England	103[a]	110	108	102	104
Middle Atlantic	97	112	120	116	114
East North Central	95	102	97	97	99
South Atlantic	92	91	93	95	94
East South Central	94	88	89	91	92
West South Central	102	90	87	90	92
West North Central	104	100	99	98	96
Mountain	105	103	104	107	107
Pacific	107	109	109	107	107

[a] Mean tax burden (ratio of taxes to personal income) is set equal to 100. Values reported are mean index values for the region. Alaska not included in calculations.
Source: U.S. Bureau of Census, *Governmental Finances*, various years.

not changed. Birch's analysis makes the interesting point that economic factors cannot explain the rapid growth in certain very-high-wage SMSAs—Orlando, Houston, Denver, Seattle, Phoenix, San Diego, Los Angeles, San Francisco, Atlanta, Dallas, and Santa Barbara. To explain growth in these SMSAs, one might look to the quality of life offered.[21]

Sooner or later, forces will come into play to slow regional shifts by improving the comparative advantage of the older industrial states. As Olson has noted with reference to southern economic growth, "The advantage in economic growth which the South has enjoyed since World War II because of the differential in the levels of cartelization cannot last forever. Thus, the South will eventually lose its position as a leader in American economic growth."[22] If forces to slow sunbelt economic growth have already appeared, they are so recent that they cannot yet be detected. A more likely prospect for the 1980s is a continuation of the Sunbelt shifts of the past two decades.

Fiscal Adjustments. Regional movements of population and economic activity will pressure state and local governments to adjust their fiscal behavior. For some northern states and for some central cities in all regions, the scenario will be continued, long-term retrenchment. As a state like New York attempts to bring per capita expenditures (40 percent above the national average in 1981) into line with per capita income (9 percent above the national average in 1981), the central issue becomes how to lower the level of public services relative to other states.[23] Few states, and especially New York State, have experience with such matters.

To gain some idea of the degree of fiscal adjustment necessary in various states, an index of fiscal development has been estimated. This index, for any state i, is defined as the difference between (a) per capita current expenditures in state i as a percent of national average per capita expenditures, and (b) per capita fiscal capacity in state i as a percent of national average per capita fiscal capacity. For an index of fiscal capacity, we have used the 1979 estimates of the yield of a representative tax system as developed by the ACIR. The resulting index of fiscal development for Rhode Island is 31.6; its governments spend 27.5 percent above the national average but its fiscal capacity is about 4 percent below the national average. Rhode Island, thus, may be designated an "overdeveloped" public sector. Texas, with an index of −44.6, is an underdeveloped state and local government sector. We have arbitrarily defined a "balanced" state and local government sector as a difference of 5 percent between relative expenditures and income, and arrayed all states in Table 6-3.

The data show that all "overdeveloped" public sectors are not in the North, and not all northern states are overdeveloped. On average, however, northern and western states have larger public sectors than one would expect given their income levels, and southern and western states have smaller public sectors. Note that 10 of the 15 states with "overdeveloped" public sectors are in the north and midwest, and 5 of 23 "underdeveloped" public sectors are in the northern tier.

As was noted in Chapter 5 above, these imbalances have come about because of a failure to adjust government budgets to new economic realities. It is important to note that regardless of where a state ranks on this continuum, however, there will be serious adjustment problems. The adjustment process is naturally slow and complicated by a number of factors:

Slower real income growth cuts into an already thin margin of revenue coverage.

Table 6-3. Balance Between State and Local Government
Expenditures and Per Capita Personal Income

	Index of Fiscal Development[a]	Per Capita Fiscal Capacity Relative[b]	Average Annual Growth in Population: 1977–81
Overdeveloped			
New York	53.6	31.6	−0.4
Rhode Island	31.6	19.0	0.5
Massachusetts	23.7	8.9	0.0
Vermont	14.9	18.0	1.7
Maine	13.4	13.1	1.1
Hawaii	13.1	13.2	2.3
Wisconsin	12.8	13.4	0.5
Michigan	11.8	11.3	0.2
Oregon	10.6	20.6	2.8
Mississippi	9.7	10.3	1.4
Minnesota	8.6	7.5	0.7
Maryland	7.9	−3.2	0.7
California	6.8	9.5	2.5
Washington	6.5	2.3	3.6
New Jersey	5.8	−8.5	0.2
Balanced			
Alabama	4.4	2.3	1.5
Delaware	2.7	8.3	0.7
South Carolina	2.4	3.1	2.4
Utah	1.5	10.5	4.6
Georgia	−0.5	−2.4	2.5
North Carolina	−0.7	−0.9	1.9
Pennsylvania	−1.2	−7.8	0.2
North Dakota	−1.6	7.3	0.2
South Dakota	−2.7	5.4	−0.1
New Mexico	−2.8	21.3	2.8
Arizona	−4.3	−2.0	5.0
Underdeveloped			
Virginia	−5.5	−10.8	1.4
Tennessee	−5.8	−5.1	1.8
Arkansas	−6.3	−4.7	1.7
Connecticut	−6.7	−22.5	0.2
Nebraska	−6.8	−9.4	0.2
Kentucky	−7.7	−1.6	1.4
West Virginia	−9.2	6.3	1.2
Idaho	−9.5	−3.4	2.8
Iowa	−10.3	−3.8	0.2
Louisiana	−11.0	6.6	2.4
New Hampshire	−11.4	−9.4	2.5
Colorado	−11.9	−7.5	3.1
Montana	−12.0	9.7	1.0
Ohio	−12.3	−11.3	0.2
Kansas	−13.8	−9.6	0.6
Illinois	−15.9	−13.9	0.5
Missouri	−17.7	−14.4	0.7

	Index of Fiscal Development[a]	Per Capita Fiscal Capacity Relative[b]	Average Annual Growth in Population: 1977–81
Indiana	−20.5	−15.9	0.6
Florida	−25.5	−18.1	4.8
Oklahoma	−27.4	−11.7	2.5
Texas	−44.6	−24.5	3.6
Wyoming	−44.9	23.5	4.9
Nevada	−59.7	−5.6	7.5
Averages			
North	6.8		
South	−7.3		
West[c]	−7.7		
U.S.[c]	−3.4		

[a] $\dfrac{Ep_i}{\overline{Ep}} - \dfrac{Fp_i}{\overline{Fp}} = \text{Index},$

where

Ep = per capita current general expenditures.
Yp = per capita fiscal capacity.
$\overline{Ep}$ and $\overline{Fp}$ are rational averages.
[b] $Fp/\overline{Fp}$
[c] Excludes Alaska.

Higher rates of inflation drive up costs faster than revenues, accentuating real service level declines.

Many northern states are characterized by highly decentralized fiscal systems, and hence it is difficult for the state government to plan for or control the aggregate level of state and local government spending and taxing.

Because of jurisdictional fragmentation, the fiscal position of central cities in the declining regions is likely to be hurt a great deal more than that of suburbs; i.e., much of the cost of retrenchment will ultimately be paid for by low-income families.

There are important psychological barriers to retrenchment; residents find it much easier to adapt to lower taxes than to lower public service levels.

The strength of public employee unions, fixed debt and pension commitments, a backlog of needed infrastructure improvements, and the precarious financial condition of many cities make substantial retrenchment an especially difficult process.

The net result of all this is that while regional shifts in economic activity require that many of the formerly rich states bring their fiscal activities into line with their new, relatively low levels of income, the retrenchment process will probably involve a period of public sector atrophy in many states, particularly those in the North. This means that governments probably will not and cannot cut back service levels in the absolute, but if they do not raise tax burdens or expand the quality and quantity of services and spend just enough to keep real per capita expenditures approximately constant, in time the rest of the country will catch up. This process is long and slow and implies making public service levels relatively worse, but it is the kind of adjustment that is most likely to occur.

The growing regions, where most of the underdeveloped public sectors are located, will also face fiscal adjustment problems. On the one hand, there is the great amount of rural poverty in the South and Southwest. One could argue that this problem has first call on the revenues from growth. On the other hand, there are the pressures from a growing population to expand infrastructure, improve school and health systems, deal with water shortages and environmental problems, and control land use. Despite this menu of fiscal priorities, the growing regions would seem better equipped (than most northern states) to deal with these pressures, for a number of reasons:

Resources are growing because of regional shifts, even though national economic growth is slowing, and because state tax structures in the growing regions tend to be more income-sensitive than those in the Northeast and Midwest.

Government finances tend to be more state-dominated and therefore more controllable.

Many urban areas are not characterized by fragmented local government structures.

On the other hand, there are state and local government financial problems ahead for southern states. Much of the increase in spending could come in the form of a catch-up in average wages; hence expenditures may rise more rapidly than public service levels. Employment levels relative to population are already higher in southern than northern states, as are levels of per capita debt.

Demographic Changes

Major changes in the makeup of the national population will continue through the year 2000. Fertility and mortality rate declines have had the combined effect of pushing the nation toward a zero population growth, an increasing concentration of the elderly, and a declining proportion of school-aged children. In addition, the baby boom generation—those born between 1945 and 1960—are moving through the labor force. Concomitant with these trends has been an increasing rate of household formation. The effects of these changes on the finances of some state and local government finances could be significant. Unfortunately, this is a virtually untouched research area, hence we can but pull together some disjointed evidence and speculate about fiscal implications.

Population Growth. A slower population growth rate implies less pressure for the expansion of public services and therefore less pressure on public budgets. For some services—education, roads and streets, and water and sewer services—this outcome seems intuitively clear. On the contrary, increases in population would seem to call for more teachers, more roads, and so forth, and place an upward pressure on budgets. In fact, the situation is considerably more complicated. Consider first the growing cities and states. One would expect two effects to operate. The growing population will increase expenditure requirements—there are simply more people to be served—but some of this pressure could be offset by economies of scale. The first effect surely operates but the second is questionable. Despite a great deal of discussion about the possibility of scale economies in the provision of local public services, there is little or no hard evidence to suggest that larger cities can deliver services any more cheaply on a per person basis than can smaller cities.[24] In sum, we can guess that an increased population, *ceteris paribus,* increases expenditures, but we do not have a feel for the magnitude of that effect in different types of jurisdictions.

Conversely, the loss of city or state population does not guarantee an expenditure reduction because there are many offsetting factors, e.g., inflation, state or federal government expenditure mandates, and noncontrollable expenditures. Instead of reducing service demands, population decline may simply result in the creation of excess capacity in the city plant. Muller has shown per capita common function expenditures between 1969 and 1973 for fourteen declining cities to rise by 51 percent, as opposed to 59 percent for thirteen growing cities.[25] As a percentage of personal income, he found the growth to be even greater for the declining cities.

If the question is whether a slower versus a faster population growth rate, *ceteris paribus,* reduces the aggregate level of state and local government spending, the answer is probably that it does. A faster population growth would not only generate more service demands but would be associated with more migration. The *movement* of population, as much as the size of population, causes costs to increase, i.e., servicing a new suburban population may increase public sector costs by a greater amount than the cost reductions resulting from the out-migration of families from an old neighborhood.

The Elderly.   A growing elderly and retired population could affect public budgets by causing shifts in social service expenditures and by putting pressure on the financing of retirement needs and health care. Russell reports that 1978 expenditures on medical care for people 65 and over averaged $2026 per person compared with $764 per person between the ages of 19 and 64.[26] Even so, the pressures of an older population on health care expenditures by state and local governments may not be so severe as one might expect. While substantially more is spent on health care for the elderly than for younger age groups, less than 9 percent of total state and local government expenditures is for health and hospitals and about 85 percent of health expenditures for the elderly is aided.

A potentially more important pressure on state and local government budgets may come from the problems of financing state and local government pension plans. If a government is operating on a pay-as-you-go basis or with substantial unfunded liabilities and if the age distribution of public employees is changing in the same fashion as the demographic makeup of the community, then the taxes necessary to finance retirement expenditures could rise substantially in the 1980s.[27] Moreover, an increased claim of social security financing on the federal budget could crowd out transfer payments to state and local governments.

The changing rate of growth and composition of population will also be felt on the revenue side of state and local government budgets. This will occur indirectly, through the effects of the aging on economic growth, and through more direct effects on state and local government tax revenues. The first of these possibilities has not been thoroughly worked, and one cannot go to a developed body of literature to support speculation about how changing demographics will affect revenue flows through changes in productivity and labor force participation.[28] In terms of more direct effects, it seems a reasonable proposition that an increasing *share* of the elderly will dampen revenue growth if for no other reason than because of an income effect. Retirees earn less and therefore have less to spend on taxable consumer goods and housing. Even if one accepts the argument that the elderly are no longer "poor,"[29] a dollar of retirement income does not generate the same amount of tax revenue as a dollar of wage and salary or proprietorship income. This is in part because the elderly receive much of their income from transfer and "in-kind" payments, but also because they receive special relief from state taxes through property tax "circuit breakers," their housing choices run toward less expensive units, and they consume a greater share of income in nontaxable housing, food, and medical care.

The net fiscal effects of an aging population will not likely be great enough to compromise the aggregate fiscal position of state and local governments in the 1980s. When the baby boom generation moves to retirement after 2000, such an effect could occur, but the evidence of the 1970s suggests that the aggregate economic effects in the coming decade will not be substantial. One interesting set of projections suggests that growth in the numbers of elderly will be offset by growth in their income (from earnings and Social Security) leaving the proportion eligible for public assistance essentially unchanged over the next forty years.[30] Still, there are two good reasons to be concerned with the fiscal implications of the elderly for state and local governments. The first is that the funds to finance retirement expenditures—including social security—are drawn from the same pool of funds that finances other expenditures. If pension payments are a priority, then a growing aged population coupled with no growth in the contributing population will necessarily result in siphoning funds away from other functions.

The second issue is that all areas in the country are not equally burdened by an increasing elderly population, e.g., Florida and other sunbelt states will receive a disproportionately large amount of the elderly. It seems clear that state and local governments will be fiscally burdened by an increase in the elderly, i.e., the elderly generate less in revenue than they require in expenditure. For some cities and states, then, the effect in the 1980s could be noticeable.

Compositional Changes.   There is a bit more evidence, albeit indirect, on the fiscal effects of compositional changes in the population. Empirical work suggests that declining population densities may reduce spending for urban services such as police and fire and that a falling pupil-population ratio can lead eventually to lower education expenditures.[31] As welcome as such relief might be, one should not think too quickly about the possible uses of such savings. First, the effects of inflation will offset some of these "quantity" reductions, and, second, there will be substantial adjustment costs associated with restructuring budgets and programs to accommodate a new clientele, e.g., the shift from youth-related to elderly-related programs. Still other compositional factors might tend to offset the savings from a lower rate of population growth. The formation of new households will bid up the costs of providing sanitation and fire services, and the continuing movement of population to suburban and nonmetropolitan areas may cause the unit costs of providing services to rise.

Two of these compositional changes would seem especially important for the future. The first is that the ratio of "fiscally dependent" to "fiscally productive" individuals[32] will decline through the mid-1980s but then begin to increase with increases in the numbers of elderly and children under ten years of age. The second is the changing number of households. A taste for smaller families, the divorce rate, the postponement of marriage and childbearing, and the declining fertility rate have decreased the rate of population growth but not the formation of households. An example of the magnitude of this effect is in New York State, where official projections are for a 9 percent increase in population between 1980 and 2000 but a 25 percent increase in number of households.[33] The fiscal implications of such a dramatic change have not been carefully studied. At first blush, more households within a given size population imply more income-earning units and therefore more taxable capacity. More property *units* suggest a bouyancy for the property tax, and more households suggest that taxable income should increase and that there will be an increase in the taxable consumption share of income. The counterargument is that more young families may result in an increased stock of lower-valued housing units and consequently little effect on the property tax. The expectation that more housing units will increase the aggregate marginal propensity to consume taxable items (because younger families will go into debt to increase their purchase of durables) is debatable at best.[34]

Overall Budgetary Implications.   On an *a priori* basis, the fiscal effects of a changing rate of growth and composition of population are so unclear as to tempt one to speculate that they will be inconsequential. Moreover, the major change in the age distribution—the movement of the baby boom generation to retirement—will not be felt until well after the year 2000. Yet, some regions will realize demographic changes more than others in the 1980s, and more substantial fiscal effects could emerge in the effected cities and states. The increasing proportion of the aged and the increasing number of households are a national phenomenon, but the lower rate of national population growth, and population decline, is most pronounced in the

North and Midwest. A continuing interregional migration will tend to compensate for declining birth rates in some regions and to reinforce natural population decline in others. Particularly the central cities will feel the change in becoming older and smaller and having more households. If the fiscal consequences of demographic change turn out to be harmful, it is these cities that will be hurt most.

The Limitation Movement

Proposition 13 in California highlighted a movement to limit growth in government which was spreading across the country. Soon after Proposition 13, thirty state legislatures were considering balanced-budget amendments, as was the United States Congress, and fourteen states passed some form of tax or expenditure limitation between 1978 and 1980.[35] The mood has remained clearly in the direction of slowing the growth of government at all levels. Discretionary tax reduction became the order of the day for state and local governments in the late 1970s.

The question on the table is whether this signals a permanent reversal in the growing government share in GNP or simply an interruption in a growth trend to which the United States will eventually return. As far as state and local government is concerned, the answer is to be had in the attitudes of voters. The economic setting since 1975 has been an important influence on these attitudes. Increasing taxes are expecially objectionable during inflationary times, when real spendable earnings for most United States families have hardly increased. As long as the growth in real incomes remains low, the objections from this group of voters will remain substantial and growth in government will be resisted. In particular, rising property tax rates place onerous burdens on homeowners in that accrued worth may differ markedly from annual income. Shapiro, Puryear, and Ross argue that the high and rising property tax burden was at the heart of the Proposition 13 movement.[36] An ACIR attitudinal survey places the federal income tax (36 percent of respondents) and the local property tax (30 percent) as the most objectional.[37]

Some interesting findings have emerged from sample survey studies of voter attitudes that resulted in the passage of Proposition 13,[38] Proposition 2½ in Massachusetts,[39] and the Headlee amendment in Michigan.[40] The major features of these three programs are described in Table 6-4. Perhaps the most important issue is whether voters were simply reacting to too much government. In all three studies the answer was clearly that they were not and that, with the exception of public welfare, there was general satisfaction with the level of public services offered. A commonly cited source of discontent is what is perceived as an inefficient public sector—one that is thought to be overpaid, underworked, and not responsive to citizens' needs. The surveys confirmed that perceived inefficiencies in government were a major reason for the imposition of limitations. Courant *et al.*, in the Michigan survey also point to the "free lunch" effect, i.e., that voters believe they might be able to cut taxes without reducing services. Again, this is an extension of the feeling that there is much waste in the state and local government service delivery system.

Table 6-4. Features of Three Tax Limitation Programs

	Proposition 13	Proposition 2½	Headlee Amendment
Property tax rollback	Reduced property taxes to 1% of market value	Reduce property tax levels by 15% per year until they reach 2½% of full market value	—
Property tax growth	2% annual increase in assessed value from 1975–76 base	Maintain a 2½% maximum effective rate	Growth cannot exceed CPI
State taxes	—	—	Limit state government revenues from own sources to a constant share of state personal income

Source: Jack Citrin, "Do People Want Something for Nothing: Public Opinion on Taxes and Government Spending," *National Tax Journal*, **XXXII** (2 supplement): 113 (1979); Paul Courant, Edward Gramlich, and Daniel Rubinfeld, "Why Voters Support Tax Limitation Amendments: The Michigan Case," *National Tax Journal*, March 1980; and Helen Ladd and Julie Boatright Wilson, "Why Voters Support Tax Limitations: Evidence from Massachusetts, Proposition 2½," Sloan Working Paper 3–32, University of Maryland, January 1982.

These results leave anyone reading voter attitudes with a feeling that voters are not displeased with the scope and level of government services but that they are displeased with property taxes, welfare expenditures, and inefficiencies in government. To this list one has to add the resistance to tax increases during times of high inflation and slow real income growth. Kirlin has made the interesting observation that the limitation movement is also a reaction against a complex political system, and reflects the desire of voters to participate more directly and to shift the focus of public policy debates from specific programs to general fiscal issues.[41]

The next decade will see a slower real income growth, a setting conducive to a continued limitation movement. The property tax, because it charges wealth and not income, will remain especially burdensome and carefully watched by voters. There is no reason to believe that voters will become more favorably inclined to welfare expenditures; in times of slow national growth, the "surplus" for the poor just is not there. Although these factors set the stage for more limits on government growth, there are two important factors working in the other direction. First, the feelings about an inefficient and overpaid public sector might temper in the face of public employee layoffs and the real compensation declines of the past few years. Second, the newest federalism could dump an increasing service load on state and local governments, forcing voters to choose between giving up services (which they do not want to do) and allowing taxes to grow.

What if the limitation movement does continue? What will be its impact on the state and local government sector? One important effect will be to reduce the discretion of government decision makers in formulating new programs and taxes and in altering the timing of fiscal expansions and contractions. Even though there is an option to switch to user charge financing (a compensating device used in the aftermath of California's Proposition 13), it is clear that local fiscal planning will be more constrained and new spending initiatives will likely be bypassed to meet increased spending for noncontrollable budget items.[42] Moreover, the limitations placed on local government revenue growth in states such as Massachusetts and California will increase pressure to push service delivery and financing to the state government level. The limitation movement surely reduces local autonomy.

It is less clear what the effects on aggregate state and local government spending and taxing will be. On the surface, tying tax and expenditure growth to personal income growth suggests a dampening effect. Yet thirteen of the first fourteen states to impose such limits were in the growing regions; only two (Arizona and Hawaii) were "high taxing" states,[43] and only Michigan was a declining state. Hence even with limitations, a growth in total state and local government taxes above the national rate of income growth could occur. Would state and local government spending have grown faster without limitations? The ACIR argues that it would have, by 6 to 8 percent per capita more than in the nonlimitation states,[44] whereas Ladd argues in the opposite position.[45]

Perhaps a more significant effect on the budgets of state and local governments is the possibility of limitations at the federal level. Even without a legal indexing of federal expenditures, the tax revolt movement and the huge projected deficits of the early 1980s have brought pressure to find some way of balancing the federal budget.[46] Some of this balancing will surely result in reduced resources available for federal grant-in-aid programs and in a further dampening effect on state and local government revenues.

The tax and expenditure limitation movement creates many inequities and inefficiencies, but it does have its moments. It has called attention, in a rather dramatic way, to some features of our public financing system that a majority of the population simply does not want: too much property tax, too much welfare, and too much pay for too little work in the public sector. Federal, state, and local governments have simply responded to these voter concerns.[47]

One might speculate that the lessons have been taught and that government might now return to a path of slower growth. Moreover, while the limitation movement has gained momentum since 1978 and still more states will probably adopt varying kinds of controls on their budget growth, federal assistance cuts and slow economic growth will eventually catch up with some limitation states and stall the movement in others. State legislators and voters will eventually reason that limitations are not going to address the underlying problem of an inefficient public sector that so rankles taxpayers, nor is it clear that they will stimulate local economic development as others hope. Further, limitations may cause state and local governments to make such revenue-raising adjustments as increased use of benefit charges and the creation of special districts. The adoption of such policies as a way around a formal limitation is not likely to be in the public interest. The adjustments by state and local governments to circumvent debt limitations in the 1960s, the consequences of these adjustments, and the efficiency and controllability of these agency arrangements constitutes a lesson worth remembering.

Limitations are not without virtues. They use the political process to force governments to live within their means. Yet this discipline is accomplished at a cost of giving up substantial flexibility in fiscal decision making and may induce some inefficient behavior by the limited government. In light of these considerations, one might guess that the enthusiasm for legislated tax and spending limitations will wane in the next few years, but the consequences may be more lasting. If the message of the limitation movement has come through to government decision makers, future growth in state and local government expenditures will be slower than it otherwise would have been.

Revitalization

Some analysts and many journalists see a revitalization of central cities taking place. It is not usually made clear whether revitalization means increased city population, employment, and income; an improved economic position of the central city relative to suburbs; or simply a physical rehabilitation of certain parts of the inner city. Some, who borrow the term "gentrification" from the British, see it as the process of upgrading housing (or neighborhoods and retail districts) from working class to professional middle class.[48] Whatever the meaning, the implication is that the inner cities of the future will be much less the distressed areas that they now are and that federal policy toward cities ought to be adjusted accordingly. Indeed, some public policy is premised on the ability to attract employment and residential activity to depressed inner city areas. "Enterprise Zones" a national development bank, and tax abatements for construction investments in blighted areas are examples.

The revitalization argument is made on the basis of *a priori* reasoning, casual observation, and wishful thinking. It has several elements. First, the changing demographics may favor central cities over suburbs. Greater numbers of single people, childless couples, and elderly in the national population; the increased demand for rental housing; smaller and less expensive housing; and the convenience of city living (mass transit, walk to shopping, and so on) will bring people back to the city. The deterrent of poor public schools in central cities will be less important for families without children. Second, the energy crisis will favor the city. Workers will move closer to work—and perhaps to where mass transit is available—to avoid the longer and more expensive commute. Third, there is the bright-lights of the city argument. Cities are exciting places to live, with more cultural and social activities, and some new awareness of these benefits will bring back white collar, middle-income residents. Finally, there are the agglomeration effects that make the city a competitive location for certain types of white collar and service activities. As evidence of revitalization, proponents may give many examples: a booming Manhattan, Chicago's loop, and Capitol Hill-like neighborhood revivals in most large cities.

Acceptance of the revitalization arguments as a basis for policy making is better than wishing on a star. But not much. City populations are not increasing, their relative (to suburbs) income and employment levels are deteriorating, and there is little evidence that their disadvantaged are better off. Population in central cities declined by about 3 percent between 1970 and 1980, the central city share of metropolitan area population and employment also declined, and the city-suburb per capita income disparity has grown. If there has been a back-to-the-city movement, it has been dwarfed by the effects of those factors that stimulate decline.

Even the *a priori* arguments on revitalization seem flawed. There is some appeal to the notion that childless couples and single people see the city as a desirable location because they are not deterred by poor schools and because of proximity to amenities and work. Yet the postponement of having children does not necessarily mean that couples will remain childless or that children will not be planned for. Indeed, some have argued that the fertility rate in the United States will soon begin to increase. If this occurs, the quality of the public schools remains a major drawback to living in the city. Locations closer to amenities may also be a comparative disadvantage of cities; e.g., most cities cannot compete with the convenience and choice of suburban shopping centers and in all but a few large cities the mass transit system is not a major inducement.

The energy argument may also be questioned. There are more suburban than central city job locations; hence if the rising price of gasoline induces any population movement, it may well be to the suburbs. Moreover, if the commute to work gets too expensive, other kinds of adjustments might be made: e.g., a four-day work week or innovations in communications to minimize necessary personal contact. To the extent that movement takes place in response to commuting costs it will likely be blue collar manufacturing workers moving to suburbs. Some white collar workers might be lured to the city, but again the quality of the public schools would be an important impediment.

The bright lights argument is based on the notion that cities are exciting centers of cultural and social activity, which make city living more exciting. The impression is true enough, perhaps, for a Manhattan or a Georgetown but would hardly seem to fit a Syracuse, Wilkes-Barre, or Akron.

This is not to argue that revitalization is undesirable, that cities should not be brought back. Rather it is an argument for care in defining revitalization and for realism in assessing what can happen in cities during the next decade. Revitalization can mean a conservation of capital facilities, reinvestment in blighted areas, and a general improvement in the quality of city life. This pattern would be perfectly consistent with shrinking population and employment, the displacement of the poor from dilapidated housing in rundown neighborhoods, and the continued loss of manufacturing employment. Revitalization of cities, in this sense, may be a reasonable expectation, but it will not mean a diminished need for federal help in compensating for the economic losses, subsidizing the dispossessed, and generally getting through a tough adjustment period.

FEDERAL POLICY

The federal government will play a major role in getting state and local governments through the difficult fiscal adjustment period that lies ahead. The question is whether the federal response will be reasoned and comprehensive or ad hoc and piecemeal. It seems essential that some general guidelines for the federal response be worked out, i.e., the kind of strategy one might expect fo find in a well-thought-out statement of national urban policy. It is as important that there be some continuity to national urban policy. The dramatic shifts in programs to deal with urban policies between the Carter and Reagan administrations (and even during the Carter years) were counterproductive: Carter believed that federal policy could and should slow regional migration, Reagan is more willing to let regional shifts run their course; Carter saw cities in the pivotal role of dealing with urban problems, Reagan sees states; Carter tried to compensate distressed cities for the failure of national economic policies, Reagan has actually cut assistance to such cities. At a time when resources are scarce and there is such a premium on good fiscal planning at the state and local government level, the country can ill afford such complete turnabouts in federal policy.[49]

In assessing the impact of federal policy on the outlook for state and local finances, and especially for the fiscal health of financially pressed cities, we turn to the question of how such a policy might view the financial problems of state and local governments. Five areas of concern about the appropriate federal response to state and local government fiscal problems can be raised: (a) whether the federal government ought to attempt revitalization of declining areas or provide compensatory assistance during a period of financial adjustment; (b) how ongoing federal programs affect the comparative advantage of one region versus another; (c) whether inflation and recession ought to be viewed as a part of intergovernmental policy; (d) what role state government should play in the intergovernmental system; and (e) what will federal policy be toward the big city financial crises that may lie ahead.

Compensation Versus Revitalization

If the Carter administration's urban policy statement of 1978 took any firm position, it was toward a revitalization rather than a compensation strategy. The National Development Bank, the targeted employment tax credit, neighborhood commercial reinvestment programs, and Urban Development Action Grants (UDAG) all seemed to lean toward renovating a deteriorated economic base in distressed cities and shoring up the competitive position of the declining regions. At least the rhetoric of that federal policy implied a belief that the declining economies can be revitalized. Yet there is little evidence that such programs work or have any effect on the employment base of declining cities.

A compensation policy would take a different tack. It would accept the notion that market forces are effecting a reallocation of population and income within the country and would attempt to compensate the most financially pressed governments and families caught in this transition period. The goal would be to protect low-income families by subsidizing public service provision and temporary job opportunities while the emptying out process goes on. Public service job programs, categorical grants in the health and education area, and federal relief of welfare financing are key elements of such a program.

There is a fine line between revitalization and compensation strategies, and one wants to be careful not to confuse the latter with any program to abandon cities or declining regions. As interregional variations in the relative costs of doing business and in market size approach some new balance, movements in population and jobs will slow. A primary role of federal policy is to assist the most distressed governments during the adjustment process. Hence, subsidies to hold businesses in a region are not an appropriate part of a compensation strategy if it is known that the business will leave (or cease operations at present levels) when the subsidy is removed. Transition grants to states with an overdeveloped public sector, such as New York, are appropriate if they are tied to longer-term reductions in the level of public sector activity. Capital grants to renew the city's infrastructure are also appropriate if the infrastructure investment is based on a "shrinkage" plan. They are inappropriate if their long-run impact is to increase excess capacity in the city's capital plant. Finally, relocation grants and labor market information systems are consistent with such a strategy in that they facilitate the out-movement.

The Reagan administration approach is more in the vein of a laissez faire strategy in that it seems to argue that the process of regional economic adjustment ought to continue. But there is no plan for compensating those governments which suffer most in the process, and there are anomalies. For example, proposed enterprise zones are a small and untested exception to the absence of programs targeted on distressed areas. Moreover, Muller has estimated that the Reagan program for FY 1982—a combination of tax cuts, defense spending increases, and federal grant reductions—will favor the growing and higher income states. His results show that ". . . the Sunbelt will receive close to two-thirds of the total net flow resulting from policy shifts of the Reagan Administration."[50]

Federal Policies and Regional Development

All federal policy affecting regional movements in jobs and people is not explicitly stated. Yet, deregulation, changes in the federal tax code, regional flows of federal funds, and new federalisms all have important implications for regional development and regional variations in state and local government fiscal problems.

Federal Tax Code. Changes in the federal tax code—reductions in marginal personal income tax rates and business investment incentives, for example—can have important effects on state and local government finances. Reductions in marginal personal income tax rates will be to the advantage of all state and local governments in that they stimulate local economic activity. On the other hand, when the marginal personal income tax rate falls, taxpayers who itemize on tax returns can shift less of their state and local government tax burden onto the federal government; hence their resistance to local tax rate increases will stiffen. Since taxpayers in states with high tax burdens will lose the most in this process, one might reasonably assume that they will become more resistant to further tax increases.

Business tax relief likely will stimulate economic activity in the growing regions and accelerate the decline in the Northeast and industrial Midwest, at least in the short run. For example, the extension of the investment tax credit to structures likely has the effect of pushing forward the plant reinvestment decisions of a firm, and accelerated depreciation favors new capital over old. Since the declining regions are less likely to be the site of new plant investment and since their capital stock is older, these policies would accelerate the pace of regional movement.[51] In the long run, however, this movement could improve the competitive position of northern states by making them smaller and more capital-intensive.[52]

Regional Flow of Funds. The federal government can bias the regional distribution of economic activity by its distribution of funds. Of the many issues raised in this connection, the narrowest and most popular has to do with the regional distribution of federal grants to state and local governments. In fact, there appears to be no consistent pattern to the distribution of federal grants. Analyses of the years 1962 to 1980 show no significant relationship with personal income; i.e., federal grants appear to be neither equalizing nor counterequalizing. Neither is there a strong regional bias in the trend of per capita federal grant distributions. As may be seen in Table 6-5, the only noticeable change has been the growing per capita advantage of the western region.

A broader question is the regional net fiscal incidence of the federal budget. Such analyses attempt to estimate, for each state, the balance between total tax payment to the federal government and total expenditures received through the federal budgetary process. The methods used in making such estimates vary from study to study and are open to much questioning, for examples, how are the subcontracts counted, how are expen-

Table 6-5. Regional Distribution of Per Capita Federal Grants, 1962–80

	Mean per Capita Federal Aid			
	North	South	West[c]	ANOVA F Ratio[a]
1962	$ 40.70	$ 44.76	$ 65.34	7.56[b]
1967	67.22	83.10	114.73	10.46[b]
1972	141.01	145.24	175.71	4.22[b]
1975	216.85	213.62	249.15	3.31[b]
1976	260.73	243.88	291.86	3.03
1977	289.25	270.02	321.00	2.78
1978	321.15	305.36	352.13	1.99
1979	346.11	326.00	361.40	1.16
1980	379.59	360.14	401.07	1.23
1981	404.98	383.63	424.89	1.13

[a] Aid to the West is significantly greater than aid to the South for each year through 1977 and greater than aid to the North through 1975. Aid to the South and North never differ significantly.
[b] Significant at .05 level.
[c] Excluding Alaska.
Source: U.S. Bureau of Census, *Governmental Finances*, various years.

diture *benefits* taken into account, and where are corporate tax burdens assigned. Nevertheless, the results tend to be reasonably consistent. In his study of 1972 data, Catsambas concluded that "there is a clear pattern of net fiscal transfer from the more industrialized parts of the country—the East Coast and the Great Lakes—to the South and the Rocky Mountains."[53] Labovitz, studying 1974–76 data, concluded that the southeast, southwest, Rocky Mountain area, and Far West had federal expenditure shares exceeding their federal revenue contributions. He found the Great Lakes and mideastern regions to be contributing more in revenues than they received back in expenditures.[54] Peterson and Muller argue that a more reasonable approach to determining the influence of the federal budget on regional growth is to examine shifts in federal spending from one period to the next. They also report a bias in favor of the growing regions.[55]

The evidence suggests that there is a bias in the regional distribution of federal monies and that this bias is enhancing the comparative advantage of the growing regions. Given the gains in Congress that population growth naturally brings to growing states, one could speculate that this comparative advantage of the Sunbelt is not likely to be reversed in the near future.

New Federalism.   Every President since Lyndon Johnson has introduced a new federalism. The newest, the Reagan administration's program, began by calling for a $50 billion transfer of federal programs to states over an eight-year phased transition. The major components of this program were a swap of Medicaid in exchange for state takeover of food stamps and AFDC and a turnback of approximately forty-three federal social, health, and nutrition programs. The federal proposal was to financially support the turnback until 1987 when financial responsibility would be shifted to states. The intention of the newest federalism is quite clear: the Reagan administration sees income redistribution as an increasing responsibility of the state and local government sector, and intends to reduce the state and local government reliance on federal assistance.

State and local governments could respond to this program in one of two ways. First, they could attempt to make up for the federal aid reductions by increasing tax rates. Such an action might be taken, for example, to hold public services and public assistance benefits at present levels. If northern and midwestern state and local governments followed this strategy, however, they could worsen their competitive tax position and add to their comparative disadvantage in attracting jobs. The alternative approach would have state and local governments attempting to keep their overall levels of taxation "in line" at the expense of not making up for the loss in federal grants and, in some cases, allowing relative public service levels to fall. The "newest federalism" has placed state and local government politicians in a very difficult position.

The Business Cycle and Intergovernmental Policy

The business cycle and inflation have severe effects on the financial health of state and local governments, as noted in Chapter 4. Indeed, it was the severity of the 1975 recession that pushed New York City over the edge and brought many other local governments and at least one state government dangerously close to fiscal insolvency. Because swings in economic activity do induce substantial changes in relative fiscal health, one might argue for an explicit recognition of business cycle effects in federal intergovernmental policy.

In a sense this was done with countercyclical aid and the stepping up of other components of the Economic Stimulus Package in the last recovery, but it was done in an ad hoc manner rather than as part of a coordinated federal policy. The basic objectives of CETA were initially the training and employment of the disadvantaged and then countercyclical stimulus, and Local Public Works was meant to stimulate state and local government construction. Some argue that both became general purpose fiscal relief programs and that neither exerted a strong stimulative effect on the economy.[56] Indeed, if the primary purposes of these programs were training and economic stimulus, neither passes muster in terms of an evaluation of their success.

Apparently, little was learned from this experience about the relationship between countercyclical policy and national urban policy. The fact is that as the United States economy sunk deeper into the 1981–83 recession, there was no firm countercyclical policy. If business cycles were linked to intergovernmental policy, an essential feature of the system would have to be targeting on relatively more distressed jurisdictions. After all, the Reagan administration's choice to combat inflation and allow unemployment to rise is a national urban policy of immense significance and with a decided bias against the older cities. This raises the especially thorny problem of identifying both those communities most hurt by recession and the severity of the recession in the various regions. The evidence of the past recessions seems clear: the older manufacturing belt in the North was hit hardest.[57] The impact of the 1981–83 recession has been most severe in the Midwest, but has spread to the southern states more than did the 1975 downturn.

The Role of State Government

An ambivalence—at the federal level—about the proper role of state government in state and local government finances may exacerbate some of the problems created by inflation and a slower growing economy.[58] State governments raised 62 per-

cent of all state and local government taxes, made 40 percent
of direct expenditures, and accounted for 75 percent of federal
aid in fiscal 1977. Yet state government seems to be approaching a new crossroads—a redefinition of its fiscal role. The past
decade saw two important, but contradictory, influences on state
government financing and service delivery. The first concerns
its relationship with the federal government and its place in the
intergovernmental system. Total grants-in-aid quadrupled between 1970 and 1978, but a significant share of this growth was
in direct federal-to-local grants, with the states being bypassed.
In 1977, local governments were directly receiving 27 percent
of total federal aid to state and local governments, as compared
with 13 percent in 1970. In addition, the state government share
of general revenue sharing has been eliminated. Whether or
not state governments brought these changes on themselves by
abrogating their responsibility toward urban governments is
debatable, but the drift toward reducing the importance of state
government in the intergovernmental process has been real
enough.

The second (contradictory) way in which the state role is
changing is in the continuing shift of financial responsibility
from local to state governments. The state government share
of total state and local government taxing and spending has
increased markedly in the past two decades. Taxes collected
rose from 56 to 64 percent between 1965 and 1981, and though
the state aid share of total state expenditures remained about
constant, the state government share of health, education, and
welfare direct spending increased markedly. States may not have
done all that they should have to lift the financing burden off
the local property tax and too little may have been done about
city-suburb fiscal disparities, but the trend toward more state
fiscal responsibility has continued. A combination of local government tax or expenditure limitations, a more elastic state
government tax structure, and high rates of inflation could accentuate this trend.

The slowdown in the growth of government, and in federal
aid to state and local governments, has begun to change the
role of states in the intergovernmental system. The three major
direct federal-local assistance programs—CETA, Local Public

Works, and antirecession fiscal assistance—are history. More-over, the Reagan administration's newest federalism places state governments in a pivotal role and increases their leverage over state and local government finances. While this clarification of the roles of different levels of government in the intergovern-mental system is welcome, it raises some interesting questions about what the 1980s hold in store. It would seem that state governments have been given primary responsibility for deal-ing with urban problems, but there are no safeguards to insure that states will live up to that responsibility. Indeed, some have argued that the growth in city-suburb fiscal disparities which occurred in the 1960s and 1970s was a direct result of the fact that state governments had the fiscal leverage but were unwill-ing to assume their full responsibilities toward the urban poor.

Default and Emergency Loans

Financial emergencies could lie ahead for some cities and states. If it does nothing else, a national urban policy ought to outline the federal response to such crises. Dealing with New York City on an ad hoc basis was excusable because there had been little reason to be concerned with municipal default since the Depression. In many respects the New York City crisis of 1975 was a special case.[59] How many special cases can there be, how-ever, before a policy is developed? Cleveland and Detroit have much in common with New York City in terms of weaknesses in the underlying economy, as do many of the other cities which commonly appear on the distressed lists.

Two questions are essential in formulating a federal policy toward distressed cities. The first involves defining the condi-tions necessary for federal intervention, i.e., what avenues must be exhausted before emergency federal subsidy is warranted. The second is what adjustments the city must make as a con-dition of receiving the aid. Neither question seems to have been clearly thought through, and neither is to be found in either the Carter or Reagan administration's urban policy statement.

On the first issue, one might query the role of state govern-ment as having a prior responsibility for city financial prob-lems. Should there have been an emergency loan to New York City when New York State was running enough of a surplus to cut taxes? Some would argue that the Clevelands and Chicagos are primarily the business of the Ohios and the Illinois and that federal bailouts are a last, desperate resort. The view from the Statehouse is likely to be quite different. State governments could argue that a combination of local autonomy, federal mandates, and direct federal-to-local aid has taken much of the control over local fiscal excesses out of their hands. Federal actions stimulated the local fisc and may have created some of the risk of default; hence, the federal government should be a partner in the bailout.

The state argument was a strong one, at least so long as the federal government was ambiguous about the role of states in the intergovernmental system. The newest federalism may change all of that—the intention of the Reagan proposals seems to be to give states first claim on dealing with city fiscal emergencies. The onus, then, will be on states to define those local fiscal actions that must be taken prior to federal intervention, e.g., emergency tax levels, program and employment cutbacks, wage freezes, and debt rescheduling.

Suppose the federal government does hold to a role of borrower of last resort for cities on the brink of default. The second issue is how far local governments will be required to go in altering their fiscal behavior as a condition for continuing to receive the emergency loan or grant, and how the fiscal improvements will be monitored. The most important question to be resolved is how the federal government will opt to distribute the burden of an austerity program. Employee layoffs and wage freezes will lay much of the burden on public employees, program cutbacks and tax increases on citizens, and bond repayment stretchouts or moratoriums on bondholders. A federal policy that accommodates a bailout in a period of emergency will implicitly or explicitly make such choices.

STATE AND LOCAL GOVERNMENT POLICY

A national urban policy is essential. State and local government financial problems will materialize in the 1980s, and a reasoned federal response is imperative. The fiscal future of state and local governments will be determined largely by factors outside their control—inflation and unemployment, the performance of the national economy, and the level and distribution of federal grants. Still, state and local governments have considerable discretionary powers which they may use to influence their financial health during this period of adjustment.

The most popular reform is to offer a program for governmental productivity increases and efficiency improvements. This is popular because it does not cost the taxpayer and can be used as a basis to reward public employees and, best of all, its success or failure cannot be measured. The need for and possibilities of state and local government employee productivity increases make great discussion material, but they do not balance budgets. A related issue is whether the tone of the productivity discussion might change with rising materials and energy costs. Heretofore, much of the attention had centered on whether capital could somehow be substituted for labor, thereby increasing output and reducing the use of the relatively expensive labor factor. If materials, capital and energy costs continue to rise at present rates, relative to labor costs, the enthusiasm for new technologies in the public sector may cool.

A second strategy is the use of tax and subsidy policy to stimulate regional economic development.[60] State and local governments in both growing and declining regions attempt to improve their competitiveness as a business location by offering various kinds of subsidies, e.g., tax abatements, tax "holidays," subsidized loans, and grants of land. Whether these subsidies have actually contributed to local economic development is as debatable as the issue of whether the induced revenue gains from new business have exceeded the expenditure costs.

Probably the most important strategy in which governments in the declining regions can participate is retrenchment, i.e., the adjustment of public service levels and growth in expenditures to properly reflect capacity to finance. Retrenchment involves cuts in service levels and employment, a more realistic look at the kinds of compensation and benefit levels that can be afforded, and a careful conservation of those capital resources that are available. With respect to the last, one would

expect to see a great deal more emphasis placed on maintenance and renovation of the existing capital stock than on the
construction of new capital facilities.[61] The austerity programs
in some cities have included these kinds of adjustments, but
other public policies have, surprisingly, gone in the opposite
direction. Relative tax burdens have risen in the declining regions, the fiscal limitation movement has been most popular in
the Sunbelt, and public employment rolls in the declining regions have expanded in the past two years.

In the growing regions, local governments also face serious
adjustment problems that will require them to carefully plan
the growth in their budgets. The problems are essentially how
much a government should grow and how fast this growth
should occur. The mistakes of governments in the older region
might be avoided if the long-term expenditure implications of
fiscal decisions are evaluated against the potential long-term
growth in the local resource base. Fiscal planning and forecasting, although a relatively new art, are being used effectively in
many cities, especially those in the growing regions.[62]

The most pressing of the fiscal adjustment problems is
keeping infrastructure development in step with population and
employment growth. With rising material and capital costs and
with the prospects for less federal aid, this could become a serious bottleneck to growth. At the same time, there is the dan-
ger of allowing growth to become too rapid and uncontrolled
and to lead fiscal development to a point where there is no
possibility for careful long-term budgetary planning.

STATE AND LOCAL GOVERNMENT FINANCES:
THE NEXT DECADE

In light of these factors of restraint and push, what is likely to
happen in state and local government finances over the next
ten years? In all probability, the state and local government sector will grow more slowly than it did in the 1960s and most of
the 1970s, but under the newest federalism it may account for
an increasing share of government domestic expenditures. Beyond this generalization, the following does not seem an unrea-
sonable scenario:

The national economy will go through the current recession and begin a period of slower real growth than in the 1960s and 1970s.

As a result of the newest federalism and the fear of tax levels being too far out of line, state and local governments in the Northeast and industrial Midwest will continue to back away from their commitments to provide relatively high levels of service to low-income families.

Cities in the declining regions will continue to suffer, some to the point of being unable to meet their expenditure commitments. Continued expenditure retrenchment, reductions in the number of public employees, and service level cutbacks will probably take place. By the end of the decade, many such cities—and similarly troubled states—will have succeeded in reducing their relative public service packages to a level they can afford.

Despite the recognition of capital obsolescence problems, the quality of the capital stock, especially in the older regions, will continue to deteriorate. Higher interest rates, inflation, reduced federal aid, and pressing financial problems will push state and local governments to further defer capital construction, maintenance, and renovation.

There will be another catchup in public employee compensation rates. The lagged effect of deferred compensation increases in recent years will account for virtually all of the public expenditure increases of some jurisdictions.

Relative levels of tax burdens will rise in many states in the growing regions in response to increasing costs and service quality and will decline in the Northeast as austerity programs begin to take hold.

Federal policy toward state and local government finances will remain ad hoc, and there will be few guiding principles. The overall level of federal grants (in real terms) will likely decline, and less targeting on distressed urban areas might be expected as the growing states more forcefully make their point about rural poverty.

These guesses would be altered by a change in the direction of federal government policy toward state and local government finances or by a better-performing United States economy. In the last analysis, there could be no better national urban policy than a low inflation rate, a low unemployment rate and a strong growth in GNP.

NOTES

CHAPTER 1: INTRODUCTION

1. See, for example, Roy Bahl, Bernard Jump, Jr., and Larry Schroeder, "The Outlook for City Fiscal Performance in Declining Regions," in *The Fiscal Outlook for Cities,* edited by Roy Bahl (Syracuse, N.Y.: Syracuse University Press, 1978) and William Oakland, *Financial Relief for Troubled Cities* (Columbus, Ohio: Academy for Contemporary Problems, 1978).

2. T. D. Allman, "The Urban Crisis Leaves Town," *Harper's,* December 1978, p. 41.

CHAPTER 2: THE GROWING FISCAL AND ECONOMIC IMPORTANCE OF STATE AND LOCAL GOVERNMENT

1. Anyone studying the United States federal system is in the debt of the Advisory Commission on Intergovernmental Relations. In particular, their excellent biennial compilation *Significant Features of Fiscal Federalism* is most useful in tracking the development of state and local government finances.

2. A review of the long-term growth in public employment, by level of government, is in Jesse Burkhead and Shawna Grosskopf, "Trends in Public Employment and Compensation," in *Public Employment and State and Local Government Finances,* edited by Roy Bahl, Jesse Burkhead, and Bernard Jump, Jr. (Cambridge, Mass.: Ballinger, 1980).

3. Current data on government expenditures are regularly re-

ported by the United States Department of Commerce, Bureau of Economic Analysis in the *Survey of Current Business*.

4. We follow the usual definition of federal domestic expenditures as federal expenditures other than for national defense, international affairs and finance, space research and technology, and the estimated portion of net interest attributable to these functions. Social Security is included.

5. ACIR, *Significant Features of Fiscal Federalism 1980–81 Edition*, p. 29.

6. The term "social welfare expenditures" is used here to include all health, education, and welfare expenditures and Social Security.

7. The GNP elasticities between 1976 and 1980 are 1.19 for federal revenues, 0.82 for own-source state and local government revenues, and 0.83 for federal aid.

8. *Survey of Current Business*, April 1982, p. 13.

9. In Table 2-4, we define "average" as the unweighted mean value of the variable across the fifty states. The average percent of taxes to personal income $(\bar{T}y)$ is

$$\bar{T}y = \sum_{i=1}^{50} Ty_i \ / 50$$

This is different, of course, from

$$\bar{\bar{T}}y = \sum_{i=1}^{50} T_i \ / \sum_{i=1}^{50} Y_i$$

For our purposes, the former seems the more appropriate way of defining a benchmark against which to compare interstate variations.

10. The standard measure of relative variation used in Table 2-4 is the coefficient of variation, i.e., the standard deviation as a percent of the mean. The smaller the coefficient, the less dispersed the distribution. For example, the reduction in the coefficient for the ratio of federal aid to personal income means that the states are grouped more closely about the mean in the latter year.

11. As may be seen in Table 2-4, there was a substantial increase in the diversity of revenue effort by state and local governments; i.e., the coefficient of variation rose from 0.15 in 1976 to 0.46 in 1980. Most of this, however, was due to substantial increases in severance tax collections in Alaska. Indeed, if Alaska is omitted from the interstate distribution of revenue effort, the mean revenue effort remains constant at 14.1 between 1976 and 1980 and the coefficient of variation changes only from 0.13 to 0.17.

12. Many public finance economists have made this point. For a summary of the issues involved, see Wallace Oates, *Fiscal Federalism* (New York: Harcourt Brace Jovanovich, 1972), pp. 4–13.

13. See, for discussions of this issue, Roy Bahl, Alan Campbell and David Greytak, *Taxes, Expenditures and the Economic Base: Case Study of New York City* (New York: Praeger Publishers, 1974), and Edward Gramlich, "The New York City Crisis: What Happened and What Is To Be Done?" *American Economic Review* 66(5):415 (1976).

14. A good questioning of the conventional thinking about the local government role in income redistribution is in Richard Tresch, *Public Finance: A Normative Theory* (Plano: Texas Business Publications, 1981), Chapter 30.

15. Alvin Hansen and Harvey Perloff, *State and Local Finance in the National Economy* (New York: Norton, 1944).

16. Robert Rafuse, "Cyclical Behavior of State-Local Finances," in *Essays in Fiscal Federalism,* edited by Richard Musgrave (Washington, D.C.: Brookings Institution, 1965).

17. Ibid., p. 117.

18. ACIR, *State-Local Finances in Recession and Inflation* (Washington, D.C.: GPO, 1979) and *Countercyclical Aid and Economic Stabilization* (Washington, D.C.: GPO, 1978).

19. Edward Gramlich, "State and Local Government Budgets the Day After It Rained: Why Is the Surplus so High?" *Brookings Papers on Economic Activity* 1 (Washington, D.C.: Brookings Institution, 1978) and Edward Gramlich, "State and Local Budget Surpluses and the Effect of Federal Macroeconomic Policies," U.S. Congress, Joint Economic Committee (Washington, D.C.: GPO, 1979).

20. Robert Vogel and Robert Trost, "The Response of State Government Receipts to Economic Fluctuations and the Allocation of Countercyclical Revenue Sharing Grants," *Review of Economics and Statistics* LXI(3):389 (1979).

21. Robert Reischauer, "The Economy, the Federal Budget and the Prospects for Urban Aid," in *The Fiscal Outlook for Cities,* edited by Roy Bahl (Syracuse, N. Y.: Syracuse University Press, 1978).

22. Frank Jones and Mark Weisler, "Cyclical Variations in State and Local Government Financial Behavior and Capital Expenditures," in *Proceedings of the Seventieth Annual Conference on Taxation* (Columbus, Ohio: National Tax Association-Tax Institute of America, 1978).

23. Larry DeBoer, "The Response of State and Local Government Finances to Economic Fluctuations," Ph.D. Dissertation, Syracuse University, 1982, chapter 6.

24. These possibilities are discussed in Edward Gramlich, "Inter-

governmental Grants: A Review of the Empirical Literature," in *The Political Economy of Fiscal Federalism,* edited by Wallace Oates (Lexington, Mass.: Lexington Books, 1977).

25. *Survey of Current Business,* July 1979.

26. In 1982, President Reagan proposed a swap whereby AFDC and food stamps would be fully funded by the state and local governments and Medicaid would become a federal responsibility. A second element of the program proposed a phased turnback of more than forty federally funded programs to state and local governments. This program was first described in "The President's Federalism Initiative," White House press release, January 26, 1982.

27. For a review of the evidence on this point, see "Domestic Consequences of United States Population Change," report prepared by the House Select Committee on Population (Washington, D.C.: GPO, 1978).

28. For a good discussion of these problems, see Charles McLure, "The Theory of Expenditure Incidence," *Finanzarchiv* 30:432 (1972).

29. The standard reference on this issue is Henry Aaron, *Who Pays the Property Tax?* (Washington, D.C.: Brookings Institution, 1975).

30. Benjamin Okner and Joseph Pechman, *Who Bears the Tax Burden?* (Washington, D.C.: Brookings Institution, 1975).

31. For examples, see Serrano versus Priest, 5 Cal., 3d 584 (1971) and San Antonio Independent School District versus Rodriguez, 411 U.S. 1 (1972).

32. Some would argue that voters can send such signals to elected politicians and hence government decision makers try not to stray too far from the preferences of the median voter. This approach is reviewed in Robert Inman, "The Fiscal Performance of Local Governments: An Interpretative Review," in *Current Issues in Urban Economics,* edited by Peter Mieszkowski and Mahlon Straszheim (Baltimore: Johns Hopkins University Press, 1981). Niskanen rejects even this possibility with the argument that fiscal decisions are primarily influenced by bureaucrats whose ultimate objective is to maximize their power by maximizing the size of their bureau budget. See William Niskanen, *Bureaucracy and Representative Government* (New York: Aldine, 1971).

33. It should be noted, however, that this estimate for New York overstates the tax burden because it takes account of neither exporting nor the federal offset.

34. Arthur B. Laffer, "Statement Prepared for the Joint Economic Committee, May 20, 1977." Reprinted in Arthur B. Laffer and Jan Seymour (editors), *The Economics of the Tax Revolt: A Reader* (New York: Harcourt, Brace, Jovanovich, 1979), pp. 75–79.

35. Don Fullerton, "On the Possibility of an Inverse Relationship Between Tax Rates and Government Revenues," *Journal of Public Economics* 19 (1982):3–22.

36. Michael Boskin, "Taxation, Saving and the Rate of Interest," *Journal of Political Economy* 86(2):S3 (1978).

37. For a discussion of these alternatives, see *Federal Tax Reform: Myths and Realities,* edited by Michael Boskin (San Francisco: Institute for Contemporary Studies, 1978).

38. Simon Kuznets, "Economic Growth and Income Inequality," *American Economic Review* 45(1):1 (1955).

39. W. Irwin Gillespie, "Effects of Public Expenditures on the Distribution of Income," in *Essays in Fiscal Federalism,* edited by Richard Musgrave (Washington, D.C.: Brookings Institution, 1965).

40. Morgan Reynolds and Eugene Smolensky, "The Post-Fisc Distribution: 1961 and 1970 Compared," *National Tax Journal* 27:515 (1974).

41. Malcolm Sawyer, "Income Distribution in OECD Countries," and Mark Wasserman, "Public Sector Budget Balance," *OECD Economic Outlook,* occasional studies, July 1976.

42. It must be admitted that estimates of the distribution of expenditure benefits are based on a primitive methodology. For a careful review of this work, see Luc DeWulf, "Fiscal Incidence Studies in Developing Countries: Survey and Critique," *International Monetary Fund Staff Papers* 22(3):61 (1975).

CHAPTER 3: THE FISCAL HEALTH OF THE STATE AND LOCAL GOVERNMENT SECTOR

1. The process involves a transfer of housing from working class families to higher-income families who have rediscovered the virtues and economies of city living. A useful discussion of the process is in Peter Salins, "The Limits of Gentrification," *New York Affairs* 5(4):61 (1979).

2. For a discussion of the targeting and spreading issues, see Richard Nathan, "The Outlook for Federal Grants to Cities," in *The Fiscal Outlook for Cities,* edited by Roy Bahl (Syracuse, N.Y.: Syracuse University Press, 1978). The argument to alter the regional distribution of federal funds is made annually by Senator Daniel Moynihan. See "The Federal Government and the Economy of New York State," unpublished report by Senator Moynihan, June 15, 1977.

3. The NIA are reported monthly in *Survey of Current Business.*

4. The Joint Economic Committee used the surplus argument and

the observation that state tax revenues have grown faster than inflation to recommend that "Congress should evaluate the General Revenue Sharing Program and should consider the possibility of reducing
or eliminating the portion going to the states." *The 1979 Joint Economic
Report,* March 22, 1979, p. 30.

5. These measurement problems are covered in some detail in
Gramlich's very useful paper "State and Local Government Budget
Surpluses and the Effect of Federal Macroeconomic Policy," Joint Eco-
nomic Committee, January 12, 1979; see also Edward Gramlich, "State
and Local Budgets the Day After It Rained: Why Is the Surplus so
High?" *Brookings Papers on Economic Activity 1* (Washington, D.C.:
Brookings Institution, 1978).

6. The term "general government surplus" should not be con-
fused with a general account surplus. The former is used here to refer
to all funds other than social insurance.

7. Gramlich's method of estimation has been followed here. This
approach probably underestimates federal funding and therefore
overestimates the surplus because only grants for highways, water, and
sewers have been included and because there is no accounting for any
earmarking of user charges for capital construction purposes. He made
these simplifying assumptions, and we follow suit, because data for a
more accurate adjustment were not available.

8. Robert Bretzfelder and Howard Friedenberg, "Sensitivity of
Regional and State Nonfarm Wages and Salaries to the National Business Cycle, 1980: I–1981:II," *Survey of Current Business,* January 1982,
pp. 26–28; and Robert Bretzfelder and Howard Friedenberg, "Sensitivity of Regional and State Nonfarm Wages and Salaries to the National Business Cycles, 1948–1979," *Survey of Current Business,* May 1980,
pp. 15–27.

9. The period 1981:III–1982:III includes only the recession phase
of the cycle.

10. Indeed, it may be necessary practice. One financial analyst for
a major bond rating agency has noted that the ratio of general fund
unobligated balances to expenditures is a key financial indicator and
thinks that 5 percent is "a good solid number for a state surplus unless
you have a cyclical economy." See *Understanding the Fiscal Condition of
the States,* p. 12. Philip Dearborn also argues that liquidity in the general fund is a key indicator of fiscal strength in *Elements of Municipal
Financial Analysis, Part I: Measuring Liquidity* (New York: First Boston
Coporation, 1979).

11. Connecticut and Vermont are exceptions. However, the legal
requirement of a balanced budget depends very much on the defini-

tion of a deficit. See National Association of State Budget Officers, *Limitations on State Deficits* (Lexington, Ky.: Council of State Governments, 1976).

12. It should be noted that the NIA accounts may show a surplus or deficit for a state or local government even if the budget is in balance because NIA data are reported on a calendar year rather than a fiscal year basis.

13. The National Association of State Budget Officers mentions year-end balances of 5 to 7 percent of general fund expenditures as common for states. See *Understanding the Fiscal Condition,* p. 12.

14. David Blank, "Reform of State-Local Fiscal Relations in New York," *National Tax Journal,* December 1950, p. 106.

15. The Michigan Stabilization Fund is relatively new, and it is too early to evaluate its effectiveness. Essentially, the law establishes formulas, based on personal income growth and unemployment rates, which determine whether money will be paid into or out of the fund. For a general discussion of such an approach, see Roger Vaughan, "Inflation and Unemployment: Surviving the 1980s" (Washington, D.C.: Council of State Planning Agencies, 1980).

16. Dearborn's analysis of the financial condition of twenty-eight large cities in 1977 supports the fiscal restraint thesis. He found a general fund operating surplus (excluding New York City, Chicago, and Cleveland) of $212.8 million, or 3.2 percent of general fund expenditures. Philip Dearborn, *The Financial Health of Major U.S. Cities in Fiscal 1977* (New York: First Boston Corporation, 1978).

17. National Governors' Association and National Association of State Budget Officers, *Fiscal Survey of the States* (Washington, D.C.: GPO, 1978–79).

18. David Levin, "Receipts and Expenditures of State Governments and of Local Governments, 1959–1976," *Survey of Current Business,* May 1978. This analysis had not been repeated for a more recent year at the time of this writing.

19. Prepared statement by Stephen Farber, Director, National Governors' Association, in *Local Distress, State Surpluses, Proposition 13: Prelude to Fiscal Crisis or New Opportunities?* Hearings before the Committee on Banking, Finance and Urban Affairs, July 25 and 26, 1978, pp. 779–87.

20. An assessment of the more recent fiscal performance of state and local governments is taken up in the last section of this chapter. The results suggested here may be found in Table 3-8.

21. National Governors' Association and National Association of State Budget Officers, *Fiscal Survey of the States* (Annual).

22. U.S. Bureau of the Census, *Governmental Finances in 1980–81,* series GF78, 5 (Washington, D.C.: GPO, 1982).

23. Each July the *Survey of Current Business* includes a description of the difference between the NIA and the Census of Governments tabulation. See, for example, *Survey of Current Business,* July 1979, Table 3.18.

24. This particular 5 percent benchmark may well be an overstatement of needs for contingencies. The rule of thumb is meant to be applied to the relationship between *total* cash balances and operating expenditures, and it seems reasonable to believe that states accumulated balances throughout the 1976–78 period of economic recovery.

25. National Governors' Association, *Fiscal Survey of the States, 1978–79.*

26. Steven Gold and Karen Benker, *State Fiscal Conditions as States Entered 1982,* Legislative Finance Paper 13 (Denver: National Conference of State Legislatures, 1982).

27. Steven Gold, Karen Benker, and George Peterson, *State Budget Actions in 1982* (Denver: National Conference of State Legislatures, 1982).

28. John Mikesell, "The Cyclical Sensitivity of State Tax Revenues," School of Public and Environmental Affairs, Indiana University, November 1982.

29. Thomas Muller, *Growing and Declining Urban Areas: A Fiscal Comparison* (Washington, D.C.: Urban Institute, 1976).

30. Philip Dearborn, *Elements of Municipal Financial Analysis,* Part IV: *Condition of Major City Finances* (New York: First Boston Corporation, 1977) and *The Financial Health of Major U.S. Cities in 1978* (Washington, D.C.: Urban Institute, 1979).

31. Richard P. Nathan and Charles Adams, "Understanding Central City Hardship," *Political Science Quarterly* 91(1):47 (1976).

32. U.S. Department of the Treasury, Office of State and Local Finance, *Report on the Fiscal Impact of the Economic Stimulus Package on 48 Large Urban Governments,* January 23, 1978.

33. We have considered these criteria at some length in Roy Bahl and Bernard Jump, Jr., "Measuring the Fiscal Viability of Cities," in *Fiscal Choices,* edited by George Peterson (Washington, D.C.: Urban Institute, forthcoming).

34. For recent reviews of these studies, see Roy Bahl, Marvin Johnson, and Michael Wasylenko, "State and Local Government Expenditure Determinants: The Traditional View and a New Approach," in *Public Employment and State and Local Government Finances,* edited by Roy Bahl, Jesse Burkhead, and Bernard Jump, Jr. (Cam-

bridge, Mass.: Ballinger, 1980) and Robert Inman, "The Fiscal Performance of Local Governments: An Interpretative Review," in *Current Issues in Urban Economics,* edited by Peter Mieszkowski and Mahlon Straszheim (Baltimore: Johns Hopkins University Press, 1979).

35. A good analysis and critique of fiscal distress studies is Office of State and Local Government Finance, U.S. Treasury, "Responsiveness of State/Federal and Direct Federal Aid to Distressed Cities," Research Note IV, 1979.

36. Nathan and Adams, "Understanding Central City Hardship."

37. Richard Nathan and James Fossett, "Urban Conditions: The Future of the Federal Role," *Proceedings of the National Tax Association (1978)* (Columbus, Ohio: National Tax Association, 1979).

38. Katherine L. Bradbury, Anthony Downs, and Kenneth A. Small, *Urban Decline and the Future of American Cities* (Washington, D.C.: Brookings Institution, 1982), Chapter 3.

39. Terry Clark *et al.,* "How Many New Yorks? The New York Fiscal Crisis in Comparative Perspective," report 72 of the Comparative Study of Community Decision-Making (Chicago: University of Chicago Press, 1976).

40. Touche-Ross and Company and the First National Bank of Boston, *Urban Fiscal Stress: A Comparative Analysis of 66 U.S. Cities* (New York: Touche-Ross, 1979).

41. Gregory Schneid, Hubert Lipinsky, and Michael Palmer, *An Alternative Approach to General Revenue Sharing: A Needs Based Allocation Formula* (Washington, D.C.: Institute for the Future, 1975).

42. Harold Bunce, *An Evaluation of the Community Development Block Grant Formula* (Washington, D.C.: U.S. Department of Housing and Urban Development, 1976).

43. Congressional Budget Office, *City Need and the Responsiveness of Federal Grants Programs* (Washington, D.C.: GPO, 1978).

44. Two exceptions are the Institute for the Future and HUD studies, where a factor analysis was used to standardize and combine the variables. See Schneid, Lipinsky, and Palmer, *An Alternative Approach,* and Bunce, *An Evaluation of the Community Development Block Grant Formula.*

45. Nathan and Fossett, "Urban Conditions: The Future of the Federal Role."

46. Bradbury, Downs, and Small, *Urban Decline.*

47. Touche-Ross, *Urban Fiscal Distress.*

48. This by no means exhausts the list of fiscal distress studies. See, for example, Linn Brown and Richard Syron, "Cities Suburbs and Regions," *New England Economic Review,* January-February 1979, p. 41;

and ACIR, *Trends in Metropolitan America* (Washington, D.C.: GPO, 1977).

49. A special tabulation from the HUD study appears in *City Need and the Responsiveness of Federal Grants Programs* (Washington, D.C.: GPO, 1978) p. 37.

50. Bradbury, Downs, and Small, p. 50.

51. Marshall Kaplan, Gans and Kahn, *Growth and the Cities of the South: A Study in Diversity* (Washington, D.C.: GPO, 1978).

52. Clark *et al.*, "How Many New Yorks?"

53. Touche-Ross, *Urban Fiscal Distress,* p. 109. A good critique of the Touche-Ross study is Department of Housing and Urban Development, "The Urban Fiscal Crisis: Fact or Fantasy?" (Washington, D.C.: GPO, 1979).

54. Computed from Bradbury, Downs, and Small, Table 3-9.

55. John Kasarda, "Industry, Community and the Metropolitan Problem," in *Handbook of Urban Life* (New York: Jossey-Bass, 1978).

56. ACIR, *Fiscal Balance in the American Federal System,* Vol. II: *Metropolitan Fiscal Disparities* (Washington, D.C.: GPO, 1968); ACIR, *Trends in Metropolitan America* (1977); and Seymour Sacks, "Estimates of Current Employment Trends and Related Information for Large Cities," Metropolitan Studies Program (Syracuse, N.Y.: Syracuse University, 1978).

57. HUD, "Changing Conditions in Large Metropolitan Areas," Urban Data Reports, No. 1 (Washington, D.C.: GPO, 1979).

58. Nathan and Fossett, "Urban Conditions."

59. Nathan and Adams, "Understanding Central City Hardship."

60. Vincent Marando describes the better record of southern and western cities in "The Politics of Metropolitan Reform," in *State and Local Government: The Political Economy of Reform,* edited by Alan Campbell and Roy Bahl (New York: Free Press, 1976). See also Patricia Dusenbury *et al.,* "Suburbs in the City: Municipal Boundary Changes in the Southern States" (Research Triangle Park, N.C.: Southern Growth Policies Board, 1980).

61. A good presentation of the view of "growing" states is in David Peterson, *The Relative Need of States and Regions for Federal Aid* (Research Triangle Park, N.C.: Southern Growth Policies Board, 1979).

62. For good examples, see ACIR, *City Financial Emergencies: The Intergovernmental Dimension* (Washington, D.C.: GPO, 1973) and David Stanley, *Cities in Trouble* (Columbus, Ohio: Academy for Contemporary Problems, 1976).

63. For attempts at comparative case studies, see Committee for

Economic Development, *Fiscal Issues in the Future of Federalism,* supplementary paper 3 (New York: 1968) and ACIR, *Fiscal Balance in the American Federal System,* Vol. II, *Metropolitan Fiscal Disparities,* 1968.

64. Dearborn's initial work on this subject appeared in ACIR, *City Financial Emergencies,* 1973. During 1977 and 1978 he developed a set of indicators of financial emergencies in *Elements of Municipal Financial Analysis* (New York: First Boston Corporation, 1978). His later extensions of this work appear in "The Financial Health of Major U.S. Cities in 1978" (New York: First Boston, 1979).

65. Dearborn, "The Financial Health of Major U.S. Cities in 1978," p. 7.

66. New York City is the best known example. Both Standard & Poor's and Moody's raised New York City's rating to A in 1973 despite what all observers now concede was a drastic deterioration in the economic and fiscal condition of the city.

67. Though Moody's Investors Service assigns grades to each city it rates, it argues that the approach is not comparative: ". . . we think an examination of each credit on its own merits is the only way to evaluate the bonds issued by cities or by any other issuer." *Moody's Analytic Overview of 25 Leading U.S. Cities* (New York: Moody's, 1977), p. i.

68. The concept of a bond rating as a tax on, or negative grant to, local government is developed in Patrick Sullivan, *Municipal Bond Ratings Viewed as Implicit Grant/Tax Mechanisms,* occasional paper 30, Metropolitan Studies Program, The Maxwell School (Syracuse, N.Y.: Syracuse University, 1976).

69. Both Standard & Poor's and Moody's have recently described their rating procedures and systems. See *Standard & Poor's Ratings Guide* (New York: McGraw-Hill, 1979) and Wade Smith, *The Appraisal of Municipal Credit Risk* (New York: Moody's Investors Service, 1979).

70. These analyses are surveyed and further evidence is presented in Roy Bahl, "Measuring the Creditworthiness of State and Local Governments: Municipal Bond Ratings," *National Tax Association, Proceedings of Sixty-Fourth Annual Conference* (1972). See also John E. Petersen, *The Rating Game,* report of the Twentieth Century Fund Task Force on Municipal Bond Credit Ratings (New York: Twentieth Century Fund, 1974).

71. Standard & Poor's, *Ratings Guide,* p. 260.

72. Congressional Budget Office, *City Need,* p. 32.

73. J. Richard Aronson and Arthur E. King, "Is There a Fiscal Crisis Outside New York?" *National Tax Journal* 31(2):161 (1978).

74. J. Richard Aronson and James R. Marsden, "Duplicating Moody's Municipal Credit Ratings," *Public Finance Quarterly* 8(1):104 (1980).

75. An interesting statement of this possibility is T. D. Allman, "The Urban Crisis Leaves Town," *Harper's,* December 1978, p. 41.

76. "State and Local Government Finances and The Changing National Economy," in *State and Local Finance: Adjustments in a Changing Economy,* Vol. 7 of the Joint Economic Committee Special Study on Economic Change, December 19, 1980.

77. Birch's reading and analysis of the Dun and Bradstreet establishment data is that much of the regional shift in employment is a result of more new companies being formed in the growing regions. See David Birch, "The Job Generation Process," Economic Development Administration, U.S. Department of Commerce (Washington, D.C.: GPO, 1979). That suburbs are in effect growing regions seems clear from Sacks' analysis in "Estimates of Large Metropolitan Areas," Urban Data Reports, no. 1 (Washington, D.C.: GPO, 1980), Table 24.

78. Kathryn Nelson and Clifford Patrick, *Decentralization of Employment During the 1969–1972 Business Cycle: The National and Regional Record* (Oak Ridge, Tennessee: Oak Ridge National Laboratory, June 1975), p. 15.

79. The data in Table 3-5 describe only cities that are coterminous with their county boundaries. Employment data are not available for the subcounty unit. In one sense the comparisons in Table 3-5 may overstate the performance of central cities during the recovery because these data include the entire county. On the other hand, only covered employment is counted and hence this is only approximately a measure of private sector growth. One should be careful not to use these data for any purpose other than comparing growth rates. Even then, findings should be reported with the greatest of care.

80. Sacks, "Estimates of Large Metropolitan Areas."

81. George Peterson, "The State and Local Sector," in *The Reagan Experiment,* edited by John Polmer and Isabel Sawhill (Washington, D.C.: The Urban Institute Press, 1982), p. 159.

82. The CPI rose by 9.2 percent in calendar 1975, 5.7 percent in 1976, and 6.5 percent in 1977. If we take the average of the 1975 and 1976 CPI increases to roughly estimate the rate of inflation for FY 1975–76 and perform a similar computation for 1976–77, we find that ten of the twenty cities gave compensation increases to public employees at rates less than the general price level increase.

83. Since employment was declining in many cities, it may not be concluded that compensation increases were *not* deferred. To the ex-

tent that governments add fewer new employees or even reduce work force size, this is likely to have a disproportionate impact on younger, lower paid employees. By the nature of arithmetic averages, it is quite possible to reduce work force size and to grant no wage increases to remaining employees and still end up with an "increase" in the average wage for the workforce.

84. Mary John Miller, Marcy Avrin, Bonnie Berk, and George E. Peterson, *The Future of Boston's Capital Plant* (Washington, D.C.: The Urban Institute, 1981).

85. Mary John Miller, Marcy Avrin, Bonnie Berk, and George E. Peterson, *The Future of Oakland's Capital Plant* (Washington, D.C.: The Urban Institute, 1981).

86. George Peterson, "Capital Spending and Capital Obsolescence: The Outlook for Cities," in *The Fiscal Outlook for Cities,* edited by Roy W. Bahl (Syracuse, N.Y.: Syracuse University Press, 1979).

87. *The Condition of Urban Infrastructure in the New York-New Jersey Region: A Survival Issue for the 1980s* (New York: The Port Authority of New York and New Jersey, 1979) and David A. Grossman, *The Future of New York City's Capital Plant* (Washington, D.C.: Urban Institute, 1979).

88. Grossman, *The Future of New York City's Capital Plant.*

89. Nancy Humphrey, George Peterson, and Peter Wilson, *The Future of Cleveland's Capital Plant* (Washington, D.C.: Urban Institute, 1979).

90. Nancy Humphrey, George Peterson, and Peter Wilson, *The Future of Cincinnati's Capital Plant* (Washington, D.C.: Urban Institute, 1979).

91. Nancy Humphrey, George Peterson, and Peter Wilson, *The Future of Dallas' Capital Plant* (Washington, D.C.: Urban Institute, 1979).

92. Miller, Avrin, Berk, and Peterson, *The Future of Oakland's Capital Plant.*

93. Miller, Avrin, Berk, and Peterson, *The Future of Boston's Capital Plant.*

94. Humphrey, Peterson, and Wilson, *The Future of Cleveland's Capital Plant,* p. 75.

95. Humphrey, Peterson, and Wilson, op. cit., pp. 13–14.

96. To illustrate, during 1981 and 1982, four major magazines carried feature stories about the infrastructure problem: "The Crumbling America," *Time* (April 27, 1981); "The Decay That Threatens Economic Growth," *Business Week* (October 18, 1981); "The Decaying of America," *Newsweek* (August 2, 1982); and "To Rebuild America— 2,500,000,000 Jobs," *U.S. News and World Report* (September 27, 1982).

CHAPTER 4: THE EFFECTS OF BUSINESS CYCLES AND INFLATION

1. Except in the case of taxes with graduated rate structures, where bracket creep will increase tax burdens.

2. A graphical analysis of the possibilities is presented in Appendix A to this chapter.

3. Including supplements. See Tables 3-9 and 3-10.

4. See Jesse Burkhead and Shawna Grosskopf, "Trends in Public Employment and Compensation," in *Public Employment and State and Local Government Finances,* edited by Roy Bahl, Jesse Burkhead and Bernard Jump, Jr. (Cambridge, Mass.: Ballinger, 1980), and Shawna Grosskopf, "Public Employment Trends and Problems," in *Urban Government Finances in the 1980s,* edited by Roy Bahl (Beverly Hills, Cal.: Sage, 1981).

5. See Ronald Ehrenberg, "The Demand for State and Local Government Employees," *American Economic Review* 63:366 (June 1973).

6. See, for example, R. Ehrenberg, "Municipal Government Structure, Unionization, and the Wages of Firefighters," *Industrial and Labor Relations Review* 27:36–48 (1973).

7. The constant nonlabor share of total expenditures is studied in Thomas Borcherding and Robert Deacon, "The Demand for Services of Non-Federal Governments," *American Economic Review* 62(12):891 (1972).

8. David Greytak, Richard Gustely, and Robert J. Dinkelmeyer, "The Effects of Inflation on Local Government Expenditures," *National Tax Journal* XXVII(4):583 (1974).

9. David Greytak and Bernard Jump, Jr., "Inflation and Local Government Expenditures and Revenues: Methods and Case Studies," *Public Finance Quarterly* 5(3):275 (1977).

10. Edward M. Cupoli, William A. Peek, and C. Kurt Zorn, *An Analysis of the Effects of Inflation on Finances in Washington, D.C.*, occasional paper 36, Metropolitan Studies Program, The Maxwell School (Syracuse, N.Y.: Syracuse University, 1979).

11. Bernard Jump, Jr., "The Effects of Inflation on State and Local Government Finances, 1972–1980," Metropolitan Studies Program, Unpublished, 1983.

12. George Peterson, "Capital Spending and Capital Obsolescence: The Outlook for Cities," in *The Fiscal Outlook for Cities,* edited by Roy Bahl (Syracuse, N.Y.: Syracuse University Press, 1978).

13. Bernard Jump, Jr., "The Effects of Inflation on State and Local Government Finances, 1972–1980," Metropolitan Studies Program, Unpublished, 1983.

14. Karen Davis and Cathy Schoen, *Health and the War on Poverty:*

A Ten Year Appraisal (Washington, D.C.: Brookings Institution, 1978), Chapter 3.

15. For detail on this pattern of growth, see Ann Kalman Bixby, "Social Welfare Expenditures, Fiscal Year 1979," *Social Security Bulletin* 44(11):3 (1981).

16. Greytak, Gustely, and Dinkelmeyer, "The Effects of Inflation"; Roy Bahl, Alan Campbell, and David Greytak, *Taxes, Expenditures, and the Economic Base: A Case Study of New York City* (New York: Praeger, 1974). Chapters 3 and 4; David Greytak and Bernard Jump, Jr., *The Impact of Inflation on State and Local Government Finances, 1967–1974*, occasional paper 25, Metropolitan Studies Program, The Maxwell School (Syracuse, N.Y.: Syracuse University, 1975); Greytak and Jump, *The Impact of Inflation on the Expenditures and Revenues of Six Local Governments, 1971–1974*; Greytak and Jump, "Inflation and Local Government Expenditures and Revenues: Methods and Case Studies"; and Jump, "The Effects of Inflation on State and Local Government Finances, 1972–1980," 1983.

17. Jump, "The Effects of Inflation . . ." (1983). See also Roy Bahl, Bernard Jump, Jr., and Larry Schroeder, "The Outlook for City Fiscal Performance in Declining Regions," in *The Fiscal Outlook for Cities,* edited by Roy Bahl (Syracuse, N.Y.: Syracuse University Press, 1978).

18. Crider reached a similar conclusion with an index constructed by weighting components of local government compensation and other expenditures by the CPI and WPI. See Robert Crider, *The Impact of Inflation on State and Local Government,* Urban and Regional Development Series 5 (Columbus, Ohio: Academy for Contemporary Problems, 1978).

19. The other four local governments studied were Erie County, New York; Roanoke, Virginia; Orange County, California; and Atlanta, Georgia.

20. Jan Chaiken and Warren Walker, "Growth in Municipal Expenditures: A Case Study of Los Angeles," *The Rand Corporation,* June 1979.

21. City of Dallas, *Summary Long Range Financial Plan, 1980–81 to 1984–85* (Dallas: Office of Management Services, 1979); Roy Bahl, Larry Schroeder, and Kurt Zorn, "Local Government Revenue and Expenditure Forecasting: Dallas, Texas," occasional paper 49, Metropolitan Studies Program, The Maxwell School (Syracuse, N.Y.: Syracuse University, 1981).

22. They used constant inflation rates over the 1981–85 period, as follows: personnel, 5 percent (low) and 9 percent (high); nonpersonnel, 8 percent (low) and 12 percent (high).

23. The separation of automatic from discretionary changes and

the estimation of revenue-income elasticities for state and local governments are discussed in Roy Bahl and Larry Schroeder, *Forecasting Local Government Budgets,* occasional paper 38, Metropolitan Studies Program, The Maxwell School (Syracuse, N.Y.: Syracuse University, 1979).

24. These are reviewed in Bahl and Schroeder, "Forecasting Local Government Budgets."

25. ACIR, *State-Local Finances in Recession and Inflation* (Washington, D.C.: GPO, 1979).

26. Robert C. Vogel, "The Responsiveness of State and Local Receipts to Changes in Economic Activity: Extending the Concept of the Full Employment Budget," U.S. Congress, Joint Economic Committee, *Studies in Price Stability and Economic Growth* (Washington, D.C.: GPO, 1975); and Robert Vogel and Robert Trost, "The Response of State Government Receipts to Economic Fluctuations and the Allocation of Countercyclical Revenue Sharing Grants," *The Review of Economics and Statistics,* LXI (3):389 (1979).

27. ACIR, *State-Local Finances in Recession and Inflation,* p. 34.

28. The derivation of this $40 billion estimate is in Bahl, Jump, and Schroeder, "The Outlook for City Fiscal Performance in Declining Regions."

29. ACIR, *State-Local Finances in Recession and Inflation,* p. 38.

30. On the other hand, a lag in collective bargaining agreements would cause these expenditure effects to be overestimated. Yet, it is easier to believe that over the longer run public employee wage rates will catch up with those in the private sector than to believe that assessment lags will be eliminated.

31. Larry Schroeder, "Effects of Business Cycles on City Finances: Insiders' Views," Metropolitan Studies Program, Unpublished, 1983.

32. Roy Bahl, Alan Campbell, David Greytak, Bernard Jump, Jr., and David Puryear, "Impact of Economic Base Erosion, Inflation and Retirement Costs on Local Governments," testimony on Fiscal Relations in the American Federal System, hearings before a House Subcommittee on Government Operations, 94th Congress, 1st session, July 15, 1975.

33. David T. Stanley, "Running Short, Cutting Down: Five Cities in Financial Distress" (Washington, D.C.: Brookings Institution, 1979), unpublished manuscript.

34. Senate Committee on Government Operations, Subcommittee on Intergovernmental Relations, *Intergovernmental Anti-Recession Assistance Act of 1975,* hearings on S. 1359, 94th Congress, 1st session (Washington, D.C.: GPO, 1975); House Committee on Government

Operations, Subcommittee on Intergovernmental Relations and Human Resources, *Intergovernmental Anti-Recession Assistance Act of 1977*, hearings on H.R. 3730 and related bills, 95th Congress, 1st session (Washington, D.C.: GPO, 1977).

35. U.S. Congress, Joint Economic Committee, Subcommittee on Urban Affairs, *The Current Fiscal Position of State and Local Governments: Survey of 48 State Governments and 140 Local Governments,* 94th Congress, 1st session (Washington, D.C.: GPO, 1975).

36. Senate Committee on Governmental Affairs, Subcommittee on Intergovernmental Relations, *The Countercyclical Assistance Program: An Analysis of Its Initial Impact,* 95th Congress, 1st session (Washington, D.C.: GPO, 1977).

37. U.S. Congress, Joint Economic Committee, *Emergency Interim Survey: Fiscal Condition of 48 Large Cities,* 97th Congress, 1st session (Washington, D.C.: GPO, 1982).

38. Preliminary results reported in *Resources in Review* (Washington, D.C.: Municipal Finance Officers Association, 1982), p. 11.

39. Steven Gold and Karen Benker, *State Fiscal Conditions as States Entered 1982* (Denver: National Conference of State Legislatures, 1982).

40. Tax Foundation, *Tax Review* XLII (8):1 (1981).

41. Kathryn Nelson and Clifford Patrick, *Decentralization of Employment During the 1969–1972 Business Cycle: The National and Regional Record* (Oak Ridge, Tenn.: Oak Ridge National Laboratory, 1975), p. 15.

42. John C. Zamzow, "The Current Recession: Its Regional Impact," testimony for Subcommittee on Fiscal and Intergovernmental Policy of the Joint Economic Committee, October 16, 1979; and Bahl, Jump, and Schroeder, "The Outlook for City Fiscal Performance in Declining Regions."

43. U.S. Congress, *The Current Fiscal Position of State and Local Governments.*

44. U.S. Congress, Joint Economic Committee, Subcommittees on Economic Growth and Stabilization and on Fiscal and Intergovernmental Policy, *The Current Fiscal Condition of Cities: A Survey of 67 of the 75 Largest Cities,* 95th Congress, 1st session (Washington, D.C.: GPO, 1977).

45. U.S. Congress, Joint Economic Committee, *Emergency Interim Survey: Fiscal Condition of 48 Large Cities.*

46. *State Fiscal Survey Fiscal Years 1975, 1976, and 1977, Summary Report* (Lexington, Ky.: National Association of State Budget Officers, 1977), p. 3.

47. Comptroller General of the United States, report to Congress,

Antirecession Assistance Is Helping but Distribution Formula Needs Reassessment (Washington, D.C.: General Accounting Office, 1977). For more details, see The Comptroller General of the United States, *Impact of Antirecession Assistance on 15 State Governments, Impact of Antirecession Assistance on 16 County Governments,* and *Impact of Antirecession Assistance on 21 City Governments* (Washington, D.C.: General Accounting Office, 1978).

48. U.S. President, *Economic Report of the President,* 1977.

49. Vogel, "The Responsiveness of State and Local Receipts," and Vogel and Trost, "The Response of State Government Receipts."

50. Crider, *The Impact of Recession on State and Local Finance.*

51. Vogel's estimated equation is

$$\ln R = 3.04 + 0.0151 \ln R + 1.39 \ln P + 0.37 \ln GAP$$
$$\quad\quad\quad (61.2) \quad\quad\quad (34.7) \quad\quad (10.4)$$

$$R^2 = .99 \quad\quad DW = 1.27$$

The ACIR equation is shown as equation 4-4 above.

52. Bahl, Jump, and Schroeder, "The Outlook for City Fiscal Performance in Declining Regions."

53. ACIR, *State-Local Finances in Recession and Inflation,* pp. 80–81.

54. Crider, *The Impact of Recession on State and Local Finance.*

55. Schroeder, "The Effects of Business Cycles . . ." (1983)

56. ACIR, *State-Local Finances in Recession and Inflation,* pp. 80–81. It should be noted that they caution and demonstrate that this conclusion does not hold for all states.

Appendix 4B

1. The conceptual problems with defining and using price indexes to measure inflation in the public sector are considerably more complex than implied here. For a thorough discussion, see David Greytak and Bernard Jump Jr., *The Impact of Inflation on the Expenditures and Revenues of Six Local Governments, 1971–1974,* Monograph 4, Metropolitan Studies Program, The Maxwell School (Syracuse, N.Y.: Syracuse University, 1975).

2. Unfortunately, the price indexes that would be used for such construction (CPI, WPI) are available only on a national basis. Hence one might be able to account for the different mix of expenditures of different local governments but not for the differential rates of price increase in different regions of the country.

3. See, for example, Bureau of Labor Statistics, "Autumn 1976 Urban Family Budgets and Comparative Indexes for Selected Urban Areas" (Washington, D.C.: GPO, 1977).

4. Greytak and Jump, *The Impact of Inflation.*

5. *Multi-Year Financial Plan FY 1979–80,* District of Columbia Government, September 1977; and Roy Bahl, Larry Schroeder, Marla Share, and Anne Hoffman, "Local Government Revenue and Expenditure Forecasting: Washington, D.C.," occasional paper 51, Metropolitan Studies Program, The Maxwell School (Syracuse, N.Y.: Syracuse University, 1981).

CHAPTER 5: THE EFFECTS OF REGIONAL SHIFTS IN POPULATION AND ECONOMIC ACTIVITY

1. See, for example, William H. Miernyk, "The Northeast Isn't What It Used To Be," in *Balanced Growth for the Northeast* (Albany: New York State Senate, 1975); Lawrence K. Lynch and E. Evan Brunson, "Comparative Growth and Structure: The South and the Nation," in *The Economics of Southern Growth,* edited by E. Blaine Liner and Lawrence K. Lynch (Durham, N.C.: The Southern Growth Policies Board, 1977); and David Puryear and Roy Bahl, *Economic Problems of a Mature Economy,* occasional paper 27, Metropolitan Studies Program, The Maxwell School (Syracuse, N.Y.: Syracuse University, 1976).

2. See, for example, George E. Peterson, "Finance," in *The Urban Predicament,* edited by William Gorham and Nathan Glazer (Washington, D.C.: Urban Institute, 1976); Roy Bahl, Bernard Jump, Jr., and Larry Schroeder, "The Outlook for City Fiscal Performance in Declining Regions," in *The Fiscal Outlook for Cities,* edited by Roy Bahl (Syracuse, N.Y.: Syracuse University Press, 1978); Roy Bahl, "The Next Decade in State and Local Government Finance: A Period of Adjustment," in *Urban Government Finance: Emerging Trends,* edited by Roy Bahl (Cambridge, Mass.: Sage, 1981).

3. Notable exceptions here are Richard P. Nathan and Paul R. Dommel, "Understanding Central City Hardship," *Political Science Quarterly* 21(1):61 (1976), who argue a relationship between regional shifts and urban fiscal problems; Tom Muller, "The Declining and Growing Metropolis: A Fiscal Comparison," in *Post-Industrial America: Metropolitan Decline and Regional Job Shifts,* edited by George Sternlieb and James W. Hughes (New Brunswick, N.J.: The Center for Urban Policy Research, State University of New Jersey, 1975), who argues that population decline is a reasonable proxy for fiscal distress; and Roy Bahl, Alan Campbell, and David Greytak, *Taxes, Expenditures and*

the Economic Base: A Case Study of New York City (New York: Praeger, 1974).

4. This chapter is an extension of my previous research on this subject. Earlier versions are "Effects of Regional Shifts in Population and Economic Activity on the Finances of State and Local Governments: Implications for Public Policy" in *National Policy Toward Regional Change,* edited by Victor Arnold (Lexington, Mass.: Lexington Books, 1981); "Regional Shifts in Economic Activity and Government Finances in Growing and Declining States" in *Tax Reform and Southern Economic Development,* edited by Bernard Weinstein (Research Triangle Park, N.C.: Southern Growth Policies Board, 1979); and Roy Bahl and Larry Schroeder, "Fiscal Adjustments in Declining States," in *Cities Under Stress,* edited by Robert Burchell and David Listokin (New Brunswick, N.J.: Rutgers University Press, 1981).

5. The states included in each region are enumerated in Table 5-3. Some authors exclude certain states in these regions on grounds that they are qualitatively different in terms of economic base. For example, Jusenius and Ledebur exclude Maine, Vermont, and New Hampshire from the northern region because the industrial bases of these states differ in kind and degree from those of the rest of the region. See C. L. Jusenius and L. C. Ledebur, *A Myth in the Making: The Southern Economic Challenge and the Northern Economic Decline,* Economic Development Administration, U.S. Department of Commerce (Washington, D.C.: GPO, 1976), p. 2.

6. A brief and useful discussion of regional breakdowns is Chapter 1 in Gregory Jackson, George Masnick, Roger Bolton, Susan Bartlett, and John Pitkin, *Regional Diversity: Growth in the United States, 1960–1990* (Boston: Auburn House, 1981).

7. Much of the text in this chapter refers only to regional averages, but comparable state-by-state data are presented in my papers "Effects of Regional Shifts in Population" and "Regional Shifts in Economic Activity."

8. ACIR, *Federal Grants: Their Effects on State-Local Expenditures, Employment Levels, Wage Rates* (Washington, D.C.: GPO, 1977).

9. To better understand the nature of these regional variations, we performed an analysis of variance on the state government financing and spending shares. State responsibility for taxing in the North is 4.25 percentage points lower than in the South and 2.12 points lower than in the West. All differences are significantly different from zero at the .01 level. There are no statistically significant differences between regions for spending responsibility.

10. Sacks has been tracking changes in city-suburb disparities for

several years. See Department of Housing and Urban Development, *Changing Conditions in Metropolitan Areas,* Urban Data Reports, No. 1 (Washington, D.C.: Office of Policy Development and Research, 1979).

11. Sacks' East and Midwest correspond approximately to our northern tier and his southern region to our southern tier, with the following exceptions: in the Midwest he includes Des Moines, Wichita, Minneapolis, Kansas City, St. Louis, and Omaha and in the East he includes Washington, D.C.

12. Vincent Marando, "The Politics of Metropolitan Reform," in *State and Local Government: The Political Economy of Reform,* edited by Alan Campbell and Roy Bahl (New York: Free Press, 1976).

13. *Final Report of the Southern Growth Policies Board Task Force on Southern Cities* (Research Triangle Park, N.C.: SGPB, 1981), pp. 13–16.

14. In comparing economic and fiscal performance among regions, there is the problem of selecting the appropriate average. Assuming, as we do, that the arithmetic mean is a better measure of central tendency than the median, there remains the choice between the average value for the entire region and the average state performance. The average state performance measure has the disadvantage of giving the same weight to all states in determining the regional average and may be a misleading indicator if there are wide variations in population size within the region. This leads us to use the average value for the entire region when computing a regional average.

15. The share of federal financing of welfare was, in 1980, 55.8 percent in the North, 64.4 percent in the South, and 53.8 percent in the West.

16. Muller, "The Declining and Growing Metropolis," pp. 203–6.

17. Another possible explanation is that such comparisons are not valid because of data and conceptual measurement problems. There are no good disaggregated data on the wage levels of public employees at various levels of seniority or in various occupations. The estimates presented in Table 5-3 are of average payroll per full-time equivalent employee. This measure misses the wide variation in pay levels by class of employees, and since October payrolls are used, mixes nine-month employees (teachers) with twelve-month employees. Moreover, the inclusion of total payroll but only full-time equivalent employees introduces distortions created by payments to part-time employees. The variation in this distortion across states is unknown.

18. For a discussion of these measurement problems, see Bernard Jump, Jr., "Public Employment, Collective Bargaining and Employee Wages and Pensions," in *State and Local Government Finance and Finan-*

cial Management (Washington, D.C.: Municipal Finance Officers Association, 1978).

19. HUD has established fair market rent levels for 3100 areas throughout the nation in conjunction with their Section Eight Lease Housing Program. One might support the use of these data to construct a cost-of-living index because (a) housing costs make up a large proportion of total consumption and (b) much of the variance in living costs might be attributed to housing. Following this procedure, we have taken the indexes computed for 501 formula cities under the HUD community development block grant program, aggregated by state, and averaged to an index. For a discussion of the potential use of the HUD index as a cost-of-living measure in another context, see Comptroller General of the United States, "Why the Formula for Allocating Community Development Block Grant Funds Should Be Improved" (Washington, D.C.: General Accounting Office, 1976).

20. There are no adequate deflators for this purpose. The choices here were between the BLS levels of living for low-, intermediate-, and high-income families and the HUD index of rent. We chose the latter because the BLS data are available only for 41 metropolitan areas. See Bureau of Labor Statistics, "Autumn 1976 Urban Family Budgets and Comparative Indexes for Selected Urban Areas" (Washington, D.C.: GPO, 1977).

21. David Greytak and Bernard Jump, Jr., "Inflation and Local Government Expenditures and Revenues: Method and Case Studies," *Public Finance Quarterly* 5(3):275 (1977).

22. Richard P. Nathan and Paul R. Dommel, "The Strong Sunbelt Cities and the Weak Cold Belt Cities," hearings before the Subcommittee on the City of the House Committee on Banking, Finance and Urban Affairs, *Toward a National Urban Policy*, 95th Congress (Washington, D.C.: GPO, 1977), pp. 19–26; and "Understanding Central City Hardship," *Policital Science Quarterly* 21(1):61 (1976).

23. HUD, *Changing Conditions in Metropolitan Areas.*

24. For a parallel analysis of the New York State economy and fisc, see my papers, "The Long-Term Fiscal Outlook for New York State," in *The Declining Northeast,* edited by Benjamin Chinitz (New York: Praeger, 1978); and *The New York State Economy: 1960–1978 and the Outlook,* occasional paper 37, Metropolitan Studies Program, The Maxwell School (Syracuse, N.Y.: Syracuse University, 1979).

25. Jusenius and Ledebur, *A Myth in the Making.*

26. Jackson *et al., Regional Diversity.*

27. Michael R. Greenberg and Nicholas J. Valente, "Recent Economic Trends in the Major Northeastern Metropolises," in *Post-Indus-*

trial America: Metropolitan Decline and Inter-Regional Job Shifts, edited by
George Sternlieb and James Hughes (New Brunswick, N.J.: Rutgers
University Press, 1975).

28. Daniel Garnick, "The Northeast States in the Context of the
Nation," in *The Declining Northeast,* edited by Benjamin Chinitz (New
York: Praeger, 1978).

29. Congressional Budget Office, *Troubled Local Economies and the
Distribution of Federal Dollars* (Washington, D.C.: GPO, 1977).

30. The convergence in per capita income levels is a national trend
of the past two decades. The relative variation (mean as a percent of
standard deviation) among forty-nine states (excluding Alaska) declined from 19.0 percent in 1962 to 12.9 percent in 1980.

31. These possibilities are examined for New York City in Roy
Bahl and David Greytak, "The Response of City Government Revenues to Changes in Employment Structure," *Land Economics* 52(4):415
(1976).

32. Garnick, "The Northeast States in the Context of the Nation,"
p. 158.

33. Puryear and Bahl, *Economic Problems of a Mature Economy,* and
Roy Bahl, "The Prospects for Urban Government Finances in the
1980s," paper presented at the American Federation of State, County
and Municipal Employees Conference, Glen Cove, N.Y.: December
11, 1979.

34. Puryear and Bahl, *Economic Problems of a Mature Economy.*

35. Unweighted averages computed from Sacks, *Changing Conditions in Metropolitan Areas,* Table 24.

36. Michael J. Greenwood, "Research on Internal Migration in the
United States: A Survey," *Journal of Economic Literature,* June 1975, p.
406; and Larry H. Long, "Migration Differentials by Education and
Occupation: Trends and Variations," *Demography,* May 1973, p. 245.

37. Bernard Weinstein and Robert Firestine, *Regional Growth and
Decline in the U.S.* (New York: Praeger, 1978).

38. Roy Bahl, Marvin Johnson, and Michael Wasylenko, "State and
Local Government Expenditure Determinants: The Traditional View
and a New Approach," in *Public Employment and State and Local Government Finance,* edited by Roy Bahl, Jesse Burkhead, and Bernard Jump,
Jr. (Cambridge, Mass.: Ballinger, 1980).

39. Jusenius and Ledebur, *A Myth in the Making,* pp. 1–5.

40. For some evidence, see Julie DaVanzo, "U.S. Internal Migration: Who Moves and Why," in *Consequence of Changing U.S. Population,*
hearings before the Select Committee on Population, June 6, 1978.

41. Peter A. Morrison, "Current Demographic Change in Regions

of the United States," in *Alternatives to Confrontation*, edited by Victor Arnold (Lexington, Mass.: Lexington Books, 1980).

42. Sacks, *Changing Conditions in Metropolitan Areas*.

43. Expenditure-income elasticity is the percent increase in expenditures divided by the percent increase in personal income.

44. It is interesting to consider the consequences of indexed expenditures in this light. What if each state's expenditure increase (financed from own sources) since 1962 had been tied to its personal income increase? Assuming no change in the distribution of federal grants, the actual and hypothetical positions in 1980 would compare as follows:

| | Per Capita Expenditures from Own Sources | | Unweighted Average | | | Revenues from Own Sources as Percent of Personal Income | |
| | | | Per Capita Federal Grants | Per Capital Total Expenditures | | | |
	Actual	Indexed		Actual	Indexed	Actual	Indexed
Northern tier	$1,247	$872	$380	$1,627	$1,252	13.5	9.1
Southern tier	1,065	838	360	1,425	1,198	13.2	10.1
Western tier	1,315	1,069	401	1,716	1,470	15.0	11.4
North-South disparity							
Amount	182	34	20	202	54	0.3	−1.0
Percent	17.1	4.1	5.6	14.2	4.5	—	—
North-West disparity							
Amount	−68	−197	−21	−89	−218	−1.5	−2.3
Percent	−5.2	−18.4	−5.2	−5.2	−14.8	—	—

45. R. G. Ehrenberg, "The Demand for State and Local Government Employees," *American Economic Review* 63(3):366 (1973); T. E. Borcherding and R. T. Deacon, "The Demand for Services of Non-Federal Governments," *American Economic Review* 62(5):891 (1972); and Roy Bahl, Richard Gustely, and Michael Wasylenko, "The Determinants of Local Government Police Expenditures: A Public Employment Approach," *National Tax Journal* 31(1):67 (1978).

46. It is important to reemphasize that the rates of increase of average wages measure not total compensation but only direct wage and salary payments. To the extent that there are regional differences in the pension and benefit component of compensation *increases,* these comparisons are distorted.

47. ACIR, *Measuring the Fiscal Blood Pressure of the States* (Washington, D.C.: GPO, 1977); and ACIR, *Tax Capacity of the Fifty States: Methodology and Estimates* (Washington, D.C.: GPO, 1982).

48. Revenue-income elasticity is the percent increase in revenue divided by the percent increase in personal income. A more rigorous

measure of revenue-income elasticity requires adjusting the revenue data for discretionary changes in both the rates and bases of the tax systems. For a review of applications of various "cleaning" approaches, see Roy Bahl and Larry Schroeder, *Forecasting Local Government Budgets,* occasional paper 38, Metropolitan Studies Program, The Maxwell School (Syracuse, N.Y.: Syracuse University, 1979).

49. That this should be the case is more than a bit ironic. States such as New York and Massachusetts financed the increase in their public sectors with relatively progressive taxes and spent the proceeds lavishly (relative to other states) on redistributive services. With the need to reduce the relative size of the public sector, this same spirit of northern liberalism has led to regressive cuts in the personal income tax (in New York State) and pressures to reduce the real levels of redistributive services in several states.

50. Yet there have been some impressive attempts to show how one might improve the effectiveness of a given level of outlays. See, for example, Harry Hatry *et al., Efficiency Measurement for Local Government Services: Some Initial Suggestions* (Washington, D.C.: Urban Institute, 1979).

51. A review of the issues surrounding productivity measurement and improvement is presented in Jesse Burkhead and John P. Ross, *Productivity in the Local Government Sector* (Lexington, Mass.: Heath, 1974); and Jesse Burkhead and John P. Ross, "Local Government Productivity," in *Public Employment and State and Local Government Finances,* edited by Roy Bahl, Jesse Burkhead, and Bernard Jump, Jr. (Cambridge, Mass.: Ballinger, 1980).

52. Felix Rohatyn and John C. Sawhill, *Urgently Needed—A Northeast Energy Development Corporation* (New York: CONEG Policy Research Center, 1979).

53. The Coalition of Northeast Governors, *An Agenda for Action in the Northeast* (New York: 1976).

CHAPTER 6: THE NEXT DECADE IN STATE AND LOCAL
GOVERNMENT FINANCE: A PERIOD OF ADJUSTMENT

1. *Budget of the United States Government, Fiscal Year 1983,* pp. 2–5 and 27; and *Economic Report of the President,* transmitted to Congress, February 1983, pp. 143–45.

2. Norman C. Saunders, "The U.S. Economy to 1990: Two Projections for Growth," in *Employment Projections for the 1980s,* Bureau of Labor Statistics Bulletin 2030 (Washington, D.C.: GPO, 1979).

3. Congressional Budget Office, *The Outlook for Economic Recovery,*

Report to the Senate and House Committees on the Budget, Part I (Washington, D.C.: GPO, February 1983), p. 4–8.

4. *1982 Joint Economic Report,* Report 97-436 (Washington, D.C.: GPO, 1982), p. 22.

5. "Regional and State Projections of Income, Employment and Population to the Year 2000," *Survey of Current Business,* November 1980.

6. Saunders, "The U.S. Economy to 1990."

7. *1982 Joint Economic Report,* p. 24.

8. For state-by-state projections of this slowdown, see Roy Bahl, Marvin Johnson, and Larry DeBoer, *The Fiscal Outlook for State Governments,* paper prepared for Hamilton-Rabinovitz, Inc., October 1979.

9. Larry DeBoer, "The Response of State and Local Government Finances to Economic Fluctuations," Syracuse University, Ph.D. dissertation, 1982.

10. Water Resources Council, "1972 OBERS Projections (Series E Population)" (Washington, D.C.: GPO, 1974); Bureau of Economic Analysis, Regional Economic Analysis Division, "Population, Personal Income and Earnings by State: Projections to 2000" (Washington, D.C.: GPO, 1977); and "Regional and State Projections of Income, Employment and Population to the Year 2000," *Survey of Current Business,* November 1980.

11. Henry Herzog, David Bjornstad, and Dana Stuckwish, *Long-Term Projections of Population and Employment for Regions of the United States* (Oak Ridge, Tenn.: Oak Ridge National Laboratory, 1981); and R. Olsen *et al., MULTIREGION: A Simulation-Forecasting Model of BEA Area Population and Employment* (Oak Ridge, Tenn.: Oak Ridge National Laboratory, 1977).

12. Bureau of the Census, "Population Projections of the U.S.: 1977–2050," *Current Population Reports,* Series P25, 704 (Washington, D.C.: GPO, 1977).

13. Gregory Jackson, George Masnick, Roger Bolton, Susan Bartlett, and John Pitkin, *Regional Diversity: Growth in the United States, 1960–1990* (Boston: Auburn House, 1981), Chapter II and Appendix A.

14. For example, "Sunbelt Having Trouble Living Up to Its Promise," *New York Times,* July 5, 1982, p. 1.

15. See Table 4-1, and Hans Landsberg, "The Uneven Burden of High Energy Costs," *Resources,* 70 (July 1982): 5–7.

16. Irving Hoch, "The Role of Energy in the Regional Distribution of Economic Activity," in *Alternatives to Confrontation,* edited by Victor Arnold (Lexington, Mass.: Lexington Books, 1980).

17. Bernard Weinstein, *Cost-of-Living Adjustments for Federal Grants*

in Aid: A Negative View (Research Triangle, N.C.: Southern Growth Policies Board, 1979).

18. David Birch, "Regional Differences in Factor Costs: Labor, Land, Capital, and Transportation," in *Alternatives to Confrontation,* edited by Victor Arnold (Lexington, Mass.: Lexington Books, 1980).

19. Ibid., p. 150.

20. A 1980 ACIR estimate of relative tax effort has twelve of seventeen northern states but none of fourteen southern states above the national average. ACIR, *Tax Capacity of the Fifty States, Supplement: 1980 Estimates* (Washington, D.C.: GPO, 1982), p. 13.

21. Birch, pp. 138–39.

22. Mancur Olson, "The South Will Fall Again: The South as Leader and Laggard in Economic Growth," *Southern Economic Journal* 49(4) (1983): 932.

23. Roy Bahl and Larry Schroeder, *Projecting and Planning State and Local Government Fiscal Activity in a Declining Region: The New York Case,* monograph 5, Metropolitan Studies Program, The Maxwell School (Syracuse, N.Y.: Syracuse University, 1980).

24. For a review of this literature see Roy Bahl, Marvin Johnson, and Michael Wasylenko, "State and Local Government Expenditure Determinants: The Traditional View and a New Approach," in *Public Employment and State and Local Government Finance,* edited by Roy Bahl, Jesse Burkhead and Bernard Jump, Jr. (Cambridge, Mass.: Ballinger, 1980).

25. Thomas Muller, *Growing and Declining Urban Areas: A Fiscal Comparison* (Washington, D.C.: Urban Institute, 1976), pp. 82–83.

26. Louise Russell, *The Baby Boom Generation and the Economy* (Washington, D.C.: Brookings Institution, 1982), p. 132.

27. A good discussion of the implications of changing demographics on public pensions is Alicia Munnell, *Pensions for Public Employees* (Washington, D.C.: National Planning Association, 1979), Chapter 3; see also Comptroller General of the United States, *An Actuarial and Economic Analysis of State and Local Government Pension Plans* (Washington, D.C.: GPO, 1980).

28. There are, however, some good discussions of the possibilities. See Robert L. Clark and John A. Menefee, "Economic Responses to Demographic Fluctuations," Special Study on Economic Change of the Joint Economic Committee, Washington, D.C., 1980; Lawrence Olson, Christopher Caton, and Morton Duffy, *The Elderly and the Future Economy* (Lexington, Mass.: Lexington Books, 1981); and Russell, *The Baby Boom Generation and the Economy.*

29. A 1977 CBO study estimated that less than 5 percent of el-

derly families were below the poverty line after adjustment for taxes and in-kind payments. Congressional Budget Office, "Poverty Status of Families Under Alternative Definitions of Income," Background Paper No. 17 (Washington, D.C.: GPO, February 1977).

30. John Goodman, "The Future's Poor: Projecting the Population Eligible for Federal Housing Assistance," *Socio-Economic Planning Sciences* 13:117 (1979).

31. Stephen M. Barro, *The Urban Impacts of Federal Policies, Fiscal Conditions* (Santa Monica, Cal.: Rand Corporation, 1978).

32. A "fiscally dependent" individual is one who requires more in expenditures than he generates in revenue.

33. *1978 Official Household Projections for New York State Counties,* New York State Economic Development Board, April 1978.

34. The consumption literature has reached no consensus about the effects of a changing age distribution on the marginal or average propensity to consume. For a good summary, see Louise Russell, "The Macroeconomic Effects of Changes in the Age Structure of the Population," *Economic Perspectives: An Annual Survey of Economics,* Vol. 1 (New York: Harwood Academic, 1979).

35. These are reviewed in Deborah Matz, "The Tax and Expenditure Limitation Movement," in *Urban Government Finances in the 1980s,* edited by Roy Bahl (Beverly Hills, Cal.: Sage, 1981).

36. Perry Shapiro, David Puryear, and John Ross, "Tax and Expenditure Limitations in Retrospect and in Prospect," *National Tax Journal* (supplement) XXXII(2):1 (1979).

37. ACIR, *Changing Public Attitudes on Governments and Taxes, 1982* (Washington, D.C.: GPO, 1982), pp. 3–5.

38. Jack Citrin, "Do People Want Something for Nothing: Public Opinion on Taxes and Government Spending," *National Tax Journal* (supplement) XXXII(2):113 (1979).

39. Helen Ladd and Julie Boatright Wilson, "Why Voters Support Tax Limitations: Evidence From Massachusetts, Proposition 2½," Sloan Working Paper 3-82, University of Maryland, January 1982.

40. Paul Courant, Edward Gramlich, and Daniel Rubinfeld, "Why Voters Support Tax Limitation Amendments: The Michigan Case," *National Tax Journal* (1980).

41. John J. Kirlin, *The Political Economy of Fiscal Limits* (Lexington, Mass.: Lexington Books, 1982), chapter 1.

42. These efficiency losses are explored in Helen Ladd, "An Economic Evaluation of State Limitations on Local Taxing and Spending Power," *National Tax Journal* XXXI(1):1 (1979).

43. John Shannon, "The Great Slowdown in State and Local

Spending in the United States: 1976–1984" (Washington, D.C.: ACIR, 1981).

44. ACIR, *State Limitations on Local Taxes and Expenditures* (Washington, D.C.: GPO, 1977).

45. Ladd, "An Economic Evaluation."

46. For an interesting discussion, see Jesse Burkhead, "Balance the Federal Budget," *Public Affairs Comment,* LBJ School of Public Affairs (Austin: University of Texas, 1979).

47. Robert Inman makes an interesting case for limitations as a valuable policy instrument in "The Economic Case for Limits to Government," *American Economic Review* 72(2):176 (1982).

48. A useful discussion of the process is in Peter Salins, "The Limits of Gentrification," *New York Affairs* 5(4):3 (1979). For a very optimistic view of urban conditions, see T. D. Allman, "The Urban Crisis Leaves Town," *Harper's,* December 1978, p. 41.

49. The Carter administration's urban policy is outlined in "New Partnership to Conserve America's Communities," reprinted in *The Fiscal Outlook for Cities: Implications of a National Urban Policy,* edited by Roy Bahl (Syracuse, N.Y.: Syracuse University Press, 1979); the Reagan program is reported in U.S. Department of Housing and Urban Development, *The President's National Urban Policy Report, 1982* (Washington, D.C.: GPO, 1982).

50. Thomas Muller, "Regional Impacts," in *The Reagan Experiment,* edited by John Palmer and Isabel Sawhill (Washington, D.C.: The Urban Institute Press, 1982), p. 454.

51. Kathy Jean Hayes and David Puryear, "The Urban Impacts of the Revenue Act of 1978" in *The Urban Impacts of Federal Policies,* edited by Norman Glickman (Baltimore: Johns Hopkins University Press, 1980).

52. Paul Courant, "On the Effects of Federal Capital Taxation on Growing and Declining Areas," Institute of Public Policy Studies discussion paper 170, University of Michigan, January 1981; and Robert Schwab, "The Regional Effects of Investment Incentives," Sloan Workshop in Urban and Public Economics, working paper 2–82, University of Maryland, 1982.

53. Thanos Catsambas, *Regional Impacts of Federal Fiscal Policy* (Lexington, Mass.: Lexington Books, 1978), p. 97.

54. ACIR, *Regional Growth: Growth of Federal Funds, 1952–76* (Washington, D.C.: GPO, 1980), p. 16.

55. George Peterson and Thomas Muller, "Regional Impact of Federal Tax and Spending Policies" in *Alternatives to Confrontation;* and Muller, "Regional Impacts."

56. Evaluation of CETA programs is reviewed in Robert Cook, "Fiscal Implications of CETA Public Service Employment" in *Fiscal Crises in American Cities: The Federal Response,* edited by Kenneth Hubbell (Cambridge, Mass.: Ballinger, 1979). The stimulative impact of local public works is analyzed in Edward Gramlich, "State and Local Government Budgets the Day After It Rained: Why Is the Surplus so High?" *Brookings Papers on Economic Activity* 1 (Washington, D.C.: Brookings Institution 1978).

57. Kathryn Nelson and Clifford Patrick, *Decentralization of Employment During the 1969–1972 Business Cycle: The National and Regional Record* (Oak Ridge, Tenn.: Oak Ridge National Laboratory, 1975) and Richard Rosen, "Identifying States and Areas Prone to High and Low Unemployment," *Monthly Labor Review* 103(3):20 (1980).

58. See also the discussion by George Break, "Intergovernmental Fiscal Relations" in *Setting National Priorities: Agenda for the 1980s* (Washington, D.C.: Brookings Institution, 1980).

59. New York City is unique in terms of its size, the broad range of functions for which it has responsibility, and the excesses in its financial management, particularly its short-term borrowing practices. On the other hand, New York City is not at all unique in terms of its declining economic base, loss of population, rising dependent population, and slow-growing tax base. For a discussion of the uniqueness of New York during this period, see Roy Bahl, Alan Campbell, David Greytak, Bernard Jump, Jr., and David Puryear, "Impact of Economic Base Erosion, Inflation, and Retirement Costs on Local Governments," hearings before a House Subcommittee on Government Operations, July 15, 1975 (Washington, D.C.: GPO, 1975).

60. For surveys of state and local government tax incentive programs and studies of their effectiveness, see Larry Schroeder and Paul Blackley, "State and Local Government Locational Incentive Programs and Small Business in Region II," paper prepared for the Small Business Administration Project "The Regional Environments for Small Business and Entrepreneurship," Metropolitan Studies Program, Syracuse University, September 1979; Roger Schmenner, *The Manufacturing Location Decision: Evidence from Cincinnati and New England* (Cambridge, Mass.: Harvard Business School and Harvard-MIT Joint Center for Urban Studies, 1978); and Michael Wasylenko, "The Role of Taxes and Fiscal Incentives in the Location of Firms" in *Urban Government Finances in the 1980s,* edited by Roy Bahl (Beverly Hills, Cal.: Sage, 1981).

61. For an example of the results of a careful management of the capital stock in a declining city see Nancy Humphrey, George Peter-

son, and Peter Wilson, *The Future of Cincinnati's Capital Plant* (Washington, D.C.: Urban Institute, 1979).

62. Roy Bahl and Larry Schroeder, *Forecasting Local Government Budgets*, occasional paper 38, Metropolitan Studies Program, The Maxwell School (Syracuse, N.Y.: Syracuse University, 1979).

BIBLIOGRAPHY

Henry Aaron, *Who Pays the Property Tax?* Washington, D.C.: Brookings Institution, 1975.

Charles Adams and Richard P. Nathan, "Understanding Central City Hardship," *Political Science Quarterly* **91**(1):XX (1976):61–62.

Advisory Commission on Intergovernmental Relations, *Changing Public Attitudes on Governments and Taxes, 1982*. Washington, D.C.: GPO, 1982, pp. 3–5.

———, *City Financial Emergencies: The Intergovernmental Dimension*. Washington, D.C.: GPO, 1973.

———, *Countercyclical Aid and Economic Stabilization*. Washington, D.C.: GPO, 1978.

———, *Federal Grants: Their Effects on State-Local Expenditures, Employment Levels, Wage Rates*. Washington, D.C.: GPO, 1977.

———, *Fiscal Balance in the American Federal System*, Vol. II: *Metrolpolitan Fiscal Disparities*. Washington, D.C.: GPO, 1968.

———, *Measuring the Fiscal Blood Pressure of the States*. Washington, D.C.: GPO, 1977.

———, *Regional Growth: Close of Federal Funds, 1952–76*. Washington, D.C.: GPO, 1980.

———, *Significant Features of Fiscal Federalism*. Washington, D.C.: GPO, 1981.

———, *State Limitations on Local Taxes and Expenditures*. Washington, D.C.: GPO, 1977.

———, *State-Local Finances in Recession and Inflation*. Washington, D.C.: GPO, 1979.

———, *Tax Capacity of the Fifty States: Methodology and Estimates.* Washington, D.C.: GPO, 1982.

———, *Tax Capacity of the Fifty States,* Supplement: *1980 Estimates.* Washington, D.C.: GPO, 1982.

———, *Trends in Metropolitan America.* Washington, D.C.: GPO, 1977.

T. D. Allman, "The Urban Crisis Leaves Town," *Harper's,* December 1978, p. 41.

Anonymous, "The President's Federalism Initiative." White House press release, January 26, 1982.

Richard J. Aronson and Arthur E. King, "Is There a Fiscal Crisis Outside New York?" *National Tax Journal* 31(2):XX (1978):153–64.

——— and James R. Marsden, "Duplicating Moody's Municipal Credit Ratings," *Public Finance Quarterly* 8(1):XX (1980):97–106.

Roy Bahl, "Effects of Regional Shifts in Population and Economic Activity on the Finances of State and Local Governments: Implications for Public Policy," in *National Policy Toward Regional Change,* edited by Victor Arnold. Lexington, Mass.: Lexington Books, 1981.

———, "The Long-Term Fiscal Outlook for New York State," in *The Declining Northeast,* edited by Benjamin Chinitz. New York: Praeger, 1978.

———, "Measuring the Creditworthiness of State and Local Governments: Municipal Bond Ratings," in *Proceedings of Sixty-fourth Annual Conference.* Kansas City: National Tax Association, 1972.

———, *The New York State Economy: 1960–1978 and the Outlook,* occasional paper 37, Metropolitan Studies Program, The Maxwell School. Syracuse, N.Y.: Syracuse University, 1979.

———, "The Next Decade in State and Local Government Finance: A Period of Adjustment," in *Urban Government Finance: Emerging Trends,* edited by Roy Bahl. Cambridge, Mass.: Sage, 1981.

———, "The Prospects for Urban Government Finances in the 1980s," paper presented at the American Federation of State, County, and Municipal Employees Conference, Glen Cove, N.Y., December 11, 1979.

———, "Regional Shifts in Economic Activity and Government Finances in Growing and Declining States," in *Tax Reform and Southern Economic Development,* edited by Bernard Weinstein. Research Triangle Park, N.C.: Southern Growth Policies Board, 1979.

———, "State and Local Government Finances and the Changing National Economy," testimony before the Special Study on Economic Change of the Joint Economic Committee, July 28, 1980.

——, Alan Campbell, and David Greytak, *Taxes, Expenditures, and the Economic Base: A Case Study of New York City.* New York: Praeger, 1974.

——, ——, ——, B. Jump, Jr., and D. Puryear, "Impact of Economic Base Erosion, Inflation and Retirement Costs on Local Governments," testimony on Fiscal Relations in the American Federal System, hearings before the House Subcommittee on Government Operations, July 15, 1975.

—— and David Greytak, "The Response of City Government Revenues to Changes in Employment Structure," *Land Economics* **52**:415 (1976).

——, Richard Gustely, and Michael Wasylenko, "The Determinants of Local Government Police Expenditures: A Public Employment Approach," *National Tax Journal* **XXXI**: (1978):67–79.

——, A. Hoffman, L. Schroeder, and M. Share, *Local Government Revenue and Expenditure Forecasting: Washington, D.C.*, occasional paper 51, Metropolitan Studies Program, The Maxwell School. Syracuse, N.Y.: Syracuse University, 1981.

——, Marvin Johnson, and Lawrence P. DeBoer Jr., *The Fiscal Outlook for State Governments,* report prepared for Hamilton-Rabinovitz, Inc., under a grant from Aetna Foundation, 1979.

——, ——, and Michael Wasylenko, "State and Local Government Expenditure Determinants: The Traditional View and a New Approach," in *Public Employment and State and Local Government Finances,* edited by Roy Bahl, Jesse Burkhead, and Bernard Jump, Jr. Cambridge, Mass.: Ballinger, 1980.

—— and Bernard Jump, Jr., "Measuring the Fiscal Viability of Cities," in *Fiscal Choices,* edited by George Peterson. Washington, D.C.: Urban Institute, forthcoming.

Roy Bahl, Bernard Jump, Jr. and Larry Schroeder. "The Outlook for City Fiscal Performance in Declining Regions," In *The Fiscal Outlook for Cities.* edited by Roy Bahl. Syracuse, NY: Syracuse University Press, 1978.

—— and David Puryear, *Economic Problems of a Mature Economy,* occasional paper 27, Metropolitan Studies Program, The Maxwell School. Syracuse, N.Y.: Syracuse University, 1976.

—— and Larry Schroeder, "Fiscal Adjustments in Declining States," in *Cities Under Stress,* edited by Robert Burchell and David Listokin. New Brunswick, N.J.: Rutgers University Press, 1981.

—— and ——, *Forecasting Local Government Budgets,* occasional paper 38, Metropolitan Studies Program, The Maxwell School. Syracuse, N.Y.: Syracuse University, 1979.

———— and ————, *Projecting and Planning State and Local Government Fiscal Activity in a Declining Region: The New York Case,* monograph 5, Metropolitan Studies Program, The Maxwell School. Syracuse, N.Y.: Syracuse University, 1980.

————, ————, and Kurt Zorn, *Local Government Revenue and Expenditure Forecasting: Dallas, Texas,* occasional paper 49, Metropolitan Studies Program, The Maxwell School. Syracuse, N.Y.: Syracuse University, 1981.

Stephen M. Barro, *The Urban Impacts of Federal Policies,* Vol. III: *Fiscal Conditions.* Santa Monica, Cal.: Rand Corporation, 1978.

Susan Bartlett, R. Bolton, G. Jackson, G. Masnick, and J. Pitkin, *Regional Diversity: Growth in the United States, 1960–1990.* Boston: Auburn House, 1981.

Karen Benker and Steven Gold, *State Fiscal Conditions as States Entered 1982,* legislative finance paper 13. Denver: National Conference of State Legislatures, 1982.

David Birch, "The Job Generation Process," Economic Development Administration, U.S. Department of Commerce. Washington, D.C.: GPO, 1979.

————, "Regional Differences in Factor Costs: Labor, Land, Capital and Transportation," in *Alternatives to Confrontation,* edited by Victor Arnold. Lexington, Mass.: Lexington Books, 1980.

Ann Kalman Bixby, "Social Welfare Expenditures, Fiscal Year 1979," *Social Security Bulletin* **44**(11):3 (1981).

David Bjornstad, Henry Herzog, and Dana Stuckwish, *Long-Term Projections of Population and Employment for Regions of the United States.* Oak Ridge, Tenn.: Oak Ridge National Laboratory, 1981.

Paul Blackley and Larry Schroeder, "State and Local Government Locational Incentive Programs and Small Business in Region II," paper prepared for the Small Business Administration project "The Regional Environments for Small Business and Entrepreneurship," Metropolitan Studies Program, Syracuse University, September 1979.

David Blank, "Reform of State-Local Fiscal Relations in New York," *National Tax Journal* **III**(12):106 (1950).

Thomas Borcherding and Robert Deacon, "The Demand for Services of Nonfederal Governments," *American Economic Review* **62**(12):891 (1972).

Michael Boskin, ed., *Federal Tax Reform: Myths and Realities.* San Francisco: Institute for Contemporary Studies, 1978.

————, "Taxation, Saving and the Rate of Interest," *Journal of Political Economy* **86**(2):23 (1978).

Katherine L. Bradbury, Anthony Downs, and Kenneth A. Small, *Urban Decline and the Future of American Cities*. Washington, D.C.: Brookings Institution, 1982.

George Break, "Intergovernmental Fiscal Relations," in *Setting National Priorities: Agenda for the 1980s*. Washington, D.C.: Brookings Institution, 1980.

Robert Bretzfelder and Howard Friedenberg, "Sensitivity of Regional and State Nonform Wages and Salaries to the National Business Cycle, 1980:I - 1981:II," *Survey of Current Business,* January 1982, 26–29.

Linn Brown and Richard Syron, "Cities, Suburbs and Regions," *New England Economic Review,* January-February 1979, p. 41.

E. Evan Brunson and Lawrence K. Lynch, "Comparative Growth and Structure: The South and the Nation," in *The Economics of Southern Growth,* edited by E. Blaine Liner and Lawrence K. Lynch. Durham, N.C.: Southern Growth Policies Board, 1977.

Budget of the United States Government, Fiscal Year 1983. Washington, D.C.: GPO, 1982.

Harold Bunce, *An Evaluation of the Community Development Block Grant Formula*. Washington, D.C.: U.S. Department of Housing and Urban Development, 1976.

Jesse Burkhead, "Balance the Federal Budget," *Public Affairs Comment*. Austin: LBJ School of Public Affairs, University of Texas, 1979.

———— and Shawna Grosskopf, "Trends in Public Employment and Compensation," in *Public Employment and State and Local Government Finances,* edited by Roy Bahl, Jesse Burkhead, and Bernard Jump, Jr. Cambridge, Mass.: Ballinger, 1980.

———— and John P. Ross, "Local Government Productivity," in *Public Employment and State and Local Government Finances,* edited by Roy Bahl, Jesse Burkhead, and Bernard Jump, Jr. Cambridge, Mass.: Ballinger, 1980.

———— and ————, *Productivity in the Local Government Sector*. Lexington, Mass.: Heath, 1974.

Thanos Catsambas, *Regional Impacts of Federal Fiscal Policy*. Lexington, Mass.: Lexington Books, 1978.

Jan Chaiken and Warren Walker, *Growth in Municipal Expenditures: A Case Study of Los Angeles*. Santa Monica, Cal.: Rand Corporation, 1979.

Jack Citrin, "Do People Want Something for Nothing? Public Opinion on Taxes and Government Spending," *National Tax Journal* **XXXII** (supplement):113 (1979).

City of Dallas, *Summary Long-Range Financial Plan, 1979–80 to 1983–84.* Dallas: Office of Management Services, 1979.

Robert L. Clark and John A. Menefee, *Economic Responses to Demographic Fluctuations,* Special Study on Economic Change of the Joint Economic Committee. Washington, D.C.: GPO, 1980.

Terry Clark, "How Many New Yorks? The New York Fiscal Crisis in Comparative Perspective," report 72 of the Comparative Study of Community Decision-Making. Chicago: University of Chicago, 1976.

The Condition of Urban Infrastructure in the New York–New Jersey Region: A Survival Issue for the 1980s. New York: The Port Authority of New York and New Jersey, 1979.

Congressional Budget Office, *City Need and the Responsiveness of Federal Grants Programs.* Washington, D.C.: GPO, 1978.

———, "Poverty Status of Families Under Alternative Definitions of Income," background paper 17. Washington, D.C.: GPO, 1977.

———, *Troubled Local Economies and the Distribution of Federal Dollars.* Washington, D.C.: GPO, 1977.

Robert Cook, "Fiscal Implications of CETA Public Service Employment," in *Fiscal Crisis in American Cities: The Federal Response,* edited by Kenneth Hubbell. Cambridge, Mass.: Ballinger, 1979.

Paul Courant, "On the Effects of Federal Capital Taxation on Growing and Declining Areas," discussion paper 170. Ann Arbor: Institute of Public Policy Studies, University of Michigan, 1981.

———, Edward Gramlich, and Daniel Rubinfeld, "Why Voters Support Tax Limitation Amendments: The Michigan Case," *National Tax Journal* **XXXIII** (3):1 (1980).

Robert Crider, *The Impact of Inflation on State and Local Government,* Urban and Regional Development Series 5. Columbus, Ohio: Academy for Contemporary Problems, 1978.

Edward M. Cupoli, William A. Peek, and C. Kurt Zorn, *An Analysis of the Effects of Inflation on Finances in Washington, D.C.,* occasional paper 36, Metropolitan Studies Program, The Maxwell School. Syracuse, N.Y.: Syracuse University, 1979.

Julie DaVanzo, "U.S. Internal Migration: Who Moves and Why," in *Consequence of Changing U.S. Population.* Washington, D.C.: GPO, 1978.

Karen Davis and Cathy Schoen, *Health and War on Poverty: A Ten Year Appraisal.* Washington, D.C.: Brookings Institution, 1978.

Philip Dearborn, *Elements of Municipal Financial Analysis.* New York: First Boston, 1978.

————, *Elements of Municipal Financial Analysis,* Part I: *Measuring Liquidity.* New York: First Boston, 1977.

————, *Elements of Municipal Financial Analysis,* Part IV: *Condition of Major City Finances.* New York: First Boston, 1977.

————, *The Financial Health of Major U.S. Cities in Fiscal 1977.* New York: First Boston, 1978.

————, *The Financial Health of Major U.S. Cities in 1978,* working paper. Washington, D.C.: Urban Institute, 1979.

Larry DeBoer, "The Response of State and Local Government Finances to Economic Fluctuations," Ph.D. dissertation, Syracuse University, 1982.

Luc DeWulf, "Fiscal Incidence Studies in Developing Countries: Survey and Critique," *International Monetary Fund Staff Papers* **22**(3):61 (1975).

Robert J. Dinkelmeyer, David Greytak, and Richard Gustely, "The Effects of Inflation on Local Government Expenditures," *National Tax Journal* **XXVII**(12):583 (1974).

Patricia Dusenbury, *Suburbs in the City: Municipal Boundary Changes in the Southern States.* Research Triangle Park, N.C.: Southern Growth Policies Board, 1980.

R. G. Ehrenberg, "The Demand for State and Local Government Employees," *American Economic Review* **63**(6):366 (1973).

————, "Municipal Government Structure, Unionization, and the Wages of Firefighters," *Industrial and Labor Relations Review* **27**(1):XX (1973) 36–48.

Stephen Farber in *Local Distress, State Surpluses, Proposition 13: Prelude to Fiscal Crisis or New Opportunities?* Hearings before the Committee on Banking, Finance and Urban Affairs, July 25 and 26, 1978.

"The Federal Government and the Economy of New York State," unpublished report from office of Senator Daniel Moynihan, June 15, 1977.

Robert Firestine and Bernard Weinstein, *Regional Growth and Decline in the U.S.* New York: Praeger, 1978.

Fiscal Issues in the Future of Federalism, supplemental paper 3. New York: Committee for Economic Development, 1968.

James Fossett and Richard Nathan, "Urban Conditions: The Future of the Federal Role," in *Proceedings of the National Tax Association (1978).* Columbus: National Tax Association, 1979.

Howard Friedenberg and Robert Bretzfelder, "Sensitivity of Regional and State Nonform Wages and Salaries to National Business Cycles, 1948–1979," *Survey of Current Business,* May 1980, 15–27.

Don Fullerton, "On the Possibility of an Inverse Relationship Between Tax Rates and Government Revenues," *Journal of Public Economics* 19(1982):3–22.

David Garnick, "The Northeast States in the Context of the Nation," in *The Declining Northeast,* edited by Benjamin Chinitz. New York: Praeger, 1978.

W. Irwin Gillespie, "Effects of Public Expenditures on the Distribution of Income," in *Essays in Fiscal Federalism,* edited by Richard Musgrave. Washington, D.C.: Brookings Institution, 1965.

Steven Gold, Karen Benker, and George Peterson, *State Budget Actions in 1982,* National Conference of State Legislatures, July 1982.

John Goodman, "The Future's Poor: Projecting the Population Eligible for Federal Housing Assistance," *Socio-Economic Planning Sciences* **13**:117 (1979).

Edward Gramlich, "Intergovernmental Grant: A Review of the Empirical Literature," in *The Political Economy of Fiscal Federalism,* edited by Wallace Oates. Lexington, Mass.: Lexington Books, 1977.

―――, "The New York City Crisis: What Happened and What Is To Be Done?" *American Economic Review* **66**(5):415 (1976).

―――, "State and Local Budget Surpluses and the Effect of Federal Macroeconomic Policies," Joint Economic Committee, Congress of the United States. Washington, D.C.: GPO, 1979.

―――, "State and Local Government Budgets the Day After It Rained: Why Is the Surplus So High?" *Brookings Papers on Economic Activity* 1. Washington, D.C.: Brookings Institution, 1978.

Michael R. Greenberg and Nicholas J. Valente, "Recent Economic Trends in the Major Northeastern Metropolises," in *Post-Industrial America: Metropolitan Decline and Inter-Regional Job Shifts,* edited by George Sternlieb and James Hughes. New Brunswick, N.J.: Rutgers University Press, 1975.

Michael J. Greenwood, "Research on Internal Migration in the United States: A Survey," *Journal of Economic Literature,* June 1975, p. 406.

David Greytak and Bernard Jump, Jr., *The Impact of Inflation on the Expenditures and Revenues of Six Local Governments, 1971–1974,* monograph 4, Metropolitan Studies Program, The Maxwell School. Syracuse, N.Y.: Syracuse University, 1975.

――― and ―――, *The Impact of Inflation on State and Local Government Finances, 1967–1974,* occasional paper 25, Metropolitan Studies

Program, The Maxwell School. Syracuse, N.Y.: Syracuse University, 1975.

—— and ——, "Inflation and Local Government Expenditures and Revenues: Methods and Case Studies," *Public Finance Quarterly* **5**(7):275 (1977).

Shawna Grosskopf, "Public Employment Trends and Problems," in *Urban Government Finances in the 1980s*, edited by Roy Bahl. Beverly Hills, Cal.: Sage, 1981.

David A. Grossman, *A Future of New York City's Capital Plant*. Washington, D.C.: Urban Institute, 1979.

Alvin Hansen and Harvey Perloff, *State and Local Finance in the National Economy*. New York: Norton, 1944.

Harry Hatry, *Efficiency Measurement for Local Government Services: Some Initial Suggestions*. Washington, D.C.: Urban Institute, 1979.

Kathy Jean Hayes and David Puryear, "The Urban Impacts of the Revenue Act of 1978," in *The Urban Impacts of Federal Policies*, edited by Norman Glickman. Baltimore: Johns Hopkins University Press, 1980.

Irving Hoch, "The Role of Energy in the Regional Distribution of Economic Activity," in *Alternatives to Confrontation*, edited by Victor Arnold. Lexington, Mass.: Lexington Books, 1980.

Nancy Humphrey, George Peterson, and Peter Wilson, *The Future of Cincinnati's Capital Plant*. Washington, D.C.: Urban Institute, 1979.

——, ——, and ——, *The Future of Cleveland's Capital Plant*. Washington, D.C.: Urban Institute, 1979.

——, ——, and ——, *The Future of Dallas' Capital Plant*. Washington, D.C.: Urban Institute, 1979.

Robert Inman, "The Economic Case for Limits to Government," *American Economic Review* **72**(5):176 (1982).

——, "The Fiscal Performance of Local Governments: An Interpretative Review," in *Current Issues in Urban Economics*, edited by Peter Mieszkowski and Mahon Straszheim. Baltimore: Johns Hopkins University Press, 1979.

Frank Jones and Mark Weisler, "Cyclical Variation in State and Local Government Financial Behavior and Capital Expenditures," *Proceedings of the Seventieth Annual Conference on Taxation*. Columbus: National Tax Association, Tax Institute of America, 1978.

Bernard Jump, Jr., "Public Employment, Collective Bargaining and Employee Wages and Pensions," in *State and Local Government*

Finance and Financial Management. Washington, D.C.: Municipal Finance Officers Association, 1978.

C. L. Jusenius and L. C. Ledebur, *A Myth in the Making: The Southern Economic Challenge and the Northern Economic Decline.* Washington, D.C.: GPO, 1976.

Marshall Kaplan, *Growth and the Cities of the South: A Study in Diversity,* White House Conference, 1978.

John Kasarda, "Industry, Community and the Metropolitan Problem," in *Handbook of Urban Life,* edited by David Street and associates. San Francisco: Jossey-Bass, 1978.

John J. Kirlin, *The Political Economy of Fiscal Limits.* Lexington, Mass.: Lexington Books, 1982, chapter 1.

Simon Kuznets, "Economic Growth and Income Inequality," *American Economic Review* **45**(1)1 (1955).

Helen Ladd, "An Economic Evaluation of State Limitations on Local Taxing and Spending Power," *National Tax Journal* **XXXI**(3):1 (1979).

—— and Julie Boatright Wilson, "Why Voters Support Tax Limitations: Evidence From Massachusetts, Proposition 2½," Sloan working paper 3–82. College Park: University of Maryland Press, 1982.

Arthur B. Laffer, "Statement Prepared for the Joint Economic Committee May 20, 1977," reprinted in *The Economics of the Tax Revolt: A Reader,* edited by Arthur B. Laffer and Jan Seymour. New York: Harcourt, Brace, Jovanovich, 1979.

Hans Landsberg, "The Uneven Burden of High Energy Costs," *Resources* 70 (July 1982): 5–7.

David Levin, "Receipts and Expenditures of State Governments and of Local Governments, 1959–1976," *Survey of Current Business* **58**(5):15 (1978).

——, "State and Local Government Fiscal Position in 1979," *Survey of Current Business* **60**(1):23 (1980).

Hubert Lipinsky, Michael Palmer, and Gregory Schneid, *An Alternative Approach to General Revenue Sharing: A Needs Based Allocation Formula.* Washington, D.C.: Institute for the Future, 1975.

Larry H. Long, "Migration Differentials by Education and Occupation: Trends and Variations," *Demography* **10**(2):245 (1973).

Vincent Marando, "The Politics of Metropolitan Reform," in *State and Local Government: The Political Economy of Reform,* edited by Roy Bahl and Alan Campbell. New York: Free Press, 1976.

Deborah Matz, "The Tax and Expenditure Limitation Movement," in

Urban Government Finances in the 1980s, edited by Roy Bahl. Beverly Hills, Cal.: Sage, 1981.

Charles McLure, "The Theory of Expenditure Incidence," *Finanzarchiv* **30**:432 (1972).

John Mikesell, "The Cyclical Sensitivity of State Tax Revenues," School of Public and Environmental Affairs, Indiana University, November 1982.

William H. Miernyk, "The Northeast Isn't What It Used To Be," in *Balanced Growth for the Northeast.* Albany, N.Y.: New York State Senate, 1975.

Moody's Analytical Overview of 25 Leading U.S. Cities. New York: Moody's Investors Service, 1977.

Peter A. Morrison, "Current Demographic Change in Regions of the United States," in *Alternatives to Confrontation,* edited by Victor Arnold. Lexington, Mass.: Lexington Books, 1980.

Thomas L. Muller, "The Declining and Growing Metropolis: A Fiscal Comparison," in *Post-Industrial America: Metropolitan Decline and Regional Job Shifts,* edited by George Sternlieb and James W. Hughes. New Brunswick: Center for Urban Policy Research, State University of New Jersey, 1975.

———, *Growing and Declining Urban Areas: A Fiscal Comparison.* Washington, D.C.: Urban Institute, 1976.

———, "Regional Impacts," in *The Reagan Experiment,* edited by John Palmer and Isabel Sawhill. Washington, D.C.: Urban Institute Press, 1982, p. 454.

——— and George Peterson, "Regional Impact of Federal Tax and Spending Policies," in *Alternatives to Confrontation,* edited by Victor Arnold. Lexington, Mass.: Lexington Books, 1980.

Multi-Year Financial Plan FY 1979–83. Washington, D.C.: District of Columbia Government, 1977.

Alicia Munnell, *Pensions for Public Employees.* Washington, D.C.: National Planning Association, 1979.

Richard Musgrave, *The Theory of Public Finance.* New York: McGraw-Hill, 1959.

Richard Nathan, "The Outlook for Federal Grants to Cities," in *The Fiscal Outlook for Cities,* edited by Roy Bahl. Syracuse, N.Y.: Syracuse University Press, 1978.

——— and Paul R. Dommel, "The Strong Sunbelt Cities and the Weak Cold Belt Cities," hearings before the Subcommittee on the City of the House Committee on Banking, Finance and Urban Affairs. *Toward a National Urban Policy.* 95th Congress. Washington, D.C.: GPO, 1977.

—— and ——, "Understanding Central City Hardship," *Political Science Quarterly* **21**:61 (1976).

—— and Fossett, ——, "Urban Conditions: The Future of the Federal Role," in *Proceedings of the 71st Annual Convention of the National Tax Association-Tax Institute of America.* Columbus, Ohio: NTA, 1978.

National Association of State Budget Officers, *Limitations on State Deficits.* Lexington, Mass.: Council of State Governments, 1976.

——, *State Fiscal Survey Fiscal Years 1975, 1976, and 1977, Summary Report.* Lexington, Ky.: National Association of State Budget Officers, 1977.

——, *Understanding the Fiscal Condition of the States.* Lexington, Ky.: National Association of State Budget Officers, 1978.

National Governors' Association, *Fiscal Survey of the States, 1978–79.* Washington, D.C.: GPO, 1980.

—— and National Association of State Budget Officers, *Fiscal Survey of the States.* Washington, D.C.: GPO, 1977.

—— and ——, *Fiscal Survey of the States.* Washington, D.C.: GPO, Government, 1978–79.

Kathryn Nelson and Clifford Patrick, *Decentralization of Employment During the 1969–1972 Business Cycle: The National and Regional Record.* Oak Ridge, Tenn.: Oak Ridge National Laboratory, 1975.

"New Partnership To Conserve America's Communities," in *The Fiscal Outlook for Cities: Implications of a National Urban Policy,* edited by Roy Bahl. Syracuse, N.Y.: Syracuse University Press, 1979.

New York State Economic Development Board, *1978 Official Household Projections for New York State Counties.* Albany: NYSEDB, 1978.

William Niskanen, *Bureaucracy and Representative Government.* New York: Aldine, 1971.

William Oakland, *Financial Relief for Troubled Cities.* Columbus, Ohio: Academy for Contemporary Problems, 1978.

Wallace Oates, *Fiscal Federalism.* New York: Harcourt, Brace, Jovanovich, 1972.

Benjamin Okner and Joseph Pechman, *Who Bears the Tax Burden?* Washington, D.C.: Brookings Institution, 1975.

R. J. Olsen, G. W. Westley, H. W. Herzog, G. R. Kerley, Jr., D. J. Bjornstad, D. P. Vogt, L. G. Bray, S. T. Grady, and R. A. Nakosteen, *Multiregion: A Simulation-Forecasting Model of BEA Area Population and Employment.* Oak Ridge, Tenn.: Oak Ridge National Laboratory, 1977.

Mancur Olson, "The South Will Fall Again: The South as Leader and

Laggard in Economic Growth," *Southern Economic Journal* **49**(4):932 (1983).

David Peterson, *The Relative Need of States and Regions for Federal Aid.* Research Triangle Park, N.C.: Southern Growth Policies Board, 1979.

George Peterson, "Capital Spending and Capital Obsolescence: The Outlook for Cities," in *The Fiscal Outlook for Cities,* edited by Roy Bahl. Syracuse, N.Y.: Syracuse University Press, 1978.

———, "Finance," in *The Urban Predicament,* edited by William Gorham and Nathan Glazer. Washington, D.C.: Urban Institute, 1976.

———, "The State and Local Sector," in *The Reagan Experiment,* edited by John Palmer and Isabel Sawhill. Washington, D.C.: Urban Institute, 1982, p. 159.

John E. Petersen, *The Rating Game,* report of the Twentieth Century Fund Task Force on Municipal Bond Credit Ratings. New York: Twentieth Century Fund, 1974.

Neal Pierce, "State-Local Report/Fiscal Crises Illustrate Growing Interdependence," *The National Journal* **7**(8):280 (1975).

David Puryear, John Ross, and Perry Shapiro, "Tax and Expenditure Limitations in Retrospect and in Prospect," *National Tax Journal* **XXXIII** (supplement):1 (1979).

Robert Rafuse, "Cyclical Behavior of State and Local Government Finances," in *Essays in Fiscal Federalism,* edited by Richard Musgrave. Washington, D.C.: Brookings Institution, 1965.

Robert Reischauer, "The Economy, The Federal Budget and the Prospects for Urban Aid," in *The Fiscal Outlook for Cities,* edited by Roy Bahl. Syracuse, N.Y.: Syracuse University Press, 1978.

Resources in Review. Washington, D.C.: Municipal Finance Officers Association, 1982.

Morgan Reynolds and Eugene Smolensky, "The Post-Fisc Distribution: 1961 and 1970 Compared," *National Tax Journal* **27**:515 (1974).

Richard Rosen, "Identifying States and Areas Prone to High and Low Unemployment," *Monthly Labor Review* **103**(3):20 (1980).

Louise Russell, *The Baby Boom Generation and the Economy.* Washington, D.C.: Brookings Institution, 1982), p. 132.

———, "The Macroeconomic Effects of Changes in the Age Structure of the Population," *Economic Perspectives: An Annual Survey of Economics* **1**:23 (1979).

H.U.D., Office of Policy Development and Research, *Changing Conditions in Large Metropolitan Areas.* Washington, D.C.: GPO, 1980.

————, *Estimates of Current Employment Trends and Related Information for Large Cities.* Syracuse, N.Y.: Syracuse University Press, 1978.

————, "Estimates of Large Metropolitan Areas," Urban Data Reports, No. 1. Washington, D.C.: GPO, 1980.

Peter Salins, "The Limits of Gentrification," *New York Affairs* **5**:XX (1979):3–12.

San Antonio Independent School District *v.* Rodriques, 411 U.S. 1 (1972).

Norman C. Saunders, *Employment Projections for the 1980s.* Bureau of Labor Statistics, bulletin 2030. Washington, D.C.: GPO, 1979.

Malcolm Sawyer, "Income Distribution in OECD Countries," *OECD Economic Outlook,* occasional studies, July 1976, p. 3.

Roger Schmenner, *The Manufacturing Location Decision: Evidence from Cincinnati and New England.* Cambridge, Mass.: Harvard Business School and Harvard-MIT Joint Center for Urban Studies, 1978.

Robert Schwab, "The Regional Effects of Investment Incentives," Sloan Workshop in Urban and Public Economics, working paper 2–82. College Park: University of Maryland Press, 1982.

Serrano *v.* Priest 5 Cal., 3d 584 (1971).

John Shannon, "The Great Slowdown in State and Local Spending in the United States: 1976–1984," Washington, D.C.: ACIR, 1981.

Wade Smith, *The Appraisal of Municipal Credit Risk.* New York: Moody's Investors Service, 1979.

Southern Growth Policies Board, *Final Report of the Southern Growth Policies Board Task Force on Southern Cities.* Research Triangle Park, N.C., 1981.

Standard & Poor's, *Standard & Poor's Ratings Guide.* New York: McGraw-Hill, 1979.

David Stanley, *Cities in Trouble.* Columbus, Ohio: Academy for Contemporary Problems, 1976.

————, "Running Short, Cutting Down: Five Cities in Financial Distress." Washington, D.C.: Brookings Institution, unpublished report.

Patrick Sullivan, *Municipal Bond Ratings Viewed as Implicit Grant/Tax Mechanisms,* occasional paper 30, Metropolitan Studies Program, The Maxwell School. Syracuse, N.Y.: Syracuse University, 1976.

"Sunbelt Having Trouble Living Up to Its Promise." *New York Times,* July 5, 1982, p. 1.

Touche-Ross and First National Bank of Boston, *Urban Fiscal Stress: A Comparative Analysis of 66 U.S. Cities.* New York: Touche-Ross, 1979.

Richard Tresch, *Public Finance: A Normative Theory*, Texas, Business Publications, 1981.

Robert Trost and Robert Vogel, "The Response of State Government Receipts to Economic Fluctuations and the Allocation of Countercyclical Revenue Sharing Grants," *Review of Economics and Statistics* **XLI**(19):389 (1979).

U.S. Comptroller General, *An Actuarial and Economic Analysis of State and Local Government Pension Plans*. Washington, D.C.: GPO, 1980.

———, *Impact of Antirecession Assistance on 15 State Governments, Impact of Antirecession Assistance on 16 County Governments*, and *Impact of Antirecession Assistance on 21 City Governments*. Washington, D.C.: General Accounting Office, 1978.

———, *Antirecession Assistance Is Helping but Distribution Formula Needs Reassessment*, report to Congress. Washington, D.C.: General Accounting Office, 1977.

———, "Why the Formula for Allocating Community Development Block Grant Funds Should Be Improved." Washington, D.C.: General Accounting Office, 1976.

U.S. Congress, Congressional Budget Office, *The Prospects for Economic Recovery*, report to the Senate and House Committees on the Budget, Part I. Washington, D.C.: GPO, 1982.

U.S. Congress, Joint Economic Committee, *Emergency Interim Survey: Fiscal Condition of 48 Large Cities*, 97th Congress, 1st session. Washington, D.C.: GPO, 1982.

———, *1982 Joint Economic Report on the February 1982 Economic Report of the President*, report 97-436. Washington, D.C.: GPO, 1982.

U.S. Congress, Joint Economic Committee Special Study on Economic Change, "State and Local Government Finances and the Changing National Economy," in *State and Local Finance: Adjustments in a Changing Economy*. Washington, D.C.: GPO, 1980.

U.S. Congress, Joint Economic Committee, Subcommittee on Urban Affairs, *The Current Fiscal Position of State and Local Governments: Survey of 48 State Governments and 140 Local Governments*, 94th Congress, 1st session. Washington, D.C.: GPO, 1975.

U.S. Department of Commerce, Bureau of Economic Analysis, "Regional and State Projections of Income, Employment and Population to the Year 2000." *Survey of Current Business* **60**(11):**XX** (1980):44–70.

———, Regional Economic Analysis Division, "Population, Personal Income and Earnings by State: Projections to 2000." Washington, D.C.: GPO, 1977.

U.S. Department of Commerce, Bureau of the Census, *Governmental Finances in 1979–80,* series GF78, no. 5. Washington, D.C.: GPO, 1981.

———, "Population Projections of the U.S.: 1977–2050," in *Current Population Reports,* series P25, no. 704. Washington, D.C.: GPO, 1977.

U.S. Department of Commerce, Bureau of Economic Analysis. *Survey of Current Business* **59**(7):(July 1979).

U.S. Department of Commerce, *Survey of Current Business.* Washington, D.C.: April 1982.

U.S. Department of Housing and Urban Development, *Changing Conditions in Metropolitan Areas,* Urban Data Reports, No. 1. Washington, D.C.: Office of Policy Development and Research, 1979.

———, *City Need and the Responsiveness of Federal Grants Programs.* Washington, D.C.: GPO, 1978.

———, *The President's National Urban Policy Report, 1982.* Washington, D.C.: GPO, 1982.

———, "The Urban Fiscal Crisis: Fact or Fantasy?" Washington, D.C.: Office of Policy Development and Research, 1979.

U.S. Department of Labor, Bureau of Labor Statistics, "Autumn 1976 Urban Family Budgets and Comparative Indexes for Selected Urban Areas." Washington, D.C.: GPO, 1977.

U.S. Department of Treasury, Office of State and Local Government Finance, "Responsiveness of State/Federal and Direct Federal Aid to Distressed Cities," research Note IV. Washington, D.C.: GPO, 1979.

———, *Report on the Fiscal Impact of the Economic Stimulus Package on 40 Large Urban Governments.* Washington, D.C.: GPO, 1978.

U.S. House of Representatives, Committee on Government Operations, Subcommittee on Intergovernmental Relations and Human Resources, *Intergovernmental Anti-Recession Assistance Act of 1977,* hearings on H.R. 3730 and related bills, 95th Congress, 1st session. Washington, D.C.: GPO, 1977.

U.S. House of Representatives, Select Committee on Population, "Domestic Consequences of United States Population Change." Washington, D.C.: GPO, 1978.

U.S. President, *Economic Report of the President.* Washington, D.C.: GPO, 1977.

U.S. Senate, Committee on Governmental Affairs, Subcommittee on Intergovernmental Relations, *The Countercyclical Assistance Program: An Analysis of Its Initial Impact,* 95th Congress, 1st session. Washington, D.C.: GPO, 1977.

————, *Intergovernmental Anti-Recession Assistance Act of 1975,* hearings on S. 1359, 94th Congress, 1st session. Washington, D.C.: GPO, 1975.

U.S. Water Resources Council, "1972 OBERS Projections (Series E Population)." Washington, D.C.: GPO, 1974.

Roger Vaughan, *Inflation and Unemployment: Surviving the 1980s.* Washington, D.C.: Council of State Planning Agencies, 1980.

Robert C. Vogel, "The Responsiveness of State and Local Receipts to Change in Economic Activity: Extending the Concept of the Full Employment Budget." Joint Economic Committee of the U.S. Congress, *Studies in Price Stability and Economic Growth.* Washington, D.C.: GPO, 1975.

———— and Robert Trost, "The Response of State Government Receipts to Economic Fluctuations and the Allocation of Countercyclical Revenue Sharing Grants." *The Review of Economics and Statistics* **LXI**(8):389 (1979).

Mark Wasserman, "Public Sector Budget Balance," *OECD Economic Outlook,* occasional studies, July 1976, p. 37.

Michael Wasylenko, "The Role of Taxes and Fiscal Incentives in the Location of Firms," in *Urban Government Finances in the 1980s,* edited by Roy Bahl. Beverly Hills, Cal.: Sage, 1981.

Bernard Weinstein, *Cost of Living Adjustments for Federal Grants in Aid: A Negative View.* Research Triangle, N.C.: Southern Growth Policies Board, 1979.

John Zamzow, "The Current Recession: Its Regional Impact," hearings before the Joint Economic Committee, October 16, 1979. Washington, D.C.: GPO, 1980.

NAME INDEX

SUBJECT INDEX